Trees Call
for
What They Need

by
Melissa Kwasny

spinsters ink
minneapolis

First edition.
10-9-8-7-6-5-4-3-2-1

Spinsters Ink
P.O. Box 300170
Minneapolis, MN 55403

This is a work of fiction. Any similarity to persons living or dead is a coincidence.

You Are My Sunshine by Jimmie Davis and Charles Mitchell.
Copyright ©1940 by Peer International Corporation.
Copyright Renewed. International Copyright Secured.
All Rights Reserved. Used by Permission.

Cover art: "Bright October" by Gennie DeWeese
Cover design by: Teri Talley
Production: Melanie Cockrell   Mev Miller
                 Kay Hong   Stefanie Shiffler
                 Kelly Kager   Liz Tufte
                 Lori Loughney

Printed in the U.S.A. with soy ink on acid-free recycled paper.

Library of Congress Cataloging-in-Publication Data
Kwasny, Melissa, 1954—
      Trees call for what they need / by Melissa Kwasny—1st ed.
            p.   cm.
      ISBN 0-933216-97-1 (cloth)
      ISBN 0-933216-96-3 (pbk.)
      I. Title.
PS3561.W447T7   1993   93-26213
      813'.54—dc20   CIP

For my parents and grandparents

*I would like to thank Deloris Niendorf for her generous help
with my research on the folklore of rural healing;
Sherry Thomas, my former editor at Spinsters,
for her belief in this book;
Margaret Hunter and Anne Appleby
for their kind attention to it;
and most of all, my grandmother,
Lena Ohime, for her stories and her love.*

Chapter One

My name is Nettie and last night, I dreamt I was a tree, a funny dream where my roots grew heavy as Ma did when she'd fall asleep in her chair and I'd try to lift her up. Old roots, you can't dig 'em out, hardwood—oak or maple. They just sink like I did in this dream, lower and lower into the ground until all that's left to see are the branches. And what branches! Preachers and unionizers, waitresses aplenty, but not a single farmer left in the lot.

And where would this tree be growing? In America, of course. Same place my ma and pa are from. My grandkids poke fun at me. Before that, they want to know, expecting some fancy island or France. No, I can't tell 'em that. Seems like my folks have been here forever.

I don't blame 'em for wanting to know. If you want to call on your ancestors, it only makes sense that you call on the land they lived on. America. It always had a past look to it, by which I mean darkened, smoky, with a low wind stirring leaves and dust and all kinds of webs and pollens through the air. The New World? It never seemed new to me, no matter the season, as if it was thick with ghosts, which is what Aunt Till says it is. And she oughta know. She makes a living talking to 'em.

The Big Lakes ain't too far. Pa used to say sixty miles, but I never wanted to see 'em. Too big for me, I always said, if they're big enough to bring the weather. Which they do. Armloads of snow and wind, full to overflowing and set it down in one motion and everything stops: school and grazing and sometimes just getting out the back door. I get dizzy thinking about them lakes. I never did like the water.

Indiana was where I was born and where my husband was born and our families before that. Land of Indians. We never saw any, but it was a used land I was born into. Potowatami. Menominee. Now, don't ask me to pronounce 'em. Aunt Till says it was a cradle of civilization. I don't know about that, but in October, when the fields are dusty and the little sour McIntosh start smelling like vinegar, the skies fill with the smoke from some long-ago fire, and in the red and black forests, the rock piles someone used to mark his land—how far back, who can say—shift a little.

Hot nights with mosquitoes and lightning bugs and the smell of the fields drifting in. Big nights that grew from a circle of porch light out, the night traveling fast over the flat black soil. It used to be so rich you wanted to eat it, to crumble it like flour and butter in your hands. That was when there was still animals to come out and circle the red barns: raccoons, possum, squirrels and fox, bats flying right in the open windows. And in the winters, the huge storms that would call everything off. And in March, the furrows loosening and mud and lilacs fill the air. That is my life. That is where I'm from, same as my mother.

Don't think she didn't have her hands full, raising them fourteen children. There, that's her. That's my ma, next to Helen. You think she's fat? Well, she was fat. She was almost three hundred pounds and when she sat in a chair and leaned over, her belly would touch the floor. She ate like a bird. That weight you put on with every baby? You know, she just kept it. She weighed only ninety-four pounds when she was married. Just like I did. You don't believe me? I can see it plain as day, how my husband put his arms around me like this, from behind, and lifted me up.

I was a sickly fart when I was a kid, homeliest one of the

bunch. Stringy blond hair, always in my eyes. I haven't changed much. I was skinny. Skinny as a bean pole. Though I don't know why. We was poor, but we never lacked for food, being farmers of a sort. We had our chickens and cows, right in town. Pa worked at the lumberyard for thirty years, shoveling coal. He came with your coal in a wagon, stuck a pipe in your cellar window and shoveled it in. He made twenty dollars a week. He was always tired. And he never could remember our names. "Now, Lizzy," I'll never forget him saying that day. We was on our wide porch that faced the corn fields.

"Nettie," I said, correcting him.

"Alright, Nettie, then," he sighed, as if indulging me by calling me by my right name. "Suppose those strawberries is done in the garden?" He smiled, wide as he did in those days.

"No, Pa. Suppose there's a few left."

"Why don't you run out back and pick us a bowlful? And pour me a cup of coffee on your way back."

We was poor, but we was never hungry, even with Ma setting a table for fifteen or twenty. What with her relatives sitting on the sideboard, she'd go through two twenty-five-pound bags of flour in a weekend's baking. Still, we never picked berries for nothing and Pa couldn't afford to miss work. I picked that fruit so fast I smashed it, grabbed the sugar bowl—I didn't even remember doing it. When I met him on the porch, my eyes was wide with worry.

"Never mind about school today, Nettie," he said when he saw me glancing at the sun. I was fifteen and almost always late for school 'cause of something.

"You lose your job?" I asked.

He hadn't touched the strawberries. They settled under the spoonfuls of sugar and it seemed like a long time before the grains melted into the red. Clear and red like rubies, like my ma's name. I stared at 'em, thinking why on earth they named my ma Ruby, her so plain and all.

"You've probably noticed your ma's not well," he said.

"No, sir, I have noticed nothing of the kind," I said. I regarded him, suspicious. He never did like me going to school, what with all Ma's baking and cooking and all that wash. Ma not well? She wasn't gonna win no race, but who could after all them kids? True, she hadn't left the house since the last two, but that was because she was too big. She could barely make it to the garden and it had been a long time since her feet had felt a pair of shoes. Fifteen pounds with every kid, she told me. That would make one hundred eighty pounds since she was eighteen. I figured it once in arithmetic class when I was supposed to be fig-uring something else. I saw the picture, the one of her wedding day, when her stomach was flat under the button-down jacket, the picture of her like all the pictures of our family. Like we're scared. Like we never smile.

"She's sick, Nettie. Real sick. She asked me to talk to you."

"You're a damn liar," I said before I could hold my tongue. He didn't miss a second in backhanding me. I was tasting blood inside my mouth and I was holding my jaw.

"You listen to me before you talk back like that, sister," he said.

None of us hardly talked back to Pa and we was sorry when we did. He was a quiet man, a tired man, who never much war-ranted it, but there was something about the way he would ask me to do something in his quiet-as-steel way. As if it was a jail sen-tence. Even if you was willing, you felt something rise up in you against it. At least, I did. And I was always sorry.

I was only six months to graduating the ninth grade. I was gonna go to business college. I was gonna learn to do books and take shorthand. Maybe get a job in the bicycle factory down the street or maybe the five and dime. I was homely, it is true, but I was the smartest one of the bunch. I was gonna get my own place someday and have no kids. Maybe one. Have my own money to spend as I liked. I wasn't gonna get stuck like my ma. She didn't ever have no berries in the morning, I can tell ya that. She gave 'em away. To people younger, older, better, worse. Your life, don't they always say, is all you got. Seems like when you're a woman, you got to give that life away.

"What about Fred?" I asked, knowing it wouldn't do no good. "He's older than me. He's had more schooling."

Pa just looked at me. Him and me both knew boys didn't stay home and take care of the sick ones. "Can't I wait six months?" I said, waiting on that porch while Pa stared a hole into the bright red bowl of her namesake-colored berries, straight through the glistening sugar, him pitiful and bent and dusted with coal like he'd been grappling with the night and night had won. I knew I wasn't ever gonna do any of that other stuff I imagined. I was gonna quit school and take care of Ma.

"Nettie, you're too easy," people have always told me. As if I have ever had a choice about what I've had to do.

Each season has its sicknesses and we never had a name for most of 'em. What good's to name 'em if you know what to cure: fever, coughing, cloudy eyes, or blood. Simple. Your head aches? You soak your feet. They got names for all of 'em somewhere. Just like they got names for us. First names, last names, maiden names and married names, all registered in the courthouse. Marie says with women always losing and gaining names, it's a wonder God can remember what to call us. Marie's a bit harsh but I see what she means. I've been coming to think that naming is akin to owning something. When folks own something, they got a right to ruin it.

The land, for instance. My family's never owned a scrap of it and we have forever loved it. Them Rip van Winkle woods on the edge of our town? We've lost years in 'em, just like he did. And not just gathering wood or the spring mushrooms we cook with our new peas, though the rich who own it call us trespassers. All us kids, we learned blue was something you climbed to through trees. Or what flickered between the spreading green Ma put all her babies under to quiet 'em. Aunt Till says it's 'cause we used to live in trees that we feel so at home under 'em. I don't know about that. Preacher Warren has emphatically told me we did not.

It was in the forest that I first met Aunt Till. I was out there digging roots when she snuck up behind me. "They say Columbus knew he was nearing land because of the strong smell of sassafras," she said.

"Christ Almighty!" I shouted, dropping my shovel. "You 'bout scared the shit outa me!" I'd been hiking for hours, hunting the perfect bush between the new willows and birch, skirting the poison ivy. Which I had been in the habit of doing those years of taking over for Ma. Late afternoons when the sun hit her chair, she'd sleep and I'd be gone. "How'd you sneak up on me like that? Damn!" Since I learned to talk, I could cuss to beat the band.

She smiled. She was thin like a child but had the bearing and dark clothes of someone growing up fast. Too straight. Too serious. Her pale eyes serious, too, even while she smiled. "Making tea?" she asked.

I looked at her new laced boots. She wasn't dressed for digging. Still, if she wanted a share, she had better think twice and find her own tree. I started cutting careful at the edges to catch the young roots. "What are you doing here?" I demanded.

She was making me feel spooked, smiling and quiet like that. Though there was something that made me start feeling kinda sorry for her, her not much older than me and seeming so alone.

Thin. Like maybe she didn't have no family. "Ma calls it a spring tonic," I said, softening.

"Mmmm," she nodded.

"After a winter of fat and flour, it'll thin our blood so we can get up and dance again," I quoted. I struck a root with the blade of the shovel and the muddy, sharp smell of sassafras rose to greet us.

"You must really love your ma," she said, so low it seemed like the spring evening had come low to hear her, crowding out the day and growing dark roots of its own. I was glad it was getting dim 'cause that overpowering sassafras was bringing tears to my eyes.

I kept digging, Till just a-watching as if to make sure it was done proper, like we was in church almost, those roots like nothing you know above on earth, ragged with the spring and sorrowful of the winter, me needing her there to make sure, her, who I ain't never seen before, who snuck up behind me with boots on, even through all of them crunching maple leaves. By the time I dug all I needed, I was sobbing. If Till noticed, she didn't say nothing.

We could barely see ourselves inside them woods. Blue showing, hip-length, through the trunks to the outside. "You know of anything to make my ma well?" I whispered. Until today, I can't say why I thought to ask her that. It was long before I knew Till was a Spiritualist, long before Till knew it herself. But something was telling me that here was the smartest person I, in my life, was gonna meet.

Till closed her eyes. She didn't seem at all surprised I asked her. She stayed with her eyes closed, swaying a bit as the night moved in, blurring her long wool coat with the oaks. I was beginning to think about other things, like what Pa was gonna say when he got home to no dinner. I'm glad those somethings that always tell me what to do was telling 'cause I waited and, in a few minutes, she opened her eyes.

"Your ma's just tired," Till said. "She wants to die. Why don't you let her?"

I turned and walked back toward town. Till didn't follow and I wasn't to see her for many a long, hard day.

Ma died that summer in the high of Indiana heat, when the sky hangs wet and heavy like a rag on your neck, mid-sweetcorn and before the canning, so worn out she could barely swat the mosquitoes off her face and that year they was fierce. I let a lot go with her. Her appetite lagged and so did my washing. She gave up her legs and I gave up lifting her out of that chair and let her sleep there. It took three of us to put her onto the pot. Sometimes the boys was the only ones around to ask for help. I watched all the trying go out of her face, me lifting her dress and the boys staring straight out the window, none of us talking, them leaving the room 'til I called 'em back. Some days she'd spoil herself and it'd take half the afternoon for me to get over cleaning her up. Not the job, mind you, but that face of hers, tight-lipped and angry as hell, not at me, but at life for not letting her go easy, for making her pay for it like that.

Lord knows what those kids ate, or Pa. At first he'd try hollering at me, but soon even he gave up, seeing her in that chair, angry as hell for living. Guess it took all the kick out of him. I'd watch him boiling corn or eggs like the rest of 'em did for supper. Not your fault, I wished I woulda told him. Some place inside of him, some place deep and empty as a silo in April, he felt he was to blame. Birthing them kids takes a toll on the body and the toll-taking never stops. Finding shoes for school or even beds for us all. Getting Aunt Lou to come and stay a week, making over our clothes for the young ones. The constant fight with the salesman from Cleveland who came with the raisins and coffee, soup beans and rice. I remember when she started showing with my baby brother, Tom. Aunt Minn brought us some brand-new rag rugs. Beautiful rugs with all the colors you can name. And Ma wouldn't take 'em. "If I had rugs down, I'd just hafta pick 'em up and shake 'em," she said. With every kid, my pa's face'd be thinner and he'd talk to us less. And those fifteen pounds I told you about? They was fifteen pounds of heartache, too. Mary and Lydia, Heine—all gone before they was full grown. Pneumonia. Consumption. And the war. Sweet and long-suffering, people always said of my ma. A bad heart, the doctor said, is what finally done her in. Not a bad one, I argued. A tired one.

I could tell you how I found her, and about the funeral, how beautiful she looked. And you'd probably believe me 'cause it's what folks want to hear. People find their dead now, like it's something that happens when you ain't looking. Most dies alone nowadays. Most, only the nurses find 'em. But in those days, people was there. When my ma died, she died at home.

Her breath slowed, pushing out through her lips like the waves that hit the pier at Clear Lake, lapping back not of their own accord, and she started swelling. Dying is physical. Don't let nobody tell ya different. No one lifts up and there ain't no sound of angels. Dying is physical as speech. You can close your ears to it, but it gets inside you anyhow. The moaning of the body, not the soul, is a strange thing, deeper, lower, like mountains turning or trees uprooting. The body giving way, letting loose, makes noises, sadder in a way than a pain you can do something for. Bigger. Death is physical as speech and dangerous as birthing and us women, it seems, gotta be midwives to both.

"Lizzy," I said, "call up and ask one of them boys to spell us."

We'd both been up all night, one on each side of the bed, mopping Ma's brow with a wet rag.

"You go on to bed, Nettie. I can stay here by myself," she said.

"Where's Pa? Still on the porch smoking? And if he's sleeping, I'll have 'em wake him up," I shouted.

"Shhh. You're gonna wake *her* up," Lizzy said.

"She ain't sleeping. She hasn't slept for two days. Look at them eyes wide open."

"She can hear you, Nettie. Hush." Lizzy was sweet, like my ma, and looked at me the way Ma used to, like I was gonna be one more thing to take care of. "I can handle it myself," Lizzy said. "You go to bed."

Everybody in the house was staying away from that room. Nobody had to try to keep the little ones away. It was just me and Lizzy and sometimes Pa, who'd look in and try to say something to her and get hurt when she couldn't hear him or understand. He'd hurry out of there, stammering something about did we want him to put the kids to bed or start a fire in the cookstove or go to the store we was out of sugar. "Yes, Pa," Lizzy would say, "I think that's a real good idea."

"Lizzy, we've been up for two nights," I pleaded. "We won't leave her alone. We'll get Fred to sit with her."

"Nettie," Lizzy said, snapping the rag on the bedstand, "some people can't take it, don't you know?"

"Nobody's born able to take dying more'n another," I snapped back, but I didn't leave neither. "I have never understood taking or not taking," I mumbled. Let me tell you. My ma's hands was cold as catfish and she would not let me hold 'em.

"Is it 6:30 yet?" Ma'd ask in her delirium. "Is it raining?" Dying is not like falling asleep. Her heart was climbing stairs, her eyes was wide open and seeing. Seeing what, I don't know. Not what we was seeing. What did she hear? Rain? Birds? Or was it noisy as a wasp nest inside her head? What did she smell? Surely not what we did. The whole house—why didn't somebody tell me? I'll tell you. Death announces itself with that smell. It lodges back in your teeth and you can taste it for weeks after, when you breathe out hard or bend over. And let me tell you something else. You keep smelling it, a smell so thick it stops the currents, like somebody closed all the windows and doors.

"Open them windows, hon," my ma said. "Please. Let me get some air."

She had gray eyes. To the end, she was using 'em to look for me. She wanted the boys, to be sure. Asked about 'em. Scared for 'em. But when she was scared herself, she asked for me: Nettie-No-Feeling, Nettie-Can-Take-It. Nettie who was wiping her head with rags I kept in the ice chest. "Oh, that feels good, Nettie," she'd say and go back to her work.

I was only seventeen and I knew nothing to comfort the dying. I remember thinking there must be some leaf to soak or burn. There must be some color. Or music. Yes, music. Why'd I never think to sing something or wheel in that piano? They woulda all thought I was crazier than a hoot owl, but so what? I wished I woulda played something, one of those songs she used to hum. "In the Garden" or "The Old Rugged Cross." In fact, I wished I woulda hired the whole goddamned church choir if I coulda afforded it. And if I woulda thought of it. I was only seventeen then and I didn't know anything. I remember thinking there must be people somewhere who did.

They say each person carries their death with 'em through life, that death is hiding inside you like the pit of a peach, your face bruising and looking less peachy by the minute, even plumping up a bit before the pit starts pushing through. Pretty soon all we're seeing is that pit. All else falls by the wayside, the skin getting that soft gray fur, 'til that's all we're left with, the shock of that pit, bigger and rougher than we expected. Each death is different, they say. Some say you go out of this world like you came in. Hard to be born, hard to die. I never asked Aunt Till if that's true, but I will.

She quit eating. She quit peeing.

In no way could I have prepared, though I watched for the last breath, watched for something out of the ordinary. What did we know that was ordinary? Let me tell you. Blood came out of her mouth the color of tea and we cleaned it up like it was soup, we who gave up on healing and cut the rise and fall of our breaths to match hers. Crying seemed normal, sleep not, and staying alive was so important a job that when Pa came in, praying aloud how he wished she'd let go, we wanted to slap him for denying all the work we three was doing just to still be there.

Her hands were on fire and she would not let us hold 'em. Her hands was flying at her night clothes 'til we finally let her be, naked to the world but for her sheets. I'm telling you my ma died naked in the parlor where we laid out all our dead and dying, with me and Lizzy there on either side, 'bout scared to death she was gonna take us with her. I can't tell you the exact moment it happened 'cause it wasn't a moment, it was days for us. That is not exactly true. I can't tell you 'cause when her heart split in two, her body clenching and raising like a fist, one half got stuck in me and the other half, it stuck in Lizzy. Plugged up a part of us that'll never talk again.

Once she was dead, she didn't smell like death no more. The undertakers came. We gave 'em her Sunday dress, her panties and her rouge. Lizzy gave 'em some perfume and Pa, he gave her his wedding ring. I thought twice about the brassiere, but she never wore one in life, and I wouldn't give 'em her shoes neither. Lord, let somebody I love do this for me: Keep my shoes and my brassiere out of the hands of the undertaker!

When they brought her back, we took turns sitting with her in that parlor, shades drawn to keep out the heat. For four days and nights we waited for the relatives to make the trip. Now that she was dead, the boys and Pa would get near. Neighbors and friends came in, bringing casseroles and cakes. Neighbor Bill, he brung a whole turkey. I hardly noticed. I didn't want to talk to nobody and I didn't want them asking their stupid questions neither like how old was she and how much did she weigh. "She was my ma!" I'd shout. "What does that matter?"

Ma was buried in Wanatah Cemetery, 1926, Town of Pines, Indiana, County of LaCroix. I used to think LaCroix was some dead war hero or one of them Lutheran preachers who used to preach in that park across from Clear Lake. They was always naming streets and parks after them. It was Aunt Till who told me LaCroix wasn't German but French. Aunt Till explained it this way to me: She said LaCroix means the French found their way through here, through the thick cover of oak and chestnut, maple and pine that once stretched halfway across this nation. Half of that cover was cut down before we was born, Aunt Till said. I wished I coulda seen a sight like that, millions of trees older than Jesus. Or at least older than Luther. The Crossing, she said LaCroix meant. The whole county's full of names like this, telling you history, and what I call the memory names, those that stir you to think of what it must've been like: Trail Creek, Black Oak, Cedar Lake, Rolling Prairie, a hundred places with the word "Buffalo" in their names. Those are the names I like best. When I was a kid, we used to go visiting some of those places on Sunday and I'd think about it.

Town of Pines. They ring the five Small Lakes and there's a big grove of 'em left near the cemetery. And each of us has got at least one in our yard. We can't complain, since where the rest of 'em stood has all been cleared for farmland. And ya gotta eat, my ma always said. If there's truth to anything, it's that. All things gotta eat. I had a dream the night my ma died and I was just remembering it. I was taking her on one of those Sunday rides in the wagon. We got where we was going alright, but we realized that where we was going was right back to our hometown. Only it had changed since we started out. There was no trees anymore, none, let alone pine trees, just row after row of clapboard houses. Ma started to cry. "Why'd you bring me here?" she asked, falling to her knees. As if I'd tricked her, as if she knew I'd brought her there to die. I ran to get help, but nobody was home, not a soul in any one of them houses. And nailed to each door was a see-through wrapper, stuffed with pine needles like they was specimens or souvenirs.

It was at my ma's funeral that it was decided that I was to become a working girl at last.

We was all of us standing by the new grave, the little ones sniffling, the rest of us sad and gray as that plot of ground in Wanatah, what they called the farmers' plots. Used to be nobody could afford stones in them plots. And since the church hadn't commenced to keeping written records, we all depended on Mr. Kaminski, the old Pole who cleaned the grounds, and who kept in his memory who and where every one of ours was buried. He would walk up and down the rows, pointing and reciting the names of the deceased and never missing a one. When Mr. Kaminski himself died, a lot of the history of us poor people was lost with him.

I stood that day listening to the church ringing the funeral bell, that bell which cost us a dollar to be rung since we wasn't paying church members. It let people know the burial was over and they could quit coming to our house and bringing their pies.

Pa stood beside me. "These kids are getting big and I'm getting old," he was saying, "getting slow."

I nodded, thinking about the roses I was gonna dig up and plant where Ma's stone woulda been.

"Lumberyard says I probably won't get any faster. It's true they could get somebody a lot stronger, somebody young."

Something in the way he was talking to me caught my attention. He was talking to me for the first time businesslike, like he used to talk to Heine late at night, before Heine was killed in the war. "What they want from you?" I said.

"Say they'll agree to keep me on if I take a cut in pay. Things ain't going so well for 'em down there." I stared at him. The coal had done nothing to help my pa's breathing or his back. His face had thinned out and, with a pain in my gut, I knew I had been no help to that.

"How much?" I asked.

"Four dollars."

"A month?"

"A week."

I gasped. Everybody knew a carload of trees was arriving at Monroe Lumberyard every day, not to mention the coal from Pennsylvania, which came, some weeks, escorted by the police. Pa said it was 'cause the miners was on strike there and didn't want it delivered. Those weeks, Mr. Monroe, who didn't live in Town of Pines but in Chicago, didn't come to check on things. He sent his special police. My pa knew this, too, so I bit my tongue.

"Nettie, I been thinking," he said. "Lizzy's getting old enough now. She could be helping more around the house."

"You figure she could do ya better, huh?" I sighed.

"Fella I work with said they need help in the kitchen at the Roxy Hotel."

I stared at him blankly.

"I'm asking ya, Nettie. We can use the pay."

"Me? A cook?" I said, thinking of them boiled eggs, my lumpy gravy. I nodded. "Sure, Pa, I'll try. I'll try first thing in the morning." I tried smiling, looking for his eyes, but Pa was already frowning and motioning the others toward home. I let 'em go, Pa herding 'em like he was a sheep dog, sidestepping 'em into line, growling a bit. I stood there with my eyes wide open, alone as if I was waiting for the world. Death opens your eyes like that, like your whole being won't scab over, makes you see dying in everything, wondering how this one will go, how you'll turn this one over. Wondering whether you could take it better if you was before this one or if you'd want 'em to be with you when it's time for you to go.

"I heard the bells. Thought it might be your mother." And there was Till again, standing beside me, familiar, part of the time, though I hadn't seen her in Town of Pines since the spring. Same serious. Same proud, making me think of a bookshelf. Straight, proud, full of ideas.

"Where ya been?" I said. "I ain't seen you since the sassafras." I dropped my eyes to the piled-up mound of rocks and dirt at my feet. Pretty soon the afternoon storms would beat it back down to level and those stones would sink, leaving the grave pock-marked. "Sassafras didn't help, ya see." I laughed, kind of. "Where ya been?" I repeated.

She didn't seem like a young girl no more. I didn't seem like one neither. "I've been studying. Going to school in Chicago," she said. "I'm studying to be a preacher."

"Women ain't preachers."

"These people say I can be. Say I was called to it."

"Yeah? I never heard of it."

"Well, it's true." She was dressed even nicer than before, not rich but careful.

"Who are these people? What church?"

"No church, really. They're called Spiritualists."

"Those the folks who make the tables lift up?"

"Depends on what you believe. Mostly, it's a belief. Like believing in spirits. We believe that there's spirits everywhere, in everything." She stopped, frowned, then corrected herself. "Intelligence in everything."

I glanced at her crossways. She looked like a preacher, though I never saw a woman preacher before. Sing hymns, scold the little ones 'bout going to hell, that's what women did. Pa always said the grace, and Ma? All Ma taught us to do was pray the lightning wouldn't hit us, that Heine'd come home from the war, that it wouldn't frost before the corn was ready. Till, however, with her eyes the color of water, her clothes all tucked in, her shoes clean, she looked the part. Me with my wrinkles and my dirt, I could never be comfortable telling people how to do nothing.

"What else you believe?" I asked.

"That death is not the end of life, but merely a change in condition."

She just said it, flat out like that. "You mean my ma ain't dead? I seen it happen. My ma's in heaven if there was ever any such thing. Heaven with the music. Heaven with the angels waiting on her and she's walking again. And there's gladiolus there, white and lavender and pink and red, a whole gladiolus farm like Uncle Fritz used to have. And there's new soup pots without that burnt-on black, there's enough sugar and..." I was crying. "It sure as hell is a change in condition."

She said, in a voice that was like an arm around me, "We believe death is the door to the spirit world. Your mother's not gone. She will always be with you."

I stared at her. "Prove it."

Till was not at all stopped by my rudeness. "When you need her, just ask," she said gently. "You'll see."

"I need her now. My pa's got me indentured to that house, and now he wants me out working besides. And as kitchen help no less." But as I stood there feeling sorry for myself, damn if the whole picture didn't spread out before my eyes, like after a storm when the sky lifts and you can see Grady's farm on one end and the depot on the other. No more trips to the wash house. No more yelling at kids 'til my face turns blue. Money in my pockets and a real hotel. "Hell if I can't cook!" I shouted, then saw that Till had left my side and was already almost out of the graveyard.

"Where are you traipsing off to like a damn ghost again?" I called.

Till laughed, first time I'd seen it. "I'll be back. I'm going to open my own church soon. You'll see. Maybe you'll be one of my first members."

"I sure will. You just let me know."

I stayed up all that night, pressing my good dress, looking into the mirror. I was going out into the world! The mirror wasn't encouraging. Mousy, they called hair like mine then, which when you think of mouse hair, is fine, so fine a pin slides through it and the drab color of the dust I wipe off the sills in the spring. Cow eyes, people say I got. Moony, others tell me. Shit-colored eyes, I used to think when I'd wish for Lizzy's blue ones.

The longer I stayed awake, the more I wished I woulda paid attention when Ma was cooking and baking. In those days, nobody wrote anything down. Writing down cooking would be like writing down praying or planting. Each time you got different ingredients to work with, what with the weather changing and the moon growing and fading through the signs. I sat down at the oil-cloth-covered table, the one I had put more than my share of hot pans on, my fingers rubbing at the charred rings. If I could just remember one recipe, how to bake one thing. A coffee cake or biscuits. Can't fry a chicken in the morning. I wondered if I was supposed to bring my own pans. Crazy idea, but I was thinking if I showed up with a few pans like Fred did with his own hammer, I'd be one step ahead of the others. I was soon on my hands and knees, pulling out bread pans, soup pots, roasters and canners, casseroles, frying pans, sauce pans, angel food cake pans, making a racket that would wake the...there! My hands was trembling. Between the cookie cutouts and the cookie sheets, in the first loaf pan of the stack of Christmas pans, was a slip of lined paper, transparent with lard, and in my ma's own hand was written this note:

poor man's cake

Boil together 15 minutes and set aside 'til real cold
2 cups white sugar
4 cups water
1/2 pound raisins
1 cup lard

Then add
2 teaspoon baking powder
2 teaspoon cinnamon
1 teaspoon salt
1 teaspoon cloves
1 teaspoon nutmeg
5 cups flour. About level.

Beat hard. Put into loaf pans. Makes 4.

I woulda made it that night, but we was out of raisins. I copied it down and slipped it into my coat pocket. 'Cause the next morning, I was gonna get to the hotel before breakfast. And right off, I was gonna make 'em a cake.

Chapter Two

The boy with the hole is what her sisters and brothers used to call her in Poland and I can see why. The way she sits atop the roof of that bar, nailing just like a man. Brave as a man, that's my friend Marie, though I seem to be the only one around here who thinks that's flattering. People talk, that's true. About the way she fixes things, bricked her garage even, and the way she can hold her liquor no matter how many shots those men try to buy for her. I'll tell ya, it has caused no end of embarrassment for poor Stanley, her husband. "She walks all over Stanley," people say, meaning he listened to her, meaning she danced with whomever she felt like, even going out with other men to dinner and parties when Stanley fell ill. "She's loose," people say.

I don't think she's loose, though I don't know why I say that. My ma never so much as visited the neighbors but her husband was along. Marie being from a different country and all, maybe that was it. People say they never saw a woman so damn independent. And they always include the damn. I could tell she loved him. She even told me so and how her eyes light up when she tells how she met him in Chicago. He had "money in his pockets." He'd shown her. He could "already speak English good." Marie's just got foreign ways. She always did exactly what she wanted to do.

I met Marie soon after she came to America, way before Stanley and her opened their bar down the road, way before she even met Stanley. She said she was born in Poland, only the good Lord knows where. She never seen a map 'til I brought one out one night and those pools of blue and gold and brown told her nothing of how she got from there to here. No map designed could show that, I bet. She doesn't know how old she is either, 'cause in Poland, there's no birthday presents, no birthday party, no nothing. Least that's what she told me. No birthday. I always felt sorry for Marie for that and the first thing I did for her was pick a day, April 14, and every year since then I have baked her an angel food cake.

Marie has told me so many stories that I don't have to make up nothing to prove she is brave. She came all the way across that ocean by herself. That is something I can't fathom, me who gets dizzy near a well. She told me her folks had chickens like us and sometimes a cow. When she was growing up, soldiers came through and the girls would hide the cow and her mother would hide the girls. They didn't know what war was being fought half the time. Soldiers just always came through. I wondered if my brother Heine, who got himself killed in the war, was one of 'em.

Marie said her father was a soldier, though she wasn't sure what country he fought for or even if he got paid. All she is sure of is that they was poor all the time and she had to eat grass. And since she was a child, she'd been told stories of how in America the fences was made of smoked sausage.

Why Marie ended up in Town of Pines is a long story with a lot of little ones in between. I am still convinced she hasn't told me them all. I do know she got a job straight off at the Roxy Hotel, scrubbing dishes in the kitchen. I know, 'cause despite all my fancy ideas about baking cakes and being a chef, from the very first day they hired me, I was scrubbing pots and pans. I remember the morning they brought Marie in. I'd been there only a few months and it scared the daylights outa me thinking they'd gotten her to replace me. Marie looked some scared herself as the cook pointed out the sinks, the stoves, and then me. "Nettie," he said, "this here's Marie."

He had his arm around Marie's shoulder. Her eyes were squirming though her body didn't dare. She was almost as tall as he was, skinny but big-boned, not like me. She had the kind of build ready to fill out like a kid that's gonna grow up to be a boxer. Her dress was worn. She looked like she needed a job. Maybe more than me, I thought as I watched his hand crawling down her sleeve.

"Don't look so sorry-eyed," the cook said to me, lifting my chin with his hand. "Marie ain't here to take your job. She's indentured to us. She'll be working it off forever." With that, he smacked her on the behind. "She can hardly speak English, so just show her how to scrape that pile of dishes. And keep her busy cleaning when she's done with that."

He was an overseer if you ever saw one, red-faced from the stove, the kind of face that seems like it's just ready to boil over. About fifty, he was. He wore his apron folded down around his hips, making his gut puff out like a goiter. I spent day after day in that steamy kitchen with the man, seven to seven with a half hour for dinner, and he never once said a kind word to me. But his hands! The cook had hands there was no place in that hotel kitchen to hide from, hands hiding in corners, under tables. Hands talking, if he didn't, saying shameful things. Married hands, 'cause he didn't go to no trouble to hide the ring.

Folks ain't all bad, I know, ain't one-sided. But you got to understand, in those days, your family was who you associated with, and when you went out into the world? Men, ready to bring even the best of us down. In those situations where you gotta be where you are 'cause of money and they know it, and you're a woman with no husband and they know it, well, it just seems to bring out the one-sided in 'em.

Not that we woulda had a chance to be friends. Nobody

talked when they was working there. Nobody dared. If you wasn't quiet, you wasn't working, they figured, which is the first I learned of that idea. Way I was raised, people sang when they worked, talked about things that never come to a mind when the body's still: tall tales, religion, superstition. Stuff you don't have time for when you're not working, like how eating raisins will cure the boils or how, on the first of May, you can rub your freckles right off your face with the dew.

So, Marie, she came to work with me and it wasn't but six hours after she got there that I caught her scraping the food off the dirty plates, half into her pockets and half into her mouth. She was standing back by the garbage cans where she thought I couldn't see. "You act like you're plumb starved," I said. See, we got our dinner free, part of the job. And I'd seen her finish off a whole plateful, piled this high, not two hours beforehand. "Didn't you ever eat in that country of yours?" I said.

Marie squared off as if I'd come to steal her bone. "We ate grass," she hissed, the meat still in her fingers. I figured if the cook woulda come around the corner, she wouldn't have blinked, just stood like that, staring at me, defiant, sopping up the gravy with the bread, the potatoes, the fat and gristle, everything stuffed into those pockets like they must've been lined with wax paper. "Don't worry. I ain't gonna tell," I smiled.

In the weeks that followed, she never slowed up, but one thing I noticed. She never touched the sweets. She'd pick the meat out of the stew with her bare hands when the cook wasn't looking, but those delicious pies and coffee cakes, light as heaven, my downfall, were like poison to her.

Like I said before, the way I was raised, friends was either neighbors or kin. Still, something about working together twelve hours a day, every day, and it wasn't long before I started feeling like I'd known Marie forever. What she'd do! How she'd make me laugh! Getting chewed out was a hell of a lot easier when you knew you had somebody backing you up with a wink. Though we couldn't talk while we were working, we got good at making faces and Marie was so good at imitating, she'd act the cook to the cook and he wouldn't even notice. I thought it was funny between us at first. Something to pass the time. For Marie, though, it was more than fun. It was revenge. She hated him. She hated his roving hands. "I no relation here," she kept repeating to me like there was something about this that I didn't yet understand. Marie'd stick slivers in the bread while it was rising, mop the floor right where he'd have to be working. Once I seen her empty half a dustpan into the soup, trying to get him fired. Marie is brave, like I told ya, and spiteful, and unforgiving as a bull.

'Cause she owed three hundred dollars for her passage to the owner, she stayed at the hotel. But part of her wages went for rent, and rent in hotels doesn't come cheap. Which meant, after paying her rent and meals, Marie didn't have a pot to piss in. And the money she owed for the boat ride? It wasn't dwindling none too fast. This made Marie wild. Money was a kind of shining light to her, even then. A couple of weeks after I met her, I started saving my dinner and slipping it to her while she ate in the back. I needed to do it only twice. "How much I owe you for this?" she asked. I explained how I hadn't been feeling hungry but she sneered at me, unbelieving. "I never been sick. I never been accident. I never been scared. 'Cause I no owe nobody nothing. I do nothing to nobody. Especially, I no take nobody's food."

Marie didn't get off work after the hotel guests ate supper like I did. She had a broom or rag or bucket in her hand from the time she got up 'til bedtime. I got the idea to ask for extra hours so I could spend time with her after the cook went home. Pa had no trouble with that. Extra hours was extra pay. He'd come and walk me home or send one of the boys. And me? I loved it.

'Cause Marie had stories. I ran out of my life in two weeks of telling and I even told my secrets like how it was really me, not Tom, who broke the jar of grape juice that ruined the dress I hated to wear. I even made some stuff up, like how I'd wanted to marry my brother Heine, only he got killed in the war. They never sent his body back, so I still might, I told her. He wasn't in small pieces they couldn't pick up. He was earning money to come back from Europe like she did.

One night, we were mopping up the dining room after a big to-do and all the help but me and Marie had gone home. Marie was hauling hot water in buckets, two at a time. She is the strongest woman I ever met with shoulders wide as a yardstick. She had her long wool skirt hitched above her knees and the men's workboots she was always wearing then. No hips, flat as the fields, from front to back, you could hardly tell what sex Marie was. She never wore make-up, but in those days neither did I. The only thing like a woman's was her hair, thick and gold, the color of old pennies, in two braids down to the middle of her back. She wove thin strips of red wool into them.

We was all alone and cleaning hard when, out of the blue, Marie stopped mopping and said to me, "I know how to stop the babies from coming."

Her English was never something to rely on, though who am I to talk? I can hardly speak my own language. Still, I never could be sure when Marie started talking if it was gonna be a real person she was mentioning or one of her characters from the stories she said her ma told her: the man who played the fiddle on the moon, the invisible ones who carried the wind. "What babies?" I asked.

Marie lowered her voice and glanced around though no one coulda been hiding in there. We'd moved all the tables and chairs to the wall ourselves. "Back home, my brother stealed book."

"What book?" I liked that she trusted me. That we were having a conspiracy. I quit mopping, too.

"The book from doctor office. My brother to our village take it. All read. Big secret we learn." Marie took the washrag from her belt and held it out in front of her. "Every time, you make the man give it to you here." She squeezed the cloth together in her palm quick, like she'd caught something. "You grab it like this and no babies coming."

By the time I figured out what she was saying, I was too shocked to do much but mutter, "This is what you talk about in your country?"

Marie frowned. "I tell you secret. Is true. From book, we read it. Save you from houseful of babies making. Like your ma."

I grabbed a chair and sat down. We'd been working since seven and here it was, almost midnight. "Marie, didn't ya ever wish you had a sweetheart? Don't ya ever think about having a baby?"

Her face darkened and her shoulders spread wide as a night hawk's wings. "If I ever have man, he better never fool with me," she said, "or he end up just like the other."

"What happened to the other?" I gasped. "Who was it? Did you kill him?"

"This close," she said, dipping her finger in the mop water and marking on the dirty floor. "I am good horseman as girl, ride for miles across fields with no one around. Then, one day, strange boy comes riding. I ride fast but his horse better. Fancy horse, maybe he race it. Oh, I am so scary. No one for miles to hearing. I think, what he want from me? When he catch up, he reach to me like this, pull me off horse to ground. Then, out of my boot, my knife I take it."

"You carried a knife in your boot?" I asked, wide-eyed. "You knifed him?"

Marie drew a long, thin knife from a sleeve inside her boot.

"Oh, his family they come to my family seeing, want me to sorry making. I visit him in hospital in town. Have to ride same horse."

"Did you apologize?"

"Never!" Marie's eyes narrowed, flashing like the glint of her knife in the dark room. "No, the boy must make sorry to me."

"We better finish this here floor. My brother's coming to get me any minute now," I said. "Marie, you never told me. You got brothers and sisters?"

"Four sister, four brother."

"Are they still in Poland?"

Marie nodded.

"Don't ya miss 'em? Weren't ya close?"

Marie was silent a minute, thinking. "When I am growing up, I do everything with the man. Horses, potatoes, in the fields working, buggy fixing, everything with the man. My brothers and sisters ask me, 'Why, girl, you do with brother or father, no house fixing, no food cook with mother?' I say I don't know. I just be like it. But I think: Why I am so different? Why I no want to babies taking care of, no dresses making? I wear pants, hat, just like the man.

"One day, I ask my father. Why I be like this? Oh, he laugh and laugh. He say when he lie down with Mother, to baby making, the rooster is sleeping with the hens. The sun come up and the rooster is caught, just like my papa was. Cuck coooo! Cucka coooo!" Marie threw her head back, imitating the sounds of roosters and hens. "Everything is mixed up when they made me. Man. No man. Woman. No woman. Is the rooster's fault."

"Ready, Nettie?" a man said. My brother Tom was standing by the banquet room door. He had his hat in his hand on account of Marie, showing his hair the color of drying corn silk. Tom's a couple and more years younger than me and has the face of a Baptist, meaning thin with a wide grin he don't use often.

Only, when he chooses to, it's like God himself chose to shine. Tom's prettier than me though he'd hate to hear that. I could feel my face turn girlish, and I hurried across the room to take his arm.

"I don't know how ya did it, Marie. I could never leave my brother nowhere," I teased.

That is when I first learned that Marie could never take a teasing. In particular if it was about her past. She glared at us across the length of the room and began to mop furiously. "I tell you one thing," she shouted, "I no come to this country unless I be hungry."

"Marie," the letter began, "my dear Siostra." The envelope arrived addressed to Marie at the hotel, and when Marie saw her sister's hand, the same hand she herself used each week to sign over her wages, the same ocean wave scribbles, she began to tremble.

"Read it! Read it!" she screamed, thrusting it into my hands.

"How the hell can I read it if you can't?" I said. "I can't read Polish."

"I never good learning," she said, tearing it out of my hands. "Laura, Laura!" she said, the paper beating against her chest like a heart.

"Wait a minute. Let me see it." Wedged between the broken lines of a foreign tongue, I picked out the word *Canada*. "Canada," I said.

"Canada," Marie repeated. "Where is Canada?"

"Look, here's another address on the bottom. This one's in Chicago. Maybe she knows somebody there. Maybe we could write to 'em."

Marie was biting her lower lip. "No. I go to Chicago on Sunday." She nodded to herself.

I lost my patience. "What the hell'd she write you for if she knows you can't read it? Besides, I thought you was the only one come over on the boat."

"I go to Chicago," Marie repeated.

"Do you know how big a city Chicago is? You can't even walk from one side of it to the other. How you going to find this place?"

"I find it."

"How you gonna pay for the train ride?"

Her face fell.

"Take this," I said, digging for a dollar out of my purse. Pa would have to understand. "Family's everything."

Marie bit her lip again. "No."

"You can pay me back, for Christ's sake."

"No."

"Look, maybe you got all the way over that ocean without help. I can't claim to know how people do things in your country. But here in America, we help each other. That means I may be in trouble someday and I count on you are gonna help me. It's not about owing. It's about living."

I put Marie on the South Shore train to Chicago the next Sunday morning and she came back Sunday night with Stanley. The way Marie tells it, he couldn't take his eyes off her. The way Marie tells it, she didn't have to ask one person for directions, that from the train-boarding on out the men took turns leading her to that door in Chicago, all the way to Pole Town, 'cross the tracks, between the meat-packing plants that stunk, she said, ripe as a sickroom, under a sky that was even then brewing with smoke from the rubber and steel plants. Man after man drawn to her like a cat in heat. Now, Marie would not take to that comparison. More like bees to the hive, she'd say. Marie ain't what you'd call pretty. Not even what we called pretty then. She's got the build of a worker, knees round as melons, hands red as clay with blood drying in the cracks and the pads worn like a wet stone. Lord have mercy if she ain't got upper arms big around as a good-sized summer squash. Fact is, Marie reminds me of a garden, sturdy and strong as a truck garden in early August.

Magnetism, Marie calls it. Magnitizmo is how she pronounces it. Personally, I think the magic's in her mouth. You know that saying about charming the rattles off of a rattlesnake? Marie's a charmer. Not sweet like some girls. Not helpless. And not a charmer like Rosetta Spaid down the road. Rosetta charmed the cancer right off my grandmother's cheek, said she'd learned how to do it from the Indians. Not a charmer like that. Marie's charm was getting people to help her and all the while them thinking she is the one who is strong.

Marie knocked at the address on her sister's letter and waltzed right into a roomful of Poles, some just over on the boats themselves, some who'd been here working in the packing plants or the canneries for years. All about the same age as Marie and all men. I can tell ya one thing. I woulda waltzed myself right back out that door. That never bothered Marie. She said that when she walked in and heard her language, the skys and the skas, the icksvas and the ocksvas, the words came tumbling out of her mouth like they was freed slaves. No, Marie didn't say that. I said that, imagining. 'Cause I can imagine it. I wish I had a roomful of people I'd open a door to and they'd speak the same words I spoke when I was a kid with my ma. Don't know what to call that language, something with time to spare in it and lots of words like home, like laughing, and soft sounds like cabbage, words reminding you of the good taste of coffee.

The Poles welcomed Marie. They fed her and nobody gawked at how much she ate like I did. Instead, they cheered her on. They didn't eat as good as us, she said, them not working in a hotel, but they had bread, good bread, and they read her sister's letter to her.

> *Dear Marie, Sister,*
>   *After you left, I was offered my passage. I am working on a farm in Canada. The farmer beats me. I am afraid he will kill me someday. Please send money to buy me out. This is the name of friends of Aunt Sophia's in Chicago. They are the only names I know. Maybe they can help us.*
>   *Laura*

How could they help her? Nobody there had much of their own, but they chipped in and paid for Marie's train ticket. Stanley rode the train back with her to Town of Pines, though, knowing Marie, if she hadn't of been upset, she woulda never let him do it. Fact is, Stanley was smitten with her. He told her he'd be back the next Sunday to take her to the pictures. When she told him how I'd loaned her the money to go to Chicago, he told her to invite me, too.

I liked Stanley right off. 'Course, you gotta like a man who'll take out a woman a good half-foot taller than him, all the while smiling like he was responsible for growing her, like she was his prize pumpkin at the county fair. Stanley said he liked a woman who made him look up at the sky, said people walked around too much with their eyes to the ground, said he might miss a rainbow, a moon rising, or the first star.

That was Stanley, a romantic through and through. He came that first Sunday to the hotel lobby bearing a store-bought rose. I hadn't ever seen one before and I swore it wasn't no rose at all. My ma and me grew roses, Michigan roses, Indiana roses, Ohio roses, Sweethearts, all kinds I have no names for, kinds we clipped and traded with any of her relatives that came to town, roses that probably go back to her great-grandmothers, passed on like quilt patterns or remedies. That rose Stanley was holding with the pink ribbon around its stem had only a shadow of what them real roses smelled like. It didn't look like a real rose neither, not ragged, not spongy. It was perfect, like it had been on a diet, like it was some movie star rose.

"This be American rose," Marie said proudly. "Big, beautiful. Cost lots of money."

Stanley had eyes like a Chinaman's that when he laughed almost shut, big cheeks the pink color of a schoolboy's. You could see Marie amused him to no end the way his eyes was almost always slanted. He kept penny candy deep in his pockets, making me and every child he saw on the street dig for it. Which made Marie mad and which made him laugh all the more. "What for you give penny away?" she'd say. Stanley's English was better than mine. Marie said it was 'cause he came ten years before she did but that don't give me no excuse. He spoke Russian, German. His father, Marie said, was a preacher in Katowice. "Katowice is big location," she bragged to me.

Every Sunday, Stanley would take the train down to Town of Pines and we'd go out. "I got no relation," Marie would explain to me when I'd suggest they go by themselves. "He got no relation." I don't know what that had to do with it but I was tickled to death to accompany 'em. He'd take us to eat or we'd buy a taxi ride through town. We neglected the picture shows after that first day 'cause Marie couldn't follow a movie story if her life depended on it. "Why I watch that for?" she'd shout. "Everybody talk like bratwurst." Which I guess meant all mixed up. It always made Marie angry if she couldn't understand something.

One day, Stanley came with a new plan. "Marie, I've been thinking. It's time you stopped looking like a servant. You're never going to get anywhere if you don't start dressing like an American."

Marie was instantly shamed and stared at the ground. I was surprised since he must've known that everything on her back was handed down from the hotel owner's wife, a stout German with bad taste whose only discards weren't fit to wrap a calf in. Marie once told me she'd brought a trunk with her to Stüttgart, full of her Christmas and Easter clothes, embroidered aprons and shawls, hand-woven and bleached shirts made by her mother. She said she'd taken one look at the women walking the streets in that city with their modern clothes and left the whole trunk right there on the sidewalk.

"I've got some lady friends in Chicago who want to take you shopping," Stanley said, beaming. "You and Nettie take the train next week and you pick out whatever you want."

"No," she said. I coulda told him she'd say that.

"Oh, Marie, let me buy you something."

Marie was vigorously shaking her head.

"Why?" Stanley pleaded, picking up one of her braids and fingering it gently.

"Never I do this kind of work," Marie said, brushing his hand away. "I no need clothes bad as that."

Well, that really got to Stanley. "Forget it," he said, turning on his heel faster than a pay truck passing a tramp, faster than I thought that round little body could move. He stalked off in the direction of the station. Marie stood right where she was. 'Course, I knew she would. When Stanley finally turned around, Marie was crying. That is the only time I was to ever see him lose his temper. He started running back and Marie started running in the opposite direction, him shouting Polish a mile a minute, loud and angry and he didn't care who heard it. And much to my surprise, Marie slowed. When he caught up with her, she even let him wipe her eyes with the handkerchief he pulled out of his suit coat. After he left, I asked Marie if that meant we was going shopping. She told me we was gonna go to Chicago and buy her a hat.

Stanley met us at the train station the next Sunday with two other women who spoke no English at all and who grabbed Marie's arms like they was sisters. They was city girls by the way they dressed, hats and gloves, lipstick and colognes. They was pure peasant underneath. Before we did anything, we had to eat, right there in the train station, those women unwrapping brown bread and head cheese and soft cheese and even hot tea in jars. I guess they figured we had to eat after our big trip and they had no idea where Town of Pines was or how long it had taken us to get there. Marie was different than I'd ever seen her, smiling in a different way, blushing even. I wish I knew what they said to her to make her blush like that 'cause it made her look more like the girls I knew than the soldier she was to me. We had our picnic, wiped our mouths, and headed to the shops, those girls jabbering all the while.

I was so busy watching Marie be happy, I don't remember what was in them shops. Though those women did make me act as their go-between. Every time I'd tell 'em a price, they'd argue over it and then *I* was supposed to dicker with the clerk. Marie was trying on hat after city hat 'cause a hat was at that time the way you showed you was modern. American women wore hats. Aunt Till says that's about the time they wiped out the wild turkey and the ostrich. I can believe it 'cause the streets was full of feathers bobbing above the crowds like the top-knots of quail who think they are hid in the fields.

Marie stood in front of those mirrors trying to fit any hat she could over that thick head of hers. She let the braids down that was pinned up on top and it still didn't fit. She had us pull down on 'em even, but still no go. Stanley used to say Marie had muscles in her head the size of those in her arms, said that's why she's so stubborn. Marie said she couldn't understand how American women could be so smart and have such dinky heads.

She was just on her way out of the store, hatless, when she spotted a shelf of hats we hadn't seen before. She went over and picked one up and hesitantly lowered it over her head. It fit. Brown and plain as mud with a pale plum band. She tried another. A Royal Stetson, it proclaimed on the silk liner. The Polish girls came running. "No, no!" they cried. I didn't have to speak their language to guess what they thought of Marie buying a gentleman's hat. Of course, once Marie had found her hat, she would not be talked out of it.

I could tell those women thought they'd hear it from Stanley 'cause the next stop we made was a dress shop. There they picked one out themselves, all outa some new fabric they was making in the factories and plum to match the band of Marie's new hat. Marie put her old clothes in the shopping bag and we hit the streets again, Marie a sight for sore eyes in her new dress and old boots. Next thing we needed was some stockings and shoes. Marie thought the thicker the stocking, the better it was made and there was no talking her into ones you could see light through. I was hoping heels was not the thing, with Stanley being so short and all. I needn't of worried. Marie picked out a nice pair of flats.

On the way back to meet Stanley, Marie asked me how come all the ladies we was passing had their long hair tucked up under their hats. I said they didn't, that they had gone and got their long hair all chopped off.

"This is true?" Marie gasped.

"Sure, it's true," I said. "In America, women wear what we want. In America, if we don't want our braids always getting caught in the wringer, we cut 'em off." I chuckled, feeling brave as if I'd done it myself. "Besides, it's modern."

I will regret saying that to this day 'cause Marie reached

down swift as lightning and pulled out her knife. "I be America woman, too," she said, slicing off each of those braids at the ear. She smiled and stuffed them into the bag with her old clothes. I started to cry. I couldn't help it. They was so gold and thick I woulda died for 'em.

We thought Stanley would throw a fit when we brought Marie back to his flat, her hair chopped off like some hobo my ma used to feed on the back stoop, and wearing that man's hat and hosiery thick as a milkmaid's. The dress must've been a good one 'cause Stanley didn't miss a beat, just grinned and claimed Marie was as beautiful as the Statue of Liberty. And would she make him a present of one of her braids?

Stanley was cleaning offices during the week at the railroad depot in Chicago. He had a good job, Marie said, a steady one. 'Course to Marie, any job was better than looking for one. He worked ten hours, six days a week, and she thought that was cake. "Used to be for dollar work very much," she told me. "I work from sun come up to sun come down and at end of day, I go to boss lady. She give me one bread, this big. My mother slice it and give each to my sister and brother." When Stanley started talking about moving to Town of Pines, applying at the Slicers or the mills, you'd think she'd be happy. Not Marie. Marie came to me with the news like somebody who done lost all their pigs to cholera.

"What are you acting so upset for?" I asked her. "I'd bet my bottom dollar it's so he can spend more time with you."

"He want me to marriage him," Marie said, bursting into tears.

"Marry him? Then what are you crying for? You can see yourself he's in love with you. Stanley's eyes are full of moon."

"Better stick in carrots you need a man," Marie said, rubbing her eyes.

"Christ, if you ain't the most vulgar woman alive! Most women hear them words and think they're hearing Gabriel. You don't marry 'em 'cause of that. What are you gonna do? Pay your own rent all your life?"

"Why not?" Marie said.

"'Cause it don't work that way here, Marie. You'll die in the poorhouse. You see a woman running this country? You see a woman sitting behind the desk giving out the money and the jobs and the places in heaven? Shit," I said, disgusted. "Who are you trying to fool? Stanley probably makes four times what you make, given they ain't cheating you out of hours and they probably is. And he'll make even more at Slicers. Do you know what that is? It's a foundry. They say it's work fit only for a black man or a Pole. It's hot and it's dangerous and he'd do that for you." I shook my head. "Where do you get these ideas anyhow?"

Marie was staring at me, her mouth open. "Nettie, I no want marriage make," she finally pleaded. "Stanley say he love me because I am old-fashioned girl. Like woman in old country. No spoiled. I no want to be like that. Nettie, I want to be America woman. In Poland, woman got no life making. Woman can be man in America, get own work, get own pay." Marie started crying again. I guess I wasn't being much of a friend.

"You could try putting him off. Tell him you'll consider it after you pay off your debt to old Roxy."

"He says I marriage him, he pay Roxy. I no more work here. Maybe soon even pay for Laura, save up money."

"He said he'd pay to get your sister off that farm? Marie, I'm afraid to say you won't never get nobody better than Stanley. Even if you do think them carrots is." I let myself chuckle. I motioned toward the spot where the cook woulda been standing if it wasn't already past time he got off work. "Besides, it'd sure solve your problems with that devil. Has he been leaving you alone since you talked to Mrs. Roxy?"

"Is worse now than when I start here. She say there is nothing she can do. He is best friend with her husband. She say I should try to stay away from him, not angry make him. Says I will cause more trouble."

"You told him you'd tell his wife?"

"He tell me he catch me someday when nobody around. Say I should go out with him so no hurt making."

"He said what?" I noticed that something had come over Marie. She wouldn't look at me no more, just stood there looking at her hands. "Listen, this ain't your fault. Did something happen already?"

"Day before today, I am in kitchen early, just when light making. Cook come up behind me and grab me around waist, act like the pigs do it. I hit and kick but he just grin, point like this his finger to his pants. It is so big, sticking out like he steal something and put it in his pants."

"Oh, Lord. We've got to do something. Maybe I could start coming earlier? 'Course, I can't. I got my own chores to do what with Pa failing and all. Did I tell ya he quit the lumberyard last week?"

"He quit?" Marie asked, horror-stricken.

"Had to, he says. Can't hardly breathe no more and they keep heaping more work on him to prove he's gotten too old for the job. Tell ya the truth, I think the old fool's kinda glad."

"What will you do?"

"Support 'em all, I guess. Tom's working, too, except, serious as he is with his new gal, I don't know how long I can count on him. He might up and marry her and then where'll I be?"

Marie was looking out the window. "Anyway, that ain't your problem," I said. "I'm gonna finish wiping this oven down and then I gotta go. I'll come here at seven sharp tomorrow morning and you don't come down outa your room 'til then, you hear? Tell 'em you don't feel so good. We'll make sure he's never around you alone."

As luck would have it, the next day I was late and I hadn't never been late a day in the two years I was working there. Now that I look back on it, it just couldn't be helped, though I sure beat myself over the head about it then. Little Dot was down with the croup and Pa was having a bad spell, coughing up black and sitting in the same chair Ma did her dying in, him pale as a fish belly and coming in and out like the sun in an eclipse, surfacing to spout some hatred or another, old feuds, old loves, yelling nigger, yelling injun. I never heard my pa talk like that, like somebody else was taking over. "You get outa that chair if you're gonna be sick!" I screamed and Lizzy 'bout jumped out of her skin.

Lizzy was the one upset this time. She always feared my pa. Loved him and feared him, which was the way it was in those days. Lizzy just followed me around like she was lost until we got him quieted, pushed his skinny old body into bed, layered him with comforters and started the goose grease and onions frying. They always say not far from the cause lies the cure. Near the bee sting is the mud. So I scooped out some of that hot coal he carried for so many years, scooped it right out of the stove and wrapped it up good to warm his chest. I put those fried onions in a worn sock and pinned it tight around his neck. I set a pail of water on the stove boiling, smelling up the whole house with whatever was green and in reach to throw into it. I opened the windows to that cold April air, waved goodbye to Lizzy, and flew out the door.

I ran all the way to Roxy's that morning and the sun already up was scolding me. I slammed open the kitchen door, my mouth so full of sorrys and excuses I knew I was gonna stumble over 'em. I had my coat off and was holding it before I realized something was wrong. There stood the cook, both feet planted like a wrestler, facing Marie and holding a bloody cloth to his arm. His face was red and his eyes was smoking. Marie was wide-eyed as a stallion, standing by the sinks. My heart sank when I saw she had that knife of hers in her hand, that Polish boot-knife, and she was still pointing it at him. Her other hand held her cheek. The cheek had blood running down it. She did not take her gaze from him.

"Jesus Christ," I mumbled under my breath.

"You see this, Nettie?" the cook yelled, pointing to his arm. "She coulda killed me. You came just in time. I caught Marie stealing food and when I told her I was gonna tell Roxy, she went and pulled that knife out and cut me."

I turned to Marie. Her hand dropped to show me the slash where a scar would grow. Her attention on the cook did not waver. "Who cut who first?"

"Nettie, there's a slew of girls just begging for that job of yours."

"Marie, what happened?" I noticed the two top buttons on her blouse was popped off and the collar was ripped and hanging by a thread.

"Roxy knows and I know there's food been missing here," the cook continued. "Marie must think we're as dumb as she is. An egg a day, two the next. We've been keeping track, ya see. A whole pound of butter gone last week. Now where do ya suppose that went?"

I felt my face flush. That pound of butter fed Pa and them kids for six days.

"Flour, a cup here, a cup there. Cornmeal. Sugar, too."

I looked him square in the eye. "Marie didn't steal no food and you know it."

The cook smiled. "Somebody's stealing it. Besides, I caught her red-handed." He picked up a sack of soup beans, showing me. "Nettie, you come to work the same time I do, don't ya? Never late, right, Nettie? Just like you told Roxy yourself last week when you asked him for that raise. Which means you must've seen everything this morning, seen me catch Marie with this sack and seen her pull that knife."

Marie looked at me for the first time, then quickly looked away. She knew I had no choice.

"What's gonna happen to Marie?"

"Well, I guess that'll be up to them fellows at Immigration, won't it? Getting fired for stealing and carrying on with men all the way to Chicago? Ain't you girls ever heard of the Immorality Clause? Maybe they'll send her back. Maybe I'll talk to Roxy, tell him I think we should give her another chance. 'Course whether I do that or not is really between her and me."

"Never!" Marie hissed.

"What's it gonna be, Nettie?" he said.

Marie was right. I didn't have no choice. I took a deep breath. "I seen the beans. I seen the knife. And I ain't seen nothing else."

Marie's last day of work at the Roxy, there was three girls waiting in line at the door to take her place. I nodded to each of 'em as they was escorted through the kitchen and up to Mr. Roxy's office. They didn't nod back. In fact, they made believe they'd never seen me do it, just in case somebody saw they was on employment's side. I knew whose side they was on, the same side of the tracks I was, same side heard about a job two hours after a person left it and was there asking for it in two hours and a half. Some I knew from school, some I didn't. I watched how the cook made sure who wore a ring and who walked 'em to the hotel, his neck sticking out the back door like a cowlick. I smiled at 'em when they came and I smiled at 'em when they left.

You may think that was bad of me for letting Marie take the blame. I had a twinge or two over that myself. But what is important to know is that this wasn't between Marie and me and this wasn't about thieving. This was about Marie not giving in to that poor excuse of a man. I don't know if I coulda kept saying no in her position. I didn't know if those girls, smiling, desperate as I was for a job, would keep saying no either.

Marie didn't leave 'cause Mr. Roxy fired her. He was smarter than that. Immigration wasn't gonna give him the $300 she owed him if he sent her back to Poland, and without a job Marie wasn't gonna pay him back. And so, the day after the knifing, Mr. Roxy, who never appeared in the kitchen, appeared there in that suit he greeted his guests in and with that starched handkerchief that looked like he never took it out and he right away recited, one by one, every item and more than ever found its way into my cupboards at home and the price of each. When he was through, he tallied the cost of the missing food and added it to what Marie still owed him for her passage. I watched as they made her sign the piece of paper.

I don't know who Marie got to write a note to Stanley. He came right down. He didn't come to the kitchen, he marched straight to Mr. Roxy's office, plunked the $356.26 on the desk and said he'd come to pay for Marie. There was nothing they could say, just give him a receipt like he'd just bought a cow and point toward the stall which was the kitchen.

"Go up and get your things," Stanley said to Marie.

I was as shocked to see him there as the cook was, out of context, midweek, with his hair all slicked back and his hat in his hand like he was at church. The cook stood there, his face sweating and turning pale. "What the hell are you doing in my kitchen?" he shouted. "And who the hell do you think you are, ordering my help around?"

The cook loomed a good six inches above Stanley. Stanley

held his own with a poker face that didn't betray he was holding a winning hand. "Marie is no longer your help. Marie is going to be my wife." Stanley handed over the receipt.

I was staring at Marie in surprise. She was staring at the floor. The bandage must've covered most of her right cheek. I wondered if Stanley had expected it.

"I am marriage make it," she said quietly, her eyes meeting mine. The look we exchanged was split-second but it was all-knowing, resigned as creek water that is making a turn to the sea. I will never forget it.

"What's your last name gonna be now, Marie?" I remembered to ask her. "Just so I can find you."

She looked at Stanley. "Bernaki," he said proudly.

Marie took off her apron. "And your maiden name?" I called to her as she headed toward her room. "I never asked you that before."

She smiled. "Chmura," she said, whispering it. "Means white cloud. Means good weather coming."

Marie left and it wasn't an hour and a half before them other girls started showing up at the hotel, waiting to take her place.

In the photograph of Marie's wedding, she is sitting on a low stool, surrounded by men standing. Low as she is, her legs must've been bent at right angles under her skirts. She said it was the photographer who thought of that. He disapproved of how much taller Marie was than her husband. In the picture, Marie looks happy enough. Knowing her, she wouldn't of smiled like that if she didn't want to. She liked men, she always did, and there she was, surrounded by 'em, twenty butchers and bakers, foundry men and meat-packers, pressed and so clean they must've drained a well to get the smell out of 'em. That's not why Marie is so happy. Marie's happy because she got her way after suffering through the worst three weeks of her life, the three weeks when, Marie swears, she lost her soul and almost landed on the moon.

I didn't know a thing about any of it 'til later. For all I knew, Marie and Stanley left the Roxy kitchen without once looking back, walked to the courthouse, and was pronounced man and wife. I shoulda known it wasn't gonna be that easy. "I got no relation. He got no relation," she kept saying. What did that mean to me whose family goes on and on like railroad cars and just as connected? Turn around and bump into a Guelzo or a Bartz. There's godchildren and godmothers, nieces, nephews, cousins. Sometimes it seemed like you couldn't be constipated without announcing it to the whole damned reunion committee. If Marie didn't have a sister or brother to stand up for her, no father or mother to give her away, much less a parish, much less a priest, I didn't give it no thought.

The taxi was waiting outside the hotel, ready to take 'em straight to Pole Town where there was a widow by the name of Mrs. Wozniak who had agreed to take them in. Marie was to change, pretty up, and they'd still have time to meet the J.P. before closing. Stanley already had the marriage license in his pocket. He had it all figured. Mrs. Wozniak would meet 'em at the door, speaking the kitchen Polish Marie grew up on, not like Stanley who learned it written from his father. When he spoke like that, Marie'd get so angry! She said it made her feel like they was from different countries. She said it wasn't Polish at all. Mrs. Wozniak, Stanley figured, would make a nervous bride feel right at home.

Mrs. Wozniak met 'em with a babushka on her head and an apron round her thick waist. Marie frowned at Mrs. Wozniak and Mrs. Wozniak frowned back. The old woman showed her upstairs, eyeing Marie's short hair and the scar running down her right cheek, which could only have been made with a knife, with disapproval, touching the silk stockings Marie wore until Marie slapped her hands away. Mrs. Wozniak finally left her alone, clucking all the way down the steps, and Marie collapsed on the bed.

It wasn't exactly the wedding suite a bride dreams of. No furniture but a hard bed, so narrow a scarecrow's elbows would stick out of it, bare floors, and only a pail of cold water for washing. No mirrors like she was used to in the hotel, no pillows, and it was colder to boot. Still, there was a lake outside, Fish Lake, a dirt road circling it, and another circle of maple trees beyond that, smoking with just enough green to let her know spring was coming. There was the smoke of corn cobs burning in five or six chimneys and a few old men pushing a rowboat into the water. Marie said she stared out that window for a long time and I'd like to think the lake was a comfort to her. After all, she'd lost her family, her country, got a job and lost it, too, had the hands of a stranger down her blouse and up her skirt and lucky, managed to lose him. She coulda ended up in jail and instead here she was, her debts paid, the possibility of freeing Laura, and, in an hour, her name would be Bernaki.

The lake was calm, collecting shadows. It was the dark of the moon, if I remember, March. I remember 'cause Marie said the spring-cleaning had just been done: Dark of the moon, March, so's later you don't get moths. Marie stood, looking at the lake, listening to Stanley and Mrs. Wozniak arguing in Polish downstairs, only holding their voices close to 'em like her parents used to do so she couldn't hear. They was probably arguing about her. Past the lake was the forests cut down for grain. Bald fields going on and on forever, just like in Poland. Her grandmother used to tell her stories about them forests as if they was gods and how she had watched the men come with axes just when she was old enough to enter them alone. Marie was beginning to wonder if she'd left anything behind.

She splashed cold water on her face and changed into her one good Chicago dress. Above the bed, in an ornate, carved frame, was a painting of the Lady of Czestochowa. Marianna. Poland's queen. She was surprised she hadn't noticed it before but not surprised Mrs. Wozniak had hung it there. Every home in Poland had one. The Black Madonna, they called her, only she ain't black like Mrs. Thomas or Mrs. Jones, Marie says. She's brown like a chestnut, sad, alone, even if she is holding the baby Jesus. What makes her black is the scars running deep down her right cheek in two rays, each long as a finger. Marie said robbers slashed her when they tried to steal her. What with Marie's new scars it must've been like finding the mirror she was looking for.

Mrs. Wozniak took one look at Marie's tight dress and her face screwed up like her tit got caught in a wringer. Marie just laughed, switching her hips. Stanley and her left, walking arm in arm to town, Stanley flushed and singing folk tunes, so full of joy he was like a girl. Marie couldn't help but be caught up in it. They entered the courthouse, Stanley showed the J.P. his citizenship papers and license, and they got married while Marie was still searching out the window for the church.

When they returned to Pole Town, Stanley's rent money was still on the table where he'd laid it. "What is this?" Stanley joked. "My money has holes in it?" He swung Mrs. Wozniak in a small dance. "Where is the vodka for the toast?"

Mrs. Wozniak spat and motioned him into her kitchen. "This is marriage making in America?" Marie heard her say. "Where is ring?"

"There'll be a ring later. I told you I spent all my money to pay Mr. Roxy off."

"I no believe you. Let me see license."

That was all Marie needed to hear. She came bounding into

the kitchen, waving the ten she picked up off the table in the old woman's face, demanding, "How much my husband pay you for room and for insult?"

"Now, Marie," Stanley said.

"You get no money back for sinning," Mrs. Wozniak shouted, snatching the bill out of Marie's hand.

"You keep it rent money. We go somewhere else sleep having," Marie shouted back. She shoved Mrs. Wozniak aside, grabbed a bottle of milk from the ice chest, and took the loaf of bread on the counter in her hand. She sniffed it. "Not too fresh but we take it. Fair exchange." Mrs. Wozniak and Stanley stared in wonder. Marie took Stanley's arm and began pulling. "Come, Stanley, we some place better finding."

And ya know what happened next? Mrs. Wozniak laughed. Laughed right out loud with her hands on her belly and her head thrown back. "You got your hands full with this one," she said, however you say that in Polish. "This girl is like a stallion. You're going to have to cut off her balls."

Marie was half out the yard and Stanley had a hell of a time talking her back in, although in that yellow March twilight the first star was signalling. She must've known there wasn't no other place to stay and it was getting late. Still, it took Mrs. Wozniak and Stanley every trick in the book to get Marie to stay, though she refused to eat with the family, even for free. Stanley and Marie broke brown bread on their wedding night, sitting side by side on the bed, and shared that stolen milk straight out of the bottle.

Late that night, Marie left the bed and headed down to the lake alone. A thumbnail of a moon was rising. Something was rising in her, too, something that would not let her sleep, something stirred up from the sex and Mrs. Wozniak and Mr. Roxy, stirred up with the moon. There was something wrong. She could feel it.

To calm herself, she told herself a story, an old story she'd heard as a child. In it there was a man in Poland, a soft man a lot like Stanley, with not too much ambition, a man who liked to play the violin. He was a good man, her mother had told her, and she knew which were and which weren't, a farming man like her father. He worked and worked 'til the flesh about came off his bones and the more he worked, the poorer he got. Sounds a lot like me, don't it? Well, one night this man has a dream. In it, a voice tells him he will find gold and silver and sweetbreads and fruit and strong wool thread of every color. All he's gotta do is open the door in the morning and haul it in. He wakes up the next day and what do ya know? Right there, a pile of riches. And the next day, there's more. More and more for seven days 'til the gold is stacked up to the ceiling and there's so much bread it's gonna mold. Like I woulda, he decides he better start selling it off before it spoils. He packs up a bag, but he can't carry it. He tries dragging it across the floor. He's gotta sit down. He tries lifting it to his hip like a woman does and his back cracks in half like a peanut shell. Every day he tells himself he's gonna get his strength back, but it's petering out faster than a flat tire. Pretty soon, he's dying. Pretty soon, he's dead.

He's dead and flying out of his body, leaving it packed in that hut like dressing in a turkey. And, as he's flying through the air, he notices a most beautiful light to his left, shining, not like the sun, more like a face smiling, a big round face shining into itself, pale and opaque as milk and when he thinks of milk, naturally he thinks of his mother and when he thinks of his mother, he thinks of Matka Boska and when he thinks of the Mother of God, he remembers Marianna, the Lady of Czestochowa, and shit, it all comes back to him. He never thought to ask where all those gifts were coming from or who had talked to him in the dream. He knew then the devil had tricked him. Well, of course he was sorry and I guess, 'cause he was, God with just a twist of his beard slowed him on his death flight and let him land on the bright, shining moon he was admiring. That is why, when you look at the moon, you see a man playing a violin. Which it seems everybody does but me.

Stanley and Marie decided to stay on at Mrs. Wozniak's 'til Stanley found work in Town of Pines and they could afford a place of their own. To hear Stanley tell it, Marie got stranger day by day. She quit joining the rest of 'em for supper, preferring that lakeside moon-viewing post she'd dragged an old stump to. When Stanley came home, he'd find her by the water in her old clothes and boots, chewing on a piece of bread. She began to lose weight. She refused to help Mrs. Wozniak with the chores. It was on the new moon that Stanley finally gave up.

"Here. I have lost you," he said, handing the marriage license to her. "I didn't think I would make you so unhappy."

Marie turned away.

"Whose fault?" Stanley pleaded. "Is it something I did?"

"I no smart enough for America," Marie said. "I no believe this kind marriage."

"What is wrong with our marriage? We just started."

"I don't want to but my eye, it sees it," she said suddenly, full of anger. "Cook is gone. Money coming for pay off boat trip. Laura coming. Job. Sister. Stanley, I no work for this. Where is this presents come from?"

"From me!" Stanley answered. "From me because I love you."

"Love? Pfft," she spat. "Love no buy boat ride America. Love no buy sister back." Marie's eyes narrowed. "I ask self. Where is this presents coming? From Devil."

"Devil?"

"Mrs. Wozniak, I no like her but she right. No church, no family, how I know is marriage making? This is dirty business."

"Church?" Stanley shouted. "You don't even go to church."

"Why Mr. Roxy so easy let me go? Maybe cook get me when you be tired of me. Maybe you sell story to Immigration, get big money, split with cook. No brother, no father, who is fight for me?"

"I can't believe you're saying this," Stanley said, too shocked to be angry.

"Nobody get something for nothing. Not even America."

Stanley sighed. "What kind of marriage you want? I can't afford to bring your family over here."

"Priest be at it."

"Is that all?" Stanley asked, stunned. "A priest would make you happy? A priest would make you believe me?"

"I big mistake making. Now, maybe not even on moon landing. Maybe be better I go back Poland."

Stanley's friends met Marie at the Bohemian Catholic Church in Chicago with a bagful of every fancy thing they could bribe from their wives and girlfriends, skirts and slips and even a wreath of the paper mums and roses one of the widows and her children made at night by candlelight for their living. Marie stood in front of the priest like she'd just risen from the dead, smiling, and when Stanley tells the story, he can't help but tell you how much food Marie ate at the reception.

Chapter Three

How did poor folks live during the Depression? By the Bible, the prayer book, and the Farmer's Almanac. People lived by the signs. I remember Ma telling our neighbor that he was wasting his time planting his radish seed 'cause it was the wrong size of moon. "I don't plant in the moon, I plant in the ground," he answered. He grew beautiful radish leaves alright, but not one radish developed bigger than a string. He had to eat humble pie instead of radishes and ask Ma when to plant again. A friend of mine was told to wean her baby in the sign of the heart. She did and had no problems.

Some folks never had to consult the Almanac. Some people just paid more attention. Like Stanley. If Stanley woulda stayed in Europe, I bet he'd be one of them the village people went to. Stanley always could tell you how big was the moon. He'd reach down to that soft belly of his, poke around like the moon was there inside him, and say, "Two days past full. In the lungs."

There was some things we just knew without them having to be written in a book. That you plant all your peas on Valentine's Day, especially the sweet ones, and your corn better be knee-high by you know what. And lots of the green knowledge, what to pick for this ailment or grow for that. Them things we didn't read about; we heard from one mouth to another, passing 'em down like those plant clippings the women passed down. Seems like if you wrote 'em down, they wouldn't work, that part of their curing power was in the act of saying, prescribing, sorta like the difference between reading a recipe in a cookbook and having your hands in the dough.

The Almanac told ya when to plant what and what to do about the bugs, when to wean a baby, pull your teeth, or cut your hair, when to make sauerkraut, all while the moon is moving through the body of God, from his head to his feet, hitting the loins, the groins, the arms, and all things in between. The general rule, which can save you a lot of reading, is that you plant anything that grows underground while the moon is burying itself from full and anything you want above ground like flowers while the moon is blossoming from nothing. The Almanac was a hell of a lot more fun to read than the Bible, though the prayer books always got us through our off days. You could take the Almanac to the outhouse with you, even string a rope through one of the holes they had punched in it expressly for that purpose. Hang it on the outhouse wall and it would mean no disrespect.

The Bible is another story. My people are Christians, mind you, though all I remember about the inside of a church is weddings and funerals. Pa was too tired and sick to get up on Sundays and how could Ma've brought all us little ones? I got my favorite books. Job is one of 'em because it's short and I don't understand suffering neither. I like the Psalms 'cause I'm used to 'em and there's animals and fields in 'em. And, of course, I know the commandments to Moses with their high-falutin' Thous and Shalt Nots, just like the law, designed to stack the prisons with the poor. The preachers was never good at predicting, what with their heads in the time and land of Judea. But the Farmer's Almanac was: October 29, 1929. Black Tuesday. Sun and Mars next to each other in the groins. Moon in the bowels. The poor? We could smell it coming sharp as salt pork frying from the farmhouse next door.

What I wanna know is: Where did all that money go that made men jump outa the windows onto Wall Street? It had to go somewhere.

Money was never—how should I say it—my strong suit. Two years later, I was still working at the Roxy Hotel for the same wage as when I started, supporting Pa's dying in comfort and them—excuse my French—damned doctors. Me, watching the new girls move right past me from the dishroom to the kitchen, from washing pots to chopping vegetables next to the cook. I didn't get it. I growed up thinking money was something you out-tricked, like the Devil. Ma used to see how much time could pass before anybody at home would notice she hadn't bought nothing. Sometimes Pa would grumble about being out of coffee again but three days without was three days saved, she figured. The only thing she knew was that you made money by not spending it.

It runs in the family. I had an aunt in Missouri. Uncle Odie, her husband, worked in the lead mines. She had only one light bulb in the entire house. We'd visit her and she'd screw it in the middle of the bedroom ceiling while we undressed. When we'd call we were in bed, she'd take it out and move it to her room. Once, my cousins said, they pitched in to buy her a pack of bulbs. She just put 'em in the drawer for saving and was back to one bulb again. I can understand it.

I used to think there was some mystery about money I could pass on to my grandchildren if I could learn it in time. Now, I look around to all them that is rich and I say no, I don't want that; I want them to be human. No, I ain't gonna back down on that and I ain't giving out exceptions like they give out free cheese to a few. How do you think the Joneses that people are always trying to keep up with got their money? How many black folks you know got names of Jones? Hear me out: every rich person has had slaves.

Luck had it I got a new job right at the start of the Depression. Aunt Till says luck ain't got nothing to do with women and children working for less money than the men. And it's true the men poured out of them mills, unemployed, like cake batter. Next day, the call went out to the single gals in town. There was work at the mill. I can tell ya, I didn't think twice. Marie would say it was God that got the job for me and the one Stanley got at the foundry after they fired the troublemakers there. I'll tell ya, if it was God who got the Negroes, the Poles, and the women all them jobs at the woolen mills and the foundries, we must've done something terrible wrong 'cause that work was the work of the damned.

Minute I heard the call, I dropped my apron on the sink at the Roxy and walked out the front door into the middle of town. It was mid-morning and the sun was shining like it did on the weekends. 'Cross the street was the courthouse, red brick with a steeple, and the brick jail. Aunt Till says our town square was built in the same clearing in the woods the Lutheran preachers used for meetings. The Potowatamis used it, too. That is, before they were marched to Kansas in 1838, five hundred miles in winter so you can guess how many made it. The woods have backed off considerable since then. Fact is, I could barely see 'em, standing between the only two buildings in town over three stories high. From the house, I could always see the forests, a dark ring waving from the edges of the world. When I was a kid, I thought the sun lived in the woods 'cause it came up from 'em and went down to 'em at night.

That walk out to the mills was one of the few in-betweens of my life, in between school and the kitchen, in between the kitchen and the mill. Knowing it, I took my time. Past the downtown nest of the rich, built of the same brick as the courthouse, their houses so sturdy no one can budge 'em, laid out in the grids the fellows at the courthouse say to. Next, the rows of frame houses, less sturdy, bowlegged like some of us is with rickets, past them to the ones sown like seeds from the hand and the shacks that fall down when the freights rumble through on their way to Chicago. I was long on dirt roads by then, long past the sewers, to where most of town lived. Things was getting livelier and dilapidated; animals were squawking, and it seems like there was more birds. Sows and cows, roosters and crows. A stone's throw from the Roxy and I was in my own neighborhood, the fields of timothy, red clover, sweet clover, alfalfa and soybeans ready for the blade, the blue jays and cardinals, the fat grain birds, all overflowing into our backyards.

Everybody grew something. The land's rich here and there's plenty of water. Aunt Till says them Big Lakes are what's left after the North Pole went back to where it belonged and our Indiana sun, moist and dripping heat like a peach in a canner, orange-pink, melted the ice and left five fingers like a hand of water and the land good for planting. She says there's enough in those fingers to cover the entire United States of America in ten feet of water. "Can you drink it?" I said. "Sure," she said, "it's water just like the lakes in Town of Pines." I wouldn't drink out of them lakes in town if you paid me 'cause the boys have been pissing in 'em since before I can remember. Still, they're good for something. Bass fishing, ice skating. I don't know what the Big Lakes is for. Mostly, they just sits there. Mostly, 'cause they're so big, I keep an eye in their direction.

This may sound crazy, but the world was as in between things as I was that day. There, closer to town than Pole Town and the lakes, right smack next to Abe Keller's field, Abe himself out there in the gentleman's gray hat and vest he always wore, guiding his old horse and plow through the furrows he was making for winter wheat, was the woolen mill, rising from the miles of alfalfa as if it had landed from the sky. It was nothing to look at. I stood there, feeling kinda disgusted that humans could make something so ugly and dingy with no windows to speak of, no curves or paint, just a gray plank box. I thought about how I'd never been by it much before, though I could see it from the house and we'd been watching the men go back and forth to it for years. The clouds were hanging dark and heavy above it like the patches under your eyes when the tears has set too long. When I walked up to it, I seen the grass hadn't grown back around it like grass tends to do around whatever replaces it.

There was a row of policemen from town guarding the door. As if somebody had tapped me on the shoulder, I looked to where a group of men and women stood behind a barbed wire fence, glaring in my direction. Later, some of the girls told me they'd been afraid to walk past them mill workers and their wives. Not me. I was sorry they didn't have work, but I had my own mouths to feed. After all, I wasn't the one fired 'em. I must've said as much 'cause I was hired on the spot. That night, when he got home, I told my brother what I'd done and about those people aside the road, shaking their heads. "Was I right?" I asked him. Tom stood there awhile, thinking, I suppose. "How much you gonna make there?" he finally said.

Coming from the farm, coming from the kitchen, I can't begin to tell ya what that job did to me. I started feeling just like the edges round that building the grass won't come back to. No windows, nothing to look at but my hands flipping the machines. No air moving and no break in the noise, my body not moving but standing in one place for ten hours a day, not even knowing if the day was moving outside, what with them dim lights on all day. Nowhere to go, nowhere to look, no way to listen. Kitchen work, farm work, they're different. You change what you're doing. Factory work is one long holding-in of your breath 'til the day's over and you can let it out. Sometimes I was so tired walking home I'd sit on the side of the road, lost. Do ya know that tired? Brain and body tired so a place to sit is like a throne.

Was it loud? Ask somebody who's worked in the mills and

you'll have to repeat your question to 'em. It was so loud in there with the looms you never knew if a girl was hurt 'til you saw her mouth a-screaming and her arm a bloody stump. Lots of times, our hair would get caught in the machine and necks broke left and right like a gladiolus farm before the Fourth of July. I was lucky in that. Mine never did grow past a dustmop's length. The mill's when I started chewing on the ends 'cause I couldn't get to my nails. It'd break off just like the ends of a broom, getting stubbier and stubbier. When I'd wash my hair, the bottom of the basin'd be full of chaff like the bottom of the hay wagon.

People say I got an imagination that'd be worth something if I could ever land it on one thing. "Paying attention is as easy as pointing your finger," Aunt Till would always tell me. Nobody'd believe me, least of all her, if I told 'em that it was the woolen mill what stole my attention. Hell, who would want to pay attention to that? Standing there all day, it wasn't long before my hands learned to move without me and my mind could settle on the yellow I was handling or the blue. I'd pretend what kinda yellow dress I was making for myself, every detail, like the buttons. "Button, button, who's got the button?" I'd sing, designing the waist and how this dress would bring out all the qualities in me, like my sense of humor and my strong kidneys (I could drink a gallon of sweet tea and not get up once in the night) and my hands, which are small, not thin, not piano fingers but ragtime hands.

My dresses, blue or yellow or gold, depending on what warp or weave I was working on, had all the qualities you had no business thinking dresses had and the dress was just the beginning. Pretty soon I'd be thinking how I'd be walking into somewhere grand like the movie house on Washington Street and I'd be floating through in my yellow like a big old cabbage moth with the sun shining through my wings. Everybody would admire me. And I had pink dress and green coat and magenta scarf dreams and, of course, red shoe dreams where I'd die in a snowstorm on my way across the fields to the factory and the new loom-fixer and Mr. Roxy and Pa would find me and feel sorry for me. They'd find me 'cause of them red shoes, see? I had a pocketful of scenes like boys do rocks and coins and I'd dig out one after another and spend the morning elaborating on them while I worked. It was in one of them daydreams that I dreamt Art's hands.

Art was the loom-fixer and we always had an excuse to call him over. He coulda had the pick of us, him being one of the only men in the weaving rooms beside the foreman. And God and the Devil could not be more different than the foreman and Art. 'Course, I always did get the Devil and God mixed up, what with the Devil urging you to get away with something and God with his eye on you so's you can't rest. Just like the mill foreman. Art was sweet as a cow. He had eyes the color of a work shirt, that calm blue they fade to, and he was that calm inside, never making us feel like a loom breaking was our fault. He knew each of our names and made sure he said them, which was like a blessing, I'll tell ya, in that place of no names. He had a personal smile for each of us, though Art was no flirt. He was slow and quiet, walked slow, talked slow, but he was always there when the machine stopped and could fix it faster than those who hurried. There was a lot of what we called appeal in a man who moved so slow.

Art was tall and thin and there wasn't a one of us who wouldn't of cooked her fingers to the bone to fatten him up. We could tell right off he'd lost his mother early 'cause he had that respect for women, the kind of wide-eyed longing boys have before they've grown old enough to rebel against her. He was quiet but he wasn't shy. He was the kind of man whose eyes caught on something like a bird of prey and didn't let go 'til he was sure of what it was and if he wanted it. That's how he was with me, though that don't say much for him, hunting out a muskrat-looking woman with hair like a calf sucked it. But there he was, checking on my loom when it wasn't even broken, asking if I was working Saturdays or how I was doing on the rates. You see, we got paid for how many warps we'd finish and I'd get about four done a week. Seven dollars a warp. Whenever I'd stay longer to get one done, there'd be Art, asking if he could walk me home since the girls had already left. I started taking a real interest in trying to finish five warps a week.

Art and I'd leave that ugly mill and in minutes, the quiet we was making, soft through the shadowed fields, was building up something louder than the looms, Pa's coughing, and Lizzy's complaining all put together. Art noticed things in the quiet, a red fox slipping through the furrows to the pines, sugar maples dripping. Sometimes he'd point to something and he'd have to wait minutes before I figured out what it was I was supposed to be looking at. Pretty soon I'd see it was the perfect circles the sun was making through the leaves or the crossways dark lines in water. He'd watch the sky forever 'til I'd finally give up talking and look, too, though I still can't do it long. How it's always changing makes me feel crazy. Art made me a quieter woman; not quieter for him, quieter inside. For me. Listening. I'd ask him questions, like how come the circles was round when the space between leaves is not and how come the light around stars is blue.

"I don't know, Nettie," he'd say. Which shocked the hell out of me, 'cause until then I thought men knew the answers to everything. Least they pretended to. "Good question," Art would smile at me, like we had the rest of our lives to find out. He was so patient all impatience seemed foolish. When I walked home with him, I felt like we was in a rowboat, drifting in the current, though, like I said before, lakes scare me and I never get too close to 'em.

We walked a year before he took my hands in his. Just like in my dream, his hands were cold as ice. Some folks say, "cold hands, warm heart," but there's more to it. Cold hands is good for plants. They won't burn the seedlings. Cold hands means the person's not a drinker 'cause drinking heats 'em up. Cold is for laying on the forehead or the back, is a sure sign of a healer. How do I know so much about hands? I guess hands have been as important to me as feet was to my ma. I still stir the batter with my fingers. I think people lost a lot when they picked up the fork.

"Nettie, what do ya say?" Art said.

"About what?"

"About marrying me?"

Well, I'll tell ya. When a man asks a woman to marry him, a man who up 'til then has been like the sky she's seen too little of, is who she comes out into the open under, and the warm breezes and the cool ones, carrying shreds of rain, moving her clothes so they feel different on her body and her life is all lit up with sun and a new thing at every corner...or how about this: a man who's been like a wild thing to her, like the friend she makes of a deer munching the last of the corn cobs after harvest, who lets her sit down with it. A brother, sure, but a brother who don't know nothing about her father's being sick or how much short she is gonna be on the bills, a brother she ain't mad at 'cause he's gonna waltz out that door to get married and never look back, a man who, out of all the folks she knew, was one person that didn't need a thing from her; when that man asks her to marry him, it is one bad day.

Thing about it is, we don't have a choice. There I was, walking 'cross the fields at dusk, thinking about how his hair was like the grasses and how grasses was like the earth's hair and how bad hair smelled when it was burning but not grasses. I'd think about them things when I was with Art. He gave me time to. And now, here he was, acting like it meant something if I said no when the truth of it is, it was up to him in the first place to ask me. All this is decided without us: him to ask, me to answer. Don't get me wrong. Standing there, after ten hours at the mill, Art's hands fitting into mine like they was built for 'em, I couldn't help thinking cold hands was for tucking between your legs to warm 'em up.

But marriage? Marriage was stepping on a hill of problems and all of them scurrying out like ants. It brought everything back to mind: Tom's going, if Lizzy could get a job, if anybody was able or willing to take over the house, how to pay them doctors, who'd clean up that spitting Pa had taken to, and who'd steal the sugar out of the mill office for Lizzy's tea, and with no ma there, who'd help me with my first baby? I must've stood there scowling a long time. I remember seeing the lights of town go on and the sun sink and get caught in the thin green smoke that rose above the new steel mills in Gary. The houses started moving closer to the fields, so close I could almost hear the families inside, whispering about what's she doing out so long in the dark and why don't they get married and come in with the rest of us.

"What's wrong?" I heard Art say.

"We're gonna have to talk to my pa. He's not gonna like it," I said, trying, I don't know why, to hurt him.

Art, who I never heard raise his voice louder than mine, even in that deafening mill, just stood there, holding my hands to his chest, and waiting for time to settle it. Still smiling. You may call me a sinner, Lord knows there's many who would, but I swore I'd have him right then and there, despite all them folks in the houses, their barking dogs approaching like we was escapees. I swore, just once, if I couldn't have nothing else, I'd have him in between. I'd have him outside the inside places we both knew we'd have to resign ourselves to. I was holding on to Art so fierce by then, he knew what I was thinking. Without a word we both turned, not letting go of an inch of each other, to the line of willow and scrub oak running through the fields like veins, not the windbreaks but those wooded, lasting memories of when the streams ran there. Art had no choice but to take my answer as yes.

My husband moved in with us the week I stopped menstruating, bringing with him his double-to-mine paycheck so's Pa couldn't say nothing about it. We took Tom's room since he'd already gone, which was kinda small as befitting a bachelor, but it was our own and we was both thin enough then to fit in the bed. Much to my surprise, Pa took to Art and it wasn't long before he was occupying all his time. Not that we didn't have some fine detours to the irrigation ditches or the windbreaks still, but it seems soon as Art moved in, Pa commenced his dying in earnest and the Big Lakes sent the storms of winter before we had time to take down the screens.

Pa didn't turn into cement like Ma did, getting thicker and stiff 'til you had to uncrack her knees to stand her. He turned infant, wouldn't eat, wouldn't drink. His hips stuck out like a woman's and his clothes looked like hand-me-downs. He'd just whimper, coughing up every unnatural color this world has pitched into a poor man, coal and oil and all the tar that has no business coming out of the ground, not to mention the bile of having a daughter support him and a wife die young. Mining is a curse, Aunt Till says, and I can believe it. That's why they hire somebody else to do the digging. Pa coughed up so much, there was nothing left but blood, so that came, too, and took some of his adulthood with it.

He was like a boy, and in a way, happy as one. How his eyes would light up when we'd walk in the door after work, not at me but at Art. Early on, Art had moved Pa to the sunporch. They'd sit there 'til past midnight sometimes. Smoking, for God's sake! Me, I'm the kind of person's just no good when there's nothing to be done. If I can't do, I'm irritable. But Art, he didn't have that saving thing on his mind and he was so good with Pa. He and Pa had an understanding. Like dying gave them something, gave 'em the time we never have in our hard life of working, and time is gold to a poor man. Pa read the Bible three times, both old and new chapters, and him and Art would discuss it. Art'd bring Pa stale bread they sold to the bums by the tracks and Pa'd spend his day tearing it up and having one of the kids throw it out on the snow for the birds. When we'd get home, Pa'd tell Art what birds came and how many and how he'd wished he had his gun for the squirrels. Not many of them birds come by nowadays.

I can see 'em sitting there still, Pa bedridden but sitting up in bed, Art in the straight-backed chair next to him, looking out across the fields and the woods, talking about crops or the land. What sticks in my mind is how they'd talk about the finches. Art said there was so many of 'em in Town of Pines 'cause this used to be a big white pine grove. I felt kinda sorry for 'em then, and have since, how they could keep coming back to what they once knew, hoping maybe it was all make-believe, and one time they'd return and there it'd be, the forest so big they said a squirrel could make it from the ocean to the Mississippi without touching ground.

I know what them finches are thinking. Sometimes I lean out my windows and can imagine acres and acres of those tall trees, and sometimes I long for 'em. If I've never seen 'em, how can I long for 'em? "I don't know, Nettie," Art would say. Aunt Till says it's 'cause they're all still here. It's just we can't see 'em. I say if you can't see 'em, they're gone. Marie says you can't see the wind neither but it don't mean it ain't here.

I never lived in a time when we didn't worry about the land and the animals. I never lived in a pure time. You may be surprised to hear that, thinking it is a modern problem, but we was worried way before that river caught on fire in Cleveland. Think we didn't notice how something was always sifting down outa the sky like sugar? Maybe it was poison, we thought, since we'd have to take the washing down from the line and do it over. Our breath would come labored and our hearts speed up, but who could know if that was weariness or grief? You think the farmers didn't notice how the rain came less just about the time the last trees was cut down? Don't think my grandparents didn't know trees call for what they need.

Now they're saying we can fix all these mistakes. Call back the rain and separate the good fish from the bad fish in the Big Lakes. I ain't no scientist but I'll tell ya something. You make a mistake, you made it. It's like baking. You go correcting with yeast for too much salt, salt for too much sugar, and pretty soon you got something that's never gonna rise. The more you fool with it, the more problems you got. I'll tell ya something else. Nature makes mistakes, too, but we don't know 'em. It's too big a kitchen for us to know 'em.

Same thing with Pa. Nature done what it could already. Art wasn't healing Pa, though he'd close his eyes and lay on them cold hands. He gave Pa companionship. And companionship, Ma always said, was the best you could give in life. That don't mean Pa didn't suffer, but pain is a funny thing. It comes packing its own relief. Cut yourself good and the swelling takes care of the nerves so ya don't feel the doctor sewing you. By the time Pa was coughing blood, his mind had turned in another direction, away from us and from his scarecrow body that collapsed on his bones.

Me, I was pregnant and preoccupied, my stomach so big it was pushing Art outa Tom's single bed at night. I couldn't help noticing I was growing while Pa was shrinking, growing like a squash on a vine. Somewhere I'd heard the dead will cling to what's around 'em so they can keep living, and even if it was my own pa, I wasn't gonna be taking any chances. I kept a long way from that porch. I'd get up with Lizzy at dawn, run downstairs and start the coal stove, get the eggs, feed the hens, fix the school lunches, though half the time they was getting cracklings and sugar between their bread. All without much past a hello in Pa's direction.

I'd wake Art and we'd have our coffee, then head out across the fields, climbing over and dipping under the fences, waking the town dogs, snow blowing in our faces so's by the time we got there, they'd be burning like after a day of canning. It'd take us more than thirty minutes though it didn't look that far. It was 'cause of them fences. Now there's houses shouldered up round the mills so you would never know they was ever in a field and not part of town. The factories bought up all the fields, built the houses, too, and sold 'em to their workers. Cheaper than slaves 'cause you didn't have to feed 'em. Art and I never missed a day of work. We couldn't afford to.

For once, I was glad it was freezing inside the mill 'cause I could wear my coat all day and nobody'd be the wiser 'bout me having a kid. Art'd bring me treats, hot sugar water or walnuts he'd find on the way home and spend nights with Pa shelling. Sometimes he'd just lay them cold fingers back of my neck and it didn't matter if I was on my feet too long. And those yellows and blues and greens my mind used to land on like a butterfly flitting from one clover to the next? They no longer set me dreaming. My mind was set. It was a god-awful winter and I was gonna make me a comforter big enough for me and Art and the baby to hide from it.

It wasn't like I couldn't of found enough cotton scraps around the house, though it is true every piece of clothing walked the line from apparel to apron to rag. I coulda made a quilt of dish rags and don't think folks didn't. And flour sacks and grain bags, too. But I had it in my mind I wanted a wool quilt, thick and scratchy and earth-toned as the suitings we was weaving, just like if we was sleeping under a pile of autumn leaves. My mind would light on a pattern some girl'd be making and I'd have to have it, something honeyed, dyed with butternut or pecan, something the color of squash or pumpkin, a stem-green running through it.

I bought me a real good pair of dressmaker's shears. I kept 'em in my boot like Marie did her knife. It took me the whole nine months to steal enough scraps to cover us, trimming the corners and salvage like they did before shipping 'em to the dress-makers, tucking 'em up my dress and into my panties. Even Art had no idea, though some of the girls caught on fast and would stuff my overshoes with 'em so's I had to walk on top of the cloth all the way home to not let on. One day, those girls 'bout wet their drawers when the foreman stopped me on the way out the door.

"Nettie, open that coat."

He said it so's half the mill could hear him. Art was quick to my side. "What's up, Mr. Stuart?"

"No harm intended, Art, but Nettie looks mighty big round the middle and the manager's been getting complaints there's big holes cut out of the middle of some of the weaves. I'm just checking."

"You ain't accusing my wife of stealing, are ya?"

"Art, I ain't saying that. You and Nettie is both hard workers here. But when a skinny woman starts walking out every day like she's got four bolts of fabric under her coat, I gotta check her. I ain't a stupid man."

Art leaned over and whispered in Mr. Stuart's ear. "She's having my baby, sir."

"Oh, shit," the foreman said. "Oh, Lord, Nettie, I'm sorry." He was turning red as can be. Me and the girls just stood there, enjoying it. "I didn't know," he stammered. "Why the hell doesn't somebody tell me these things?"

I tried to think of something that would make me seem embarrassed, too, but all I could do was giggle.

"Don't you worry, you two. Your secret's safe with me. Though if she passes out or something, we ain't liable, you know."

"I'm fine, sir," I said.

He glanced at me and said to Art, "How long's she gonna work?"

"'Til she can't," Art said.

Doctor said it was on account of bending over and under the quilting frame. Lizzy thought, if it was anything, it was them damn fences we always was shortcutting through. Whatever it was, I went into labor on bended knees, crying out for mercy on the Ides of March, the rains coming with a vengeance. I was screaming and Lizzy was screaming, handing me towels to gnaw on. The rain was hitting all the pots and pans laid out to catch it, the little ones whimpered, scared at my screaming, and the cook-stove roared with the boiling water atop of it, making it so hot we had to open windows and let more rain in. And, as if all hell hadn't broke loose, Pa's moaning began.

I was bleeding like a stuck pig and the house filled with the smell of it. Art was wide-eyed, sending the kids off in all directions, for the midwife and the doctor and to stay with the neighbors. Poor folks didn't have telephones in the thirties and the roads was so muddy that by the time the doctor came, it was hours. The midwife took one look at me, threw up her hands, and went in to tend Pa. The doctor shook his head at Pa and came in to me. It wasn't until many years later that Art told me the doctor had given him the choice to save the son or me.

Pa died two days after my first son did and though Art says nobody told him, I'm sure he knew. Nobody came in to tell me about Pa neither, but like with him, they didn't have to. I never asked if his eyes was open or shut or if he wanted my hand or didn't. Art said it was peaceful and I gotta believe him 'cause Art is a truthful man. We didn't have a big funeral. Nobody was up to it. Just a tiny casket and a bigger one, buried the same day and next to Ma. I was too weak. I sent Art and Lizzy instead. We felt like we had no choice but to bury the baby with Pa's name.

I don't know how it is we do it. How it is we keep going when everybody we love is gonna die. Did we agree we was just gonna keep going? Did we agree the best thing to do was to try and forget it? "Try and forget it," Lizzy kept saying to me. But what about them dreams that come half-eaten by the soil, or with a mask, Death's mask, pale green or like a nylon stocking's been stretched over their features? What about the deathbed dreams or them that take it as their duty to announce the moment of death over and over? All I wanted to know was: Where'd my baby go?

God. I never did think about God. I thought about life. You'd have to remind me of him now and then. I'd remember something somebody else said about him, if I was pushed, like he was some movie star, and us, far from Hollywood or Beverly Hills, just hearing the rumors. Not that we really cared. But, shit, death comes, ya think about God. I thought, if I met God, I'd spit in his face for taking my baby. I ain't no fool. I know he's stronger than me. He done whipped me already. Brought me to my knees. I just figured, at that time, I didn't have nothing left to lose.

My ma was gone. My pa dead. And he took with him my baby boy which I may or may not ever forgive. There was my sisters Mary and Lydia, dead before I knew 'em. Also my brother Heine. Ruby was married and moved away. So was Kate and

Helen. Lizzy was twenty and sure to marry the boy next door. There was Paul, who in six months would hop the freights and be gone forever. That left Henry, six, and Amos, seven, and the sweetest baby boy, who was Dot. Tom came back with Betty, his new wife, looking for Pa's tools and his pocket watch. Lizzy got so mad she couldn't talk, but I piled Pa's soiled overalls, his whittling knife, his half-empty pouch of tobacco, his blood-stained handkerchiefs, the pennies in his pockets, his spittoon, his chipped cup...I even threw in the stale bread he never got to throw, making a big old pile Tom had to wade through to get out the door.

Art went back to work and I stayed home. Lizzy took care of me 'til I got back on my feet. When I did, I started eating everything in sight, not tasting a thing, rather keeping-from-tasting, shoving so much in so I didn't have room to think. I started getting fat, sad-fat, not jolly-fat, you know that gray color of it? I'm a small-boned woman and it was a burden to carry. That time, too, is when my eyes started watering and they've been watering ever since. My grandkids say I'm crying, but that's not true. They're just waters. Aunt Till says even in the Mayan statues of South America, the women got tears in their eyes. They call 'em the rainmakers. I didn't feel like I was making nothing, water pouring polluted and thick as snot from my eyes.

It was just when I felt the rest of my life was gonna be a list with one person after another I loved scratched off it, when I took on this kink in my neck to ward off the blow of the next one, when I'd quit sleeping with Art, quit looking for things good 'cause I couldn't risk a tender spot to receive 'em, that Aunt Till came back into my life. It was Art that brought her.

"Nettie," he said. We was drinking our morning coffee. "There's a woman in town. I heard people talking. Says she can get you in touch with the baby."

"You're gonna be late for work," I said, clearing the plates.

Art wouldn't let me go this time. "No, I think there's something to it, Nettie. If you are opposed, I'll go by myself. But I sure would be thankful if you'd accompany me."

"Ain't no woman gonna bring him back." I poured scalding water over the cups.

"Let's try it, Nettie."

I sighed, weary. "Whatever you say, Pa."

"Nettie, please don't call me Pa."

I turned and looked at him, seemed like for the first time in a month. He looked older and younger at the same time, scared as I was and skinny as an adolescent. I wondered if he'd been looking at me the whole time I hadn't been looking at him. What fat I'd gained seemed like I stole it from him. His gaze was fixed.

"When you wanna go see this woman?" I said. "What's her name?"

"Till." Art, bless his heart, smiled. "How 'bout going tonight?"

Till met us at the door of a tiny red house near the tracks, close to where the Negroes lived, who'd been coming up in droves since the War and the strikes that had been spreading from one factory to another since the Depression started. I don't know where those people came from. Some folks say the factories paid their ways, went down to get 'em even. They was poorer, for the most part, than us.

Till's house was in a grove of its own, tall pines and maples, ivy vines and blackberry, so thick you could barely see through to know it was a house at all. If we woulda come in daytime, we'd have seen the yards of spider webs strung from branch to rooftop to eaves like some giant piece of needlework sewing the forest to Till's house. It gives ya the heebie-jeebies thinking about it, when, if you'd see it in real life, you'd see it was beautiful, airy and sparkling as Aunt Sophie's lace. Till says the whole world is like that. That we're all sewn together with everything else. We couldn't see the webs that night. When we walked through, it was like spirits was touching us, wiping across our faces like a chiffon scarf.

"Nettie," Till said, taking my coat. "I'm so glad to see you again. Come in. Come in. No one is here yet."

Since we hadn't no way of calling ahead, I thought she should be a bit more surprised to see me. "It's been years," I reminded her.

"So it has, so it has." She led us into a parlor filled with rows of folding chairs all facing in one direction. There was a picture of Jesus and, though there was a couple floor lamps turned on, it was pretty dark.

"This is my husband, Art," I said.

"Pleased to meet you, Art. And thank you for reuniting old friends."

Art looked puzzled.

"We met at my mother's funeral," I said. "I thought you was gonna open a church."

"This is my church," she said.

There was a knock on the door and two middle-aged Negro women entered, nodding to us. They was dressed to the hilt with jewelry and hats and high-heeled shoes. All of a sudden, I was aware how I'd let myself go. Me in my tight housedress and my wrinkled hose.

"Evening, ladies," Till said sweetly. "Mrs. Jones, Mrs. Thomas, I'd like you to meet Art and Nettie..."

"Gall," Art said. "Art and Nettie Gall. Pleased to meet you."

"They're gonna join us tonight," Till said.

I smiled. I ain't got nothing against Negroes, but I had never been to church with 'em. 'Course I'd never much been to church.

Next came an older German woman, so heavy she could hardly walk. Her husband held her arm while she plopped down in a chair, then he left to smoke outside 'til we was done. The more I looked at her, the more I seen it was Rosetta Spaid, the charmer who could cure a cancer or tell ya how sick you was by how many blossoms would float or sink in water. Next came that bartender from Pinola who healed Aunt Gertie's daughter of thrush. He went into a trance behind the bar and the next day the girl's mouth infection was loosening in chunks that looked like surplus kitchen cleanser. Till waited a few more minutes for any latecomers, then walked up to the front, smiling at us.

She was still so thin she had to drink dirty water so's we couldn't see through her. She seemed even thinner now with the curves and curls gone, no ribbons, not even a dress, only this outfit that woulda been a man's suit if it didn't have the long skirt. All dark as night between two houses. She'd cut her long blond hair to the quick and wore a pair of newfangled, wire-rimmed spectacles. She had the longest eyelashes, like a schoolboy's. Till looked like a schoolboy now, 'cept not like ours, rough and ragged from milking and dusted with hay. More like the boys at university I used to read about in them books about England.

"Welcome to the Spiritualist Church," Till said. "Town of Pines Chapter. As many of you know, I am Till Barnes, director, minister, and medium."

I suppose if I'd a known what to expect, I woulda been nervous. As it was, I sat there like we was listening to Preacher.

"Spiritualism," Till began, "is the science and religion of continuous life. We do not believe in dogma, but we do have a foundation for our beliefs. First of all, we believe in an infinite intelligence."

"We believe in Infinite Intelligence," the audience repeated.

"That's right," Till said. "And we believe we never die."

"Yes, Lord," Mrs. Jones echoed.

"Now, I'd like to remind our guests that Spiritualism accepts and teaches the philosophy of Jesus as we do that of others. And that we protest against every attempt to compel mankind to worship God in any particular manner." Till went on, step-by-step. "We affirm that communication with the so-called dead is a demonstrated fact. There are those of you here who have had someone you have loved die recently. I am here to tell you: be comforted. I am here to tell you there is no death. That death is not the end but only the portal to the Spirit World. The good news is: all who pass on still live."

The air in the room seemed like it was clouding up and things seemed like they was moving through it as if those spider webs had passed on inside. "We've come to the time in our service when I will see if there are any messages from our dear departed ones." Till closed her eyes calmly, more calm than I'd be if the dead was gonna come knocking on my door. "Please, pray with me and invite them here."

We waited. It was strange to be in church at night with floor lamps and folding chairs and a rug under my feet, waiting like I'd wait for the next number to be called at bingo. Till left us to our own prayers for minutes. Suddenly, she raised her head.

"Mmmm," she said, nodding as if she were listening to somebody. "I see a large woman with a beautiful face. Oh yes, you do have a beautiful face, honey," she said. "This woman says her name is Melody. She wants to let you know she loves you and is waiting for you. She says it's gonna be awhile before you see each other because you're going to recover from the illness that plagues you."

Mrs. Jones burst into tears, grabbing her friend's arm and soaking her sleeve in her outpouring. "My sister, my sister," she cried. "I'm gonna be well. Thank you, Lord."

"Now, here's a man with his hair slicked back from his

forehead. He's not walking so well. He has what looks like a sassafras stick to lean on."

"That's my pa," the bartender from Pinola said quietly.

"He says to tell you to be careful with the new calf. It's weak now but if you baby it, it's gonna turn out to be worth more than all of them put together." Till pursed her lips. "Let's see. There's lots of 'em crowding up to speak tonight. This one's holding a bundle." Till crooked her ear to the left. "A baby, yes. A pretty new baby. She calls it Jelly Beans, isn't that funny?"

I about died there on the spot. No one knew I called my baby that.

"She says to say the baby's healthy and in her arms."

"What's she look like, that woman's got my baby?" I yelled. Art was holding me back. He must've known I woulda started shaking Till.

"She says there is a project you haven't finished under your bed. Something that should be atop of it. She says to tell Nettie there's healing in the needle."

I guess it was Art who dragged me outa there that night 'cause he was who I was grabbing onto so tight.

Chapter Four

Everybody always wants to hear about Marie and who can blame 'em? "What'd she say then?" Lizzy or Art would ask me. "What would Marie think of that?" they'd say about the last freeze, the lay-offs, or the high prices. "God twists one hair on his head," Marie'd say, "one hair and the people burn up, the land freeze or river flood. He even sometime tie up the Devil." Or she'd say, "No loss hope. Ocean is big but ocean been upset too sometime. Just like United State." Used to be in Europe, Marie said, folks went out together to work in the fields and lived close enough you could hear a pin drop next door. America's not like that. "Too much work to do in America," Marie would say with pride. "No time for visit." Marie and Stanley stayed over in Pole Town in them days and it wasn't 'til Stanley's accident that we met up again.

Stanley. Some of us never took to the machines of America. Some never drove a car, never got a license, avoided fans and meat cutters and typewriters when we could. When our minds went wandering, it was on paths, not roads, and we backtracked and got lost, missed the shortest route on purpose, going clear out of our way for nothing except the sight of corn growing corn-silk early in the front lawn next to city hall or a family who hung their laundry out every Tuesday afternoon. Stanley was one of them people. Marie said she'd send him to the store and there he'd be, half an hour later, staring at the line of indigo, pink, and key-lime sheets blowing in one of the Negro yards. "Do ya really think they sleep under such colors?" he'd ask Marie in awe. Stanley never took to the radio neither and he was scared silly by photographs, said they robbed the memory of what was real. The more Stanley worked in America, the more peasant and Polish he got. It drove Marie crazy.

Stanley was soft. Soft as my upper arms and his hair was white as underneath 'em. His hair started turning when he hit thirty and he didn't lose one strand to no in-between gray. What with his blue-green eyes and long, dark lashes, he was dazzling. And he loved women. Marie said sometimes he'd stare at her from across the room looking like, if she'd let him, he'd crawl right into her lap. I'll tell you a secret. When Stanley was a boy in Poland, he wanted a doll. His pa beat him, his mother said she could see no good in dolls for boys, and his grandma made him one outa old scarves. Wool the color of apricots for the head and the rest wrapped in poppy red like a papoose. Stanley was soft as that apricot-faced doll his grandma hid under her bed. And that he carried all the way across the ocean to give to his first child. Stanley told me about it. The foundry in Town of Pines was no place for Stanley.

"Hunky," people called the Poles and Slavs back then 'cause most of 'em was. Bearish from the farms of Europe, round-shouldered, big-handed, hard workers who picked garlic from their teeth, never talked back, and lined up to work long days and overtime for nothing. Later on, hunky became "honky," meaning any white folks the black folks came in contact with, which was mostly Poles since they lived on the same side of the tracks. Some things was true. They was big and seemed dumb. They'd be the first to fall for a lie or the ruse of a choice. Though that says more bad about the liars and presenters of false choices. Still, Polacks seemed like the fools of the world. Sure, they liked to work outa respect for work itself, for the swinging of their arms and what they believed was the building of the dream of America, some giant railroad set with high-rise skyscrapers that would block our views of the sunset and rattle pictures off our walls. How was they to know they was building an America they'd never be able to afford?

I was glad Art was in the mills 'cause people got hurt in the foundries, burned on the hot iron, their feet slammed between the anvils and the hammers, or got their arms and legs caught in the chains. Men passed out regular from the heat in the summer. They'd haul 'em out back and throw cold water on 'em 'til they woke up. Men didn't talk about it for fear of complaining. No women worked in it, just worried as it belched green flames and smoke from the chimneys like it was on fire. The whistle broke up our days and rebuilt them to its timing. At six, we knew they was starting their shift and when it blew at four, we'd say a prayer for those who'd made it through another day. Even if you didn't know somebody who worked there, when the whistle blew, you'd think about them as if they was boys gone off to war. The men looked grim. I'd walk past sometimes at lunch and the men'd be spread out on their backs across the grass, most so hot and sick they'd bring their lunches home uneaten. Once I thought I saw Stanley and I waved, but he rose up on one elbow and stared as if I was from another world. And I was.

I often thought Marie woulda done better in the foundry than Stanley. She wasn't a homemaker and she wasn't much of a cook neither. Everything she made, she flavored with tomatoes and ginger ale. She'd take a swipe at cleaning, but before you'd know it, there she'd be, outside in her yard, burying rinds, skins, vegetable clippings and trimmings, pulp and cores around the trunks of every tree or spraying garlic and urine on her roses. Marie tar-papered the roof by herself and dragged stone all the way from the quarry for her garden. Stanley wore the same clothes for weeks, but the outside of his house was spotless.

It wasn't the unionizing that broke Stanley's health, though Marie would beg to differ. Marie always knew who her enemies was and, far as she was concerned, unions was evil. Unions was lazy men and weak women trying to get something for nothing. Unions was Russians and Jews with no other goal than stopping people who wanted to work from working. And in Marie's book, to have work was the best thing life had to offer. It didn't matter if Stanley came home so beat he'd have to eat his supper the next morning. Work was a gift from God. When Stanley came home with news they was starting to organize at the foundry, Marie hit the roof.

"What is this trouble Devil is making now? Everybody got home in America. Everybody got food, good to eat, plenty of it. Everybody got work."

"Marie, in America, people aren't making enough to buy groceries. They're not making a wage that keeps up with the prices. Half the country's out of bread while the other half's getting richer."

"Ocean she is big but ocean been upset sometime, too," Marie said.

"The men at work have been talking, that's all. Five dead since April. The company's not even paying for their funerals. Men throwing up from too much heat and the company saying if we don't like it, there's plenty more where we came from who will. We got to have breaks. We got to have shorter hours."

"You work short hour, you get short pay."

"We have to cool it down in there, too. Get some circulation."

"I love this country. America people be so good to me. Good people talk to me, learn me English. No union make against my country."

Stanley sighed. "It's not against the country. The country's against us."

Marie frowned. "You lose job, then what?"

"I won't lose my job unless everybody loses their job."

"So, everybody lose job. Plenty people want job. I hear young people talking." Marie lowered her voice. "Say Negro ready to foundry jobs having."

"They won't cross a picket line."

"People be hungry, they cross God. We cross ocean. We cross family, never be seeing again," Marie said fiercely. "And for what? For job!"

Stanley tried pleading. "You don't know how bad it is in there, Marie."

"Show me to boss. If he give me job, I work it. No job be bad like farm job."

"It's different work, Marie. It's nothing like you've known."

Marie slammed her fist down on the table. "How you know what I know? You grow up on pillow. You never work fields like I having to."

Some folks will say Stanley shoulda taken a strap to her. Though in the same breath, they'll say they don't believe in ever hitting a woman. Sometimes I wonder if the men don't slip those phrases into our vocabularies bit by bit so's it'll be no surprise when they let us have it. In Europe, Marie once told me, a man would just as soon slap his wife as slap his knee. That's why all the women there want to marry an American. Which is pretty funny since, in America, all the Polish men were looking for old-fashioned wives.

"What'd ya mean, Marie won't let you?" Stanley's co-workers chided him the next day. "What does she know?"

"I promised," Stanley said. "I promised her I wouldn't. I can't."

The man grabbed Stanley's arm. "In Polska, a man who lets his wife rule is the butt of jokes."

Stanley struggled free. "What does your wife think?"

"She thinks what I think," the man said. "If I was you, I'd go home tonight and knock some sense into Marie."

Marie could down Stanley in two seconds flat if she wanted to. She weighed a good twenty pounds more than he did and there wasn't an ounce of fat on her. He wouldn't know what hit him. And I can't imagine Stanley ever hitting anyone back. He was so gentle he could walk through water without making a wave. He could pick a mosquito off your sweater and not damage a wing, and once I saw a squirrel run right up his pants leg in Lincoln Park, mistaking him for a tree. Stanley came home from the foundry and told Marie that the men thought what she had said made sense and they had decided to forego any plans for a union. Three days later, one of the foremen let a hunk of steel slip from its cable as he handed it down to Stanley and three of the union leaders. Two of their backs was broke when it landed and it grazed off Stanley's rib cage on its fatal swing toward the other man.

Marie says it was the union dropped the steel 'cause Stanley wouldn't join 'em and Art says it couldn't of been a steel beam 'cause it woulda crushed Stanley, too. The foundry said it was the union that dropped it on the foreman and the union guys say Stanley was nowhere in sight. My grandkids say it didn't happen at all 'cause they looked for mention of it in the papers at the library.

"What happened next?" my grandkids are always barking, then correcting me if it don't fit in with their ideas about history. I believe in memory more than history, I tell 'em, and I do. It's easier in the beginning of your life if you keep to some kind of order, I suppose. "I'm three," you say, holding up three fingers. "Last year, I was two." You bend one down. As I get older, it gets harder to tell if what happened to Marie didn't happen to me instead or if I heard something later or if I witnessed it myself. That's why when people ask me about this date or that or what if or how come Art and Stanley and Marie and myself all ended up out of work at the same time, though Art says we didn't, that I got that one wrong, too, I can't tell 'em in a way they are satisfied with.

The facts of somebody's life would make pretty dull reading, don't ya think? Wouldn't ya think anybody's life would bore you to tears if they stuck to the events of it? Sure, we had unions and illness, bills and high prices, the outside things, but inside, boarded up so's you can't see, boarded up inside history like our broken windows would be 'til we could afford to get 'em fixed again, boarded up like the dead are in their caskets, there is life, the rich hues, a warm fire, a bunch of shared decisions I made with Art or with Lizzy when we got pushed into a corner and had only one or two ways out, the faces of my friends, sticking out in my mind bigger than the wars and the presidents. Or the hands of those who've passed on. Nothing heroic.

Take this quilt, for example. Not much to look at, then or now. Not made of silk or satin or brocade. I didn't have time to put no fancy border to it and the pattern's not the kind that makes you get eyeglasses after you finish it from all the close work. Just square next to square like the farmland is cut into. Fallow field next to a square of new shoots rising and here's the blue shadow under oaks in winter, the rockpile grays and the color of soybeans loaded in the wagon. Here's the stripes of rows of corn. Over there, a square of water, so's it must be the irrigation pond 'cause I don't think a lake was ever formed in a square. Till says if I ever went up in a plane, I'd see the whole nation's been divided like this quilt, square after military square. They even built the roads so as to patrol the edges. How did I know then that I was sewing a map of my life?

I did the quilt this way because it was easy. I ain't no artist and my patience is about as long as my little finger. I did the quilt this way, not in stars or trees or stairs, 'cause at the time I was piecing my life back together step-by-step. Till's been close when she said there was healing in the needle, though I think it wasn't in the needle, but that the needle gave me back the use of my hands. Picking it up, with its one challenge of threading a hole, after all them months of flipping levers and switches, the looms cracking so loud you would jump at the sound if it was anywhere else, gave me back something I hadn't known I was missing. I thought it was my baby that was missing, my ma and pa. And those scraps we stole? We didn't steal 'em. We wove 'em, didn't we? They was ours. I took what was mine back into my hands and I was running a needle through it.

Nights while Art was smoking or mornings after chores, I'd get out the quilting frame and talk to Jelly Beans or Ma. Just like Till said I could, and ya know what? They was there. I couldn't see 'em like she could. After all, she was trained. It's a discipline, she said, letting in only those spirits you can trust. I wasn't let-ting anybody in, just talking, like I used to, to Jelly Beans and Ma. And you know what I found out about the dead? They're kinda like women. You know, when you've been Art's wife, Tom's sister, Pa's daughter so long, when you're too busy cooking lunch to join the conversation and too used to being ignored to insist? If just one person slips in the kitchen, one person starts talking to you, asking you questions, seeing you ain't deaf and dumb, well, you start feeling more color in your cheeks, you feel your life coming into focus like a Polaroid snapshot, gathering around you whole and round and unexpected. It's like a mask falls off. A death mask. The more I talked to 'em, the nearer they'd come, stronger and more lifelike by the minute. I set a chair next to me and a pan of Epsom salts for Ma's feet. Some-times I could feel Pa there, too, though he never much liked to visit when women's work was being done.

Now, how did I know I would finish that quilt just in time to conceive my baby girl under it or was it that just as I finished it, Ivy was ready to come? Or that it'd be a cold night after Art and I had laid there talking or that we'd be talking about the unions the same time Stanley and Marie was? Or that the steel beam that flew into Stanley's ribs, starting something inside him so he couldn't work no more, was already bringing Marie and Stanley, Art and me back together again? If I've been telling these stories like I know why things happened or that they happened in some kind of order that makes sense, I'm wrong.

It was hard enough to know what to think at the time. Seemed like the whole town was crazy with talk of unions, people switching sides like a game of musical chairs. Just about the time I was ready to go back to my job at the mill, Art came home with news the ladies there was ready to strike. "They're hiring, Nettie. Word went out today. Mr. Stuart says if they get enough applying, they're gonna fire the whole kit and caboodle that's agitating there now."

"What are they striking for?"

"Same thing everybody else is. They want the eight-hour day. And they got to swallow another pay cut." Art lowered his eyes. "Mr. Stuart said to be sure and tell ya they was hiring. He asked me if you was ready to go back."

Till says there's a heaven for the workers this country struck down, the wildcatters and complainers and the fed-up ones without fingers and toes. I hope, when I pass 'em on the way to my heaven, they will forgive me my trespasses. 'Cause I can't say my people's the kind that never crossed a picket line, Art's neither. We'd cross 'em because we didn't understand 'em and 'cause nobody'd explained 'em and we'd cross 'em 'cause we dead-ended in some town without money and didn't have no food and no place else to go. Same reasons, I suppose, most poor folks crosses 'em. But these women was my friends. They stole wool for me and worked with me and they sent food home with Art when they heard about my baby dying. One Sunday, a few of 'em came to see me and brought me some homemade fudge.

"What about you?" I said to Art.

"Just the weavers so far. Nobody's asked me to join 'em yet. No need to worry. They need experienced loom-fixers."

"What we gonna do if I don't go back?"

"What we been doing, I guess."

A month later, we had more reason to worry 'cause I was three weeks late in my bleeding and the girls had called a wildcat strike.

Till was much misunderstood in Town of Pines although she could never get a grip on it. "Till," I'd say, after one more person'd stuck up their nose at her or after Preacher called her a charlatan in front of everybody at the dime store. "Till," I'd say, "most folks around here don't go around claiming they can talk to the dead."

"But it's scientifically proven," she'd say. "From ancient times, books have told of our talk with spirits."

"Well, maybe so, but folks also ain't used to women preachers. Much less ones who open up their own church."

"Why, there used to be more of us! Most of the mediums and ministers were women until the men made Spiritualism a formal religion. Most of those women did it in their homes."

"They ain't used to women going around telling 'em what they should think about things either."

When Till first came back to Town of Pines, she traveled to the different churches, to the meetings of the Elk, the Moose, and the Lions performing what she called trance speaking. She'd walk up to the speaker's platform, close her eyes, and invite the audience to ask her any question they felt like, from the politics of the coming war to the history of England, what she thought of the new immigration quotas or free love for women. And they would ask her the craziest things at first, the men trying to trip her up or embarrass her, asking about how to prevent babies or how the women was gonna vote. Once they seen Till could dance rings around any question they could throw at her, they asked better questions. Until they started not taking to her answers, and then they quit asking her to come back.

"I'm not the first woman to speak out about things. How do you think we got the vote? Sojourner Truth was a Spiritualist in her old age, you know."

I'm ashamed to tell ya I don't know who Sojourner Truth is and I ain't no more the worse for it. The vote didn't mean much to me anyway since nobody in my family was ever asked to run for election. I was more interested in driving than voting, but Art said women who got their licenses was women who never stayed home. I was disappointed even if we didn't have a car.

"Nettie, it's not me talking anyway," Till was saying. "It's the spirits. You know that and so do my audiences."

"Right," I said, "the spirits. I forgot."

Till held services on Wednesday and Sunday nights and she gave what she called private readings by appointments. There was special spirit lectures on health or the law or music, holiday services and a healing circle which met on Saturday. It was a good thing Till inherited her house. Far as I could tell, the same ones attended everything, though new people came for the readings or healings when somebody died or got sick. Till's church was not overcrowded. Art and me tried attending her services but what with Art working and Lizzy asking us to spell her so's she could go out on dates, it was too much for us. We made sure we went to the healing circles on Saturday. It wasn't long before I'd learned more about that circle of people than most people know about their own families.

Oh, it was fun! I'd bring a covered dish, my hot potato salad, wilted lettuce, or scalloped field corn. Mrs. Jones would bring the best fried chicken and Mrs. Thomas made the rice pudding. Mr. Harold Hullinger from the Pinola Tavern could bake a pie that'd make your mouth water just to look at it. Blueberry from his bushes, wild raspberry, gooseberry, fresh peach, or rhubarb simmering in real ginger and vanilla; every week something new was in season and when it started getting nippy, we'd have pumpkin and apple and sweet potato pie, banana creme with drifts of meringue. Rosetta Spaid never brought nothing but the coffee and what coffee! Tasted like she'd picked the beans herself, brewed 'em with chicory and some kind of root she dug up in the woods behind Fish Lake.

I liked Rosetta Spaid. She was past my ma's age and about as heavy. She'd been prescribing remedies for folks in Town of Pines since before I can remember. Rosetta knew every wild patch and grove left in the county, the mushrooms and poisons, the murderous bulbs you wouldn't suspect was growing right underfoot and could kill ya if they didn't cure ya. Indiana used to grow just about every medicine you can think of, ones that grow in China and Indiana and nowhere else. Like wild ginseng. Rosetta'd go south and hunt for it. She did a fine business. Rosetta Spaid: Charms and Folk Remedies. She didn't have a sign outside her door but she might as well have. People came to her with all kinds of strange illnesses they'd be frightened of 'til almost too late to show anybody: goiters and growths and sores breaking open and stones growing inside 'em, blood needing to be thinned and blood needing to be thickened.

Rosetta had a glassed-in front porch with plants hanging from the ceiling, on every sill and ledge, on the arms of wicker chairs, all of 'em coated with the dust of the dirt road outside her door and looking close to dying 'cause she never picked the dead leaves off 'em, just let 'em fall. African violets and crocheted dolls set between 'em and red, green, blue bottles filled with water and food coloring. Rosetta had the strongest basil, dark green and muscled, so's walking into her house you'd think she was always cooking a stew. She said the seeds had been passed down from her grandmothers.

Rosetta didn't look the healthiest but seems healers never do. She was covered with warts and moles though she had a reputation for being good at removing 'em. You know, them dark little animals that hide under your clothes? Ma used to tease me, pick up her breast, look underneath it and shriek, "Oh, shit, here's another one!" Scared me to death. She never went to Rosetta for moles. I guess 'cause she felt like she'd earned 'em. Rosetta was good at charming freckles off and cancers, too. Said she'd learned it from friendly Indians when she lived up by the Big Lakes. And another thing? Rosetta talked to plants and animals. She could understand 'em. She said she learned that from the Indians, too. She said that at one time we could all do it. I asked Till about it later and she said it was true. "Well, what happened?" I asked her. "How'd everything get so confounded?"

Till brought out a book that had a list in it of one sale on the Big Lakes in 1763. It was from a trading company by the name of Hudson Bay:

127,080	Beaver
110,000	Raccoon
116,512	Bear
112,428	Otter
130,325	Marten
11,276	Wolf

Till said there used to be wild turkeys, wolves, buffalo and elk, even lions here in Town of Pines, just like those clubs she speaks at are named for. She said the last buffalo was killed in 1801 at Buffalo Cross, Pennsylvania. "Would you talk to us after that?" she said. Till was always bringing out books.

Mrs. Jones and Mrs. Thomas always came together. Mrs. Thomas was the younger and she always gave Mrs. Jones her arm. Till was often invited to speak at the black churches and she told me that sometimes she went to their church. Those two ladies went to the Baptist Church and they went to Till's and they was more regular at both than anybody. And more friendly. Mrs. Jones was so easy to talk to, you felt like you could ask her anything. One Saturday, I did. "How come your people keep your dead around so long before you bury 'em?"

"Well, honey, there's two reasons," Mrs. Jones said. She had pillow breasts and heavy-lidded eyes. She was short as me and I liked that. "One reason is family. Death is important for family to see. Else they don't know it really happened. We keep 'em 'til everybody from one end of the world to another's got time to get here."

"That makes sense, Mrs. Jones."

"And the second reason is mourning. We do believe in proper mourning. Giving it your full measure."

Each of the people in the healing circle had their practices and their gifts. Mrs. Thomas and Mrs. Jones believed in prayer, to Jesus in particular, though they wasn't adverse to frequenting their own witch doctors or Rosetta Spaid. They shied away from Harold Hullinger. I suspect it was because of the drinking.

Harold would sit at the Pinola Tavern reading his Bible 'til somebody came in for a drink or a healing. Harold was a diviner. People in Town of Pines went to him with their children and to find lost things. When Rosetta's herbs seemed too strong to trust their little ones to, there was Harold, his face dark and scarred from smallpox, so quiet and effective he wouldn't touch the child at all. He could tell right off what was wrong, looking at the sick one longer'n people look at anything nowadays. Then he'd tell the parents to take the kid home and put it to bed and, no matter how long it slept, to not wake it. They'd watch, anxious, while it slept four, five, or seven hours, checking the breathing to see it hadn't died and when the child woke, it was cured. Harold, in the meantime, was out behind the bar, doing whatever it is he does, not eating, not sleeping, in some kind of a trance all day. It was hard on his married life.

Art and me? We was still learning. And with Till, we made seven. Till said it woulda been better for the currents if we had more men, but we felt lucky to have what we did. There were times we'd get to visiting, exchanging recipes and eating, having such a fine time getting to know one another, most of us would plumb forget why we came. Like I said before, there was some who never took to the machines of America. We took to other things. Things it didn't seem then that the rest of the world would find useless, though Till did her best to warn us again and again.

"There will come a time when people will abandon their ways as easily as they abandon the land here in Indiana. What they can't see, they won't believe in. Trouble is, they'll have given up seeing. And hearing, smelling, and tasting, too. The paths will become so overgrown between this world and the next that when your grandchildren say the paths were never there, you may find yourself nodding and agreeing. Remember," Till said. "It's up to us to maintain the paths."

We'd always start off with a song, if I remember right. Till would lead a prayer, we'd all hold hands, and anybody who wanted to could ask for special healing for a friend or a loved one or for themselves. We'd all try to put our best thought toward it. Till said the suggestion of health is as strong as any medicine. "Faith, hope, and kindness stimulate the life forces and promote nutrition," she said. Sometimes, Rosetta or Harold Hullinger would seek Till's help in solving a particular case they'd been working on and Till'd ask if any of the spirits was willing to give advice. I'll never forget the time the spirits singled out Art. We'd got there later than usual, so late he didn't have time to relieve himself before the seance began, and we'd been drinking coffee with Uncle Odie all morning. Just as we arrived, Till turned the lamps low, we sang, and we wasn't long into it when, out of the clear blue, Till said, "There is someone here who is deeply uncomfortable. The spirits say to let him know it is ok for him to break the circle." Sure enough, Art stood up and left the room. He never came back neither, just waited outside for me 'til we were through. Wouldn't you?

It was during one of those times when the spirits was talking to Till that she said to me, "You have a friend named Marie whose husband needs us. He is looking for a healer and can't find the way. In this instance, you are the way."

"Hell," I said to Art on the way home, "I don't even know where Marie lives anymore."

"Looks like we gotta find out since that spirit didn't leave us no address," Art said.

"Voodoo," Marie said when I finally caught up with her. "Voodoo is all he has on brain. I make appointment with doctor. I walk with him so no way lost making. What does he say when we get to door? 'Marie, you take me here to die.'" We were sitting in the front room of the house Marie and Stanley was buying, which was close to Mrs. Kaminski's at the end of a gravel road which now's the main four-lane through town. Till said all the towns are laid out like this, like a cross, one main road intersecting the other. Marie and Stanley lived on the left hand of Jesus end. It had taken me a half hour to walk to it.

"First, he want to village woman going. I tell him: there is no village woman in America. Next, he want to find someone maybe drugs giving. Last he think of is doctor. This is old-fashioned way. In America, doctor is first."

"In America, the doctor goes inside the body and cuts everything away from you. At least in Europe, the doctor takes nothing away," Stanley said.

"Why I be cursed with stubborn man?" Marie shouted.

Stanley let her calm down a bit, walked over and offered me his pocket. "Want some candy, Nettie?"

I reached in and came out with a toffee. Stanley hadn't changed a bit. We both giggled like children.

Marie, of course, didn't like that. "Better throw penny in street. Stanley feed whole town out of pocket. Better throw seed. Raise pigeon and eat it."

Stanley laughed. I did, too, 'til I seen the circles growing under his eyes, cracked fine and silver as pastry. Looked like the palm of my hand only showing on his face. People can always hide a pain until they laugh.

"What's the trouble, Stanley?"

"I'll be fine. Don't you worry."

"Blood back up from stomach. Come up with food. He pain having," Marie scolded. "Big pain."

"Guess you ain't working since you don't feel so good?" I asked him.

"Not yet. I don't have the strength for it yet. I'm going back though," Stanley said, glancing uneasy at Marie like she was gonna deny him, "real soon."

"How long you been out?"

"Month."

It wasn't my place to ask 'em how they was getting by. I didn't need to. There was Marie, no less thick-waisted, but she'd go without everything before she'd give up her new-won eggs and meat. Looked like they was living in one room to save coal. There was a pile of covers and pillows next to a sprung couch and we was sitting on three mix-matched chairs she must've found at the dump. Each had a new leg or cross piece or a board nailed over where the caning used to be. Marie could squeeze blood out of a turnip. It was dreary, nails sticking up outa the flooring and sacking for curtains. The oddest thing was that it was all staring right back at you 'cause across the entire back wall of that meager room was the finest beveled mirror I think I have ever seen.

I was sure they could feel me staring at 'em, my eyes ricocheting off the mirror behind 'em but we sat there quiet and my eyes would not let go. How many times I'd laid in my bed, staring up at the ceiling and the whole room'd be changed. I could build another life up there with new furniture, new brothers and sisters, new doors in and out. Same thing with this mirror. The more I looked, the more things seemed different than they was. Marie, her strong back to me, her hair sticking up outa her scarf since she'd taken to chopping it off herself. That prideful, angry, headstrong head, turning nervous to catch me looking at it: I seen in that mirror that she was terrified. Stanley avoided the mirror altogether. He didn't wanna see what I could plain as day, how he was getting thinner, not being able to eat but giving out candy, how you could tell by looking at him he wasn't going back to no foundry. And me, catching myself outa the corner of my eye, wondering how come I got to be joined in this picture with everybody else, all of us caught, looking and not looking.

"Why's that mirror there?" I finally said. "What'd this used to be before you moved in?"

"Tavern," Marie mumbled. Like she seen what I seen.

"We have money saved up for Laura," Stanley said, glad somebody was talking. "Marie thinks we should open some kind of business. Like the other Poles are doing. Something that doesn't need a lot of capital. Like a tavern. Maybe she's right. Though I sure feel we'll have disappointed Laura. She was counting on us."

Marie and I exchanged looks. "Stanley, what good would you be doing Laura by sending her sister out on the streets?" I said.

Stanley lowered his head. I might as well a told him what I seen in the mirror. Pried open his lids and held his face up to it. It wasn't my place to tell a man what to do with his life.

"Well, I don't see any good reason why this couldn't be a tavern again!" I said, over-cheerful to hide my shame.

Nobody said a word. In the silence, my eyes drifted back to it. I'd seen a mirror like that one before. Where was it? Did I dream it? One a bit smaller, yeah, with a stuffed owl perched huge on the counter, big enough to pick up a child, which I was, seven and staring at the jar of somebody's gallstones next to a jar of boiled eggs and another one of pickled pig's feet. "Which one you want?" the bartender said as I stood on tiptoe. He laughed and handed me the mince pie I was collecting for my grandma. There, behind the bar, was Harold Hullinger.

"I know somebody who can help you," I said, excited. "Probably got some extra equipment, too. He runs the Pinola Tavern clear on the other end of town. He's been running taverns forever. I could take Stanley to meet him on Saturday."

Marie and Stanley stared at me like I'd gone off my rocker. "Come on," I said. "We may as well get this show on the road."

Jelly Beans is the one told me Ivy was coming, way before I noticed I had missed my time of month. I didn't pay him much mind. That's one thing about the dead. They are easy to ignore. They don't send letters you can refer to, don't talk when you got a witness around, don't really talk at all in what you would call language. They talk in pictures. Pictures that fly into your head with the swiftness of a sparrow, like a shadow, whizzing by. "Images," Till calls 'em. "It's how the world speaks to us."

Now I am what you would call a slow person. They wouldn't

let me finish high school 'cause I was too dumb. I'm lying again but you wouldn't know it if ya hadn't heard how I'd had to quit. Till finished high school. That's where she read about a man named Emerson who said thoughts are like birds unlooked-for in the trees and, if you turn your attention, disappear just as easy. I always got that mixed up with what she said another man said, by the name of Thoreau. One time, a sparrow landed on his shoulder and he thought it was better than any medal he could've worn. So, what I always told people was: Thoughts is like sparrows landing on your shoulder and when ya reach out to grab hold of 'em, they're gone. Not that I ever had a sparrow or nothing land on my shoulder, leastways nothing lighter than the weight of the world. Most times I miss those messages landing and gotta go to Till to see I ain't missed too much. Till says it's just practice.

The only reason I remember Jelly Beans told me about Ivy is that when I said to myself, "Nettie, you are gonna have another child," somebody was saying it in unison with me. There are moments in life that feel like that, where everything in front of you and in back of you joins your knowing. It's a kind of music, like a bunch of bells hitting so pretty, pretty soon you can't tell what bell's being struck when.

Ivy. Where'd she come from? Not from men's gooey leavings and seed, looks like what you scrape outa the middle of a rotten pear. What you fry down for lard. And not from the blood wrapped around her in my womb to make a home. I can't believe it's as nasty in that home as the blood that comes out between my legs. Maybe it's hitting the air makes it smell sour as beer-making and just as ruddy. No, Ivy came from a quiet place, snaking into that cavity of my heart what was sealed off with thick mourning curtains, crawled right in behind 'em so's I missed her entrance, just like that Mr. Thoreau said I would.

It's a wonder I ever noticed her growing there at all, what

with all the commotion. And Ivy is still like that, letting people know that she realizes there is more important things going on in their lives besides her. How she don't get sick of all the neglect she asks for I don't know. Gathers it in with open hands, she does, begging for more when she sees the layers of it wearing thin and her own needs showing.

Commotion it was. The ladies at the mill left their looms humming and walked out down the aisles one after another like soldiers, even the little ones, twelve, eleven, following their mothers and sisters out the door, Mr. Stuart glaring at 'em, jotting down their names, no job in sight for 'em and knowing, now, none would be offered. Art stood there and watched 'em, quietlike, then went around shutting off the machines. Later, Mr. Stuart accused him of knowing about it beforehand 'cause he done it so calm. Ain't nothing the surprise to us it was to them.

I know you heard it all before. I ain't got nothing new to add to it. But have you really heard it? Did you ever wonder what happened to those women and men fighting for the eight-hour day or humane working conditions when they lost their jobs? I know, you look around this country today and the poor just keep on coming. You think there couldn't of been any mass starvation and dying. That people just made do. The history books act like the unions started in the 1960s instead of the 1900s and even my grandchildren grow up thinking unions is wrong, on their way to their eight-hour job. Say they got more sophisticated thinking, got a high-school education or college. They think less of biting the hand that feeds 'em than we did before. They think a person gives you a job like it's an expensive gift. They think them that gets rich are doing us a community service. I can't figure it. Ever since I was grown, it was plain as the nose on my face. Nobody is in business for my health.

People lived in shacks and moved in together and kids quit school to find work on the farms. Yeah, and a lot of 'em died 'cause they got sick and had no doctors and the women who was carrying lost their babies without food. Look around you. You know what happened to those people got fired? Their children and grandchildren is the poor ones, the ones straggling in school, spending generation after generation trying to make up what they lost.

They brought in the Negro women on buses to work the mills and having heard how Mr. Stuart talked about 'em before, I can imagine their life was miserable there. Mrs. Thomas had a daughter was one of 'em and she said she was scared shitless of his wrath and the apple-wood walking stick he started carrying. What most of 'em was more scared of was walking past the rows of desperate honkies, threatening 'em and calling 'em names. The company hired guards to patrol the strikers. They was sure they was gonna break 'em in a week.

Art stood it for two, walking past each one of 'em on his way in to work, ones he used to smile at, ones he knew by name, by situation, by the numbers of kids or brothers or sisters they was supporting, by how many of their family worked and where. At first they let him go by, knowing his situation, too, but ya never strike when you can afford to. Soon the women looked at him with the same scorn I reserved for Tom when he came visiting with his company clothes and car from Chicago, ate my cooking, and left without giving us a dime. On Friday, one of the women's husbands walked him home.

"You got a family, Art. A wife," he said. "And Jessie tells me Nettie's expecting again. You wouldn't want nothing to happen to her, would ya?"

Friday night, my husband came home thinking so loud the rest of the household couldn't hear each other and hushed up. He stayed thinking through dinner, barely touching the chard I'd found sprouting early by the fence. A quiet man always scared Lizzy, so she had the kids clear the dishes quick and go on to their beds. When it was just him and me, he asked me out onto the porch. Twilight, late March, the sky the watery color of the days stretching out, rain-washed for weeks and hanging out to dry. The sun'd come out strong earlier, all the snow'd disappeared with the storms and, sitting there, we could smell the pine lifting up from the needles cast down around the trunks. Imagine the smell when the sun hit an entire town of pines! We had a pine tree out front. Art and I watched it, the trunk turning all shades of purple, silver, gold, the colors changing across the bark as the light changed. The sun was going down. I shivered and went back in for my sweater. When I came back, he was smoking.

"Nettie, I wanna go farming."

Funny, I can remember how still it was, me sitting there rocking, watching the blue-green dark come snooping around the porch like a stray dog. I didn't know nothing about farming. I knew Art didn't know much either, though his pa had started out a farmer before he went to work for the railroad. I didn't know nothing about not getting a paycheck at the end of the week, about weather or no weather, or about showing up 'cause you had to, not 'cause you was supposed to. A job, I knew, not a life. I didn't know nothing about work that was life and you had to think and plan and maybe not get paid for it. "I never be farmer," Marie had once told me. "Farmer be poor forever." I looked out across them empty fields of March, the few trees holding on, the smokestacks in the distance and their flames. Wasn't it too late to be going farming? If doubts was promises, I'd still be collecting. I didn't even look at Art, just sighed a sigh poor as the winds moving the bare willows.

"If that's what you want, Art," I said.

Chapter Five

This is the land of knowing how to grow things, a holy land
the Bible didn't mention, the home of potatoes and squash.
When Columbus arrived, smelling that sassafras on shore, he
also saw people. If mankind came from Egypt, like the Bible said,
who was these? Indians, he figured. What Indiana's named after.
Indians growing peanuts, tomatoes, chiles, and beans; green
beans, wax beans, pinto beans, lima beans, red beans, white
beans, kidney beans, and corn. And if food ain't holy, what is?
When Till told me all them crops was invented in America, I
said, "Thank God. What if I was born where I couldn't eat soup
beans and ham?" Marie thinks the Cadillac is the best thing
America invented. Not me. It's the word "ain't" and soup beans
and ham.

This is the land of knowing how to do things, a land of the
hand. In the doing is the knowing. The hand moves and the
hands of anybody who ever moved like that is moving, too, backing it up. Hands reaching, five-fingered as a maple leaf or a star
rising, smoothing sheets or the hair of somebody you love, shuck-
ing an ear or shelling peas, wrapping themselves around a seed
or a child or a prayer, doing it the first time as if they done it a
million times before. And they have. Look at these. Chapped
from doing dishes and plucking too many hens, nails bitten
down for worry, open for gifts or clutched against giving, just
like everybody else's. Rubbing each other warm before grabbing

the cow's teats, holding on to each other to keep from hitting a child: hands that got a life without you. In a way, folks know that. We trust in it. That's how I was able to leave behind my old life for a new.

It was April, gray and green as the winds sweeping through the spring woods, when we found our farm. Like I said, I didn't know a thing about farming, but I'd follow Art off a cliff if that's what he wanted. Don't you have somebody in your life like that? That you don't care where you land as long as you land together? It felt like we was falling, too, when Art got notice there was a place for rent south of town. Right away, he made an appointment to see it. And he came back tickled pink. It was just our size, he said, and the house? I was gonna love it. A hundred twenty acres, four barns and a chicken coop, pasture for the cows, a milk house, and a grove of lilac. The next day, Lizzy got the neighbors to watch the kids and the three of us started walking. It was a long cliff we was walking off of, took almost an hour. The road's concrete now. Then it was pure mud.

Mrs. Rose was the landlady. Of course, I took that for a sign. Which I do everything, the letters in the names of family and the number of crows flying. Dropping a fork during dinner means you're gonna have unexpected company, and you must try to not spill salt or rock a chair with no one in it. And you don't stand near the windows during a thunderstorm, though nobody believes me. That glass don't fool the lightning. Mrs. Rose? Our new place would be a beauty, strong, delicate, giving us joy and pain because of it. Of course, I'm superstitious. All women are. We're watching too careful what's gonna happen to us next, since most times nobody tells us. Or if they do, we don't have a damn thing to say about it. Used to drive Art crazy, my superstitions. Though he'd study the same birds, clouds, and bugs when *he* was predicting the weather.

They say if you dream about a house, that house is you. If

that's true, this was the house of my dreams. It was plain and rundown and entirely unnoticeable. You know, I can't even remember what color on the outside it was and I lived there thirty-five years. I can tell you about the wallpaper, though. Mrs. Rose picked it out herself, before she moved to her mansion in town with its carriage house, four extra bedrooms, and a maid. This wallpaper was the prettiest violet color with dark green and pale green ivy growing over it, some places so thick and thin with it that it was as if the sun hit stronger on different parts of the wall. Tiny white veins running through the leaves. I used to live in town, and then I moved into a farm house with ivy growing up the insides of my walls, and sometimes it would flower when the light shone in certain corners, and sometimes the leaves would shed in pale-backed scraps to the floor.

From the time Art unlocked the door for me, the house fit me like a glove. My granddaughter tells me she can't remember anybody but me being there at all, not even herself as a body taking up room, just me, placing bowls of mashed potatoes on the table, me stemming blueberries or pulling Art's long underwear through the wringer, steaming up the kitchen. She was surprised there was room for Art in there, let alone kids. And it's true: Art never did know what to do inside. He stayed out on the porch or, if he had to be in, sat in a corner in a straight-backed chair, his hands clasped in his lap like he was praying. He wasn't praying, I can tell ya. He was just waiting for the rain to quit so he could go back outside.

This was the house my daughter Ivy was born into, the house time outgrew. We did get electricity right away and, in 1940, got a phone. It was the house she'd grow ashamed of with its outhouse in the back, its chamber pots, and the pump in the kitchen. She'd come home from school complaining how she was the only kid without indoor plumbing, how she had to take her bath in a washtub behind the coal stove. She'd stay overnight at friends' houses but her friends? She never invited them to stay with us. Later, I heard her telling somebody it wasn't just the outhouse. It was me, wearing no brassiere and no shoes if I wasn't going visiting, growing wider as I got older, just like my ma. I wasn't the best housekeeper either. If there was good food to cook or a kid to hug, why should I waste my time on dust? Ivy thinks I never noticed how she'd spend the whole day cleaning when Art took me shopping for groceries on Saturday. She'd leave the dishes in the sink to hide the polished floor.

If Art learned to farm in the fields and the barns, I learned to farm in that house. When our neighbor lady died, the undertaker asked her husband if she worked or was she just a housewife? I wished I woulda been there. He woulda got a swift kick in the pants. Till says that's just the way people's raised. God does his glory in the world, the miracles shining off his fingers like diamond rings, and God's wife inside, making the chamber pots disappear and reappear without shit in 'em. God making manna rain from heaven and God's wife inside, salting it for the winter. I worked hard on that farm, don't think I didn't. In an average day, I'd milk the cows, scrub and scald milk buckets, feed the chickens, gather their eggs, bake bread and pies, make breakfast, dinner and supper, sometimes for twenty men, mend overalls, watch children and grandchildren, wash clothes on a wringer washer, slop hogs, feed horses, and, if I was lucky, I didn't have to butcher or can and it wasn't no holiday or Sunday. But I'm getting way ahead of my story.

As I was saying, it was April, rain and seedling-colored and we'd just toured the house. Lizzy, Art, and me was standing in the yard looking across at the most striking building in the county. It was nine-sided so it looked round, with a cap on top and "TOWN OF PINES" printed in white, fading lettering above the door. To tell ya the truth, it was the first thing you noticed about the place, not the house at all. Today it's a historical landmark. Then we kept our hay in it. It was built by Mr. Ridgeway for his imported Norman and Hambletonian horses. Impressed, are ya? I'm reading it off the back of a postcard they print now, the barn shiny with a new coat of red paint, the sheep barn next to it torn down, and a field of sunflowers—of all things!—waving in front of it where the corn used to be. Not a broken-down hoe or wagon in sight. The back of the postcard don't mention Art or me, not a mention of the thirty-five years we lived there. Just Mr. Ridgeway and his Hambletonian horses. What'd they do with all our years? Wiped us out of the picture like they did the broken tools, the corn, and the people working it.

"This is your place, Nettie," Lizzy was saying, her eyes beaming. "I can just feel it. It's like a castle."

It sure was a pretty sight and more than I figured a person had a right to live on. But there was something weighing heavy on my mind. I took a deep breath and asked her, "What are we gonna do about you? We can't just leave you alone with the house and them kids."

Lizzy blushed and I followed her gaze to where the oak woods was our nearest neighbor. "Joe's asked me to marry him. It'd be real nice if we could keep living in the house. Being right next to his folks and all."

"What about the kids?" Art said.

"Don't seem right to burden a new marriage with a batch of somebody else's kids. Ya probably want to start your own family," I added.

Lizzy kicked at the dust. I could tell she wished Joe was there. Since he wasn't, she turned to Art. "What should we do?"

"What would your ma want us to do?" Art asked her gently.

The three of us stood, listening to the morning birds, wishing we could run around the back of our new house, between the barns, up the trees, run around the place while it was magic, with the fox watching from the woods, the baby mice in the attic, ghosts in the cellar off the living room and the big summertime porch, before it was a place for borrowing money and too much work and dividing households. We was thin then, like children, and so we was tempted. We was also grown and orphans, and so we stood still.

"Seems to me," Lizzy said after awhile, "you should take Dot. He's young and it's gonna be little he remembers about Ma's house. The other two is older and should stay in town for school. They're not as much trouble and they're support for one another."

I smiled. Dot was so little when Ma died and I felt like I raised him myself. He was special to me and Lizzy knew it.

"That okay with you, Nettie?" Art asked.

"That okay with you, Art?" I answered.

We borrowed five hundred dollars from Art's brother-in-law, bought a pregnant sow, a cow with calf, two horses and a plow, and enough soybeans, seed corn, oats, and alfalfa to keep Art slaving from dawn to dusk. And Mrs. Rose was standing at the end of every summer, wanting her share, which was half. It wasn't until years later that I saw my husband's face again in full daylight, and I didn't recognize him. His face wasn't shadowed with the dim before dawn and we wasn't whispering serious about money or the kids in the ten minutes before we was on to our next chore. It was 'cause I wasn't watching him snoring, the line dividing the tan below his cap from his forehead, which glowed whiter and whiter as the summer months beat down. When I was younger, I used to think about how our lives coulda been different if we wasn't leading such separate ones. If I was out there with him more. Now, I wonder if maybe men and women will grow outa being able to talk to each other anyway, if it's set up separate for a reason.

It was sad to me in a way, 'cause I loved that man when I lost him to the fields I didn't have time for. That I wasn't important as the fields no more. I got used to it. A woman gets used to anything. Even being partners instead of husband and wife, though that hurt me the most. I was a sexpot in those days, if you can believe it, and that summer was the worst. Being outside all day, the moist Indiana air clinging to my skin, bare feet and open collars, cotton skirts flirting with my legs, I was tan and flushed with the heat and work and I couldn't understand why anybody wouldn't adore me. Some days I'd greet Art almost panting, my apron pulling tight as my size grew with Ivy. "Tired, Art?" I'd ask when we finally had our supper and got to bed. Before he could answer, he'd be asleep. I tell you, though I never told another, I thought about every bachelor up and down that dirt road to town, and some of 'em I thought about twice.

There was lots of work to do and Dot helped me, taking care of the animals, the ten piglets of the sow's, growing a garden we'd have to live off of since there wasn't any money for food-buying. Dot was scrawny, sensitive, and asthmatic to boot. Art couldn't of taken him to the fields if he wanted to with all that field dust and he didn't want to. Not that he didn't treat Dot like his own son. But Dot was mine to have, we knew it, seven years old with eyes that took up a good portion of his face, so bony you could see his wings. I'd lose Dot to the schools come September, but for five long months, I had the answer to any question he cared to ask.

"What's your real name?" he asked me.

"You know my name's Nettie. Who you fooling?"

"But what's your whole name?"

"Nettie Whilamina Philamina Maria Anna Susanna Guelzo Gall," I'd say, adding one or two more when I could think of them.

He'd repeat them over and over, his eyes widening in wonder and awe. "How does a person get so many names?"

"Well, some's my Christian names and some's the names of relatives. Guelzo is my maiden name and Gall belongs to Art."

"What's a maiden name?"

"A maiden name's your name before you get married."

"What's my maiden name?"

"Silly, you don't have one. Only girls get maiden names. Then they get married ones."

"Will I get a married name?"

"Honey, only girls get married names."

"Do girls get to keep all their old names when they get married?"

"Sure, we get to keep 'em," I told him. "We're just not supposed to use 'em."

Dot loved the farm and he loved me and sometimes we'd get to laughing so hard he'd lose his breath and I'd have to put him to bed. Dot had an imagination to match mine. He'd tell me about all the red, green, yellow butterflies he'd seen landing on the ivy walls and what countries they traveled to when they could feel winter coming. He named each of the hens, both maiden names and married, and at night, listening to the great horned owls calling from the woods, he'd tell me what love poems they was reciting. It was during that summer that Dot told me about the white-haired old woman who lived under his bed.

"Is she somebody you know? Somebody you recognize?" I'd say.

"Nope," he'd say. "Never saw her."

"How come I can't see her?"

"I don't really see her. I hear her. She tells me things."

"Like what?"

"Like what she looks like. Or to be careful on my bike today."

"What else?"

"About the universe."

I didn't think much of it because he didn't seem to be scared of her. But I thought it pretty strange when, every time I'd sweep under Dot's bed, I'd be pulling out armloads of dust balls. Thinking they wasn't good for his asthma, I made it a point to sweep more than usual, but the more I swept, the more there'd be. The old lady under his bed told him where to hunt for mushrooms or when to watch for the raccoon who was gonna break into the chicken coop. Sure enough, if he hadn't mentioned something to Art, we'd a lost the whole flock that night. One day she told him he was gonna die a child. That did it for me. I moved him outa that room faster than you can shake a stick at, scrubbed that bedroom floor with enough ammonia to bleach it, and I watched him so close for the next couple years that there wasn't a skinned knee or a sniffle that escaped my attention.

That first August was one slow boil, the sweat slipping off my shoulders like lingerie, and it seemed like everything came due at once: tomatoes splitting their skins in the garden, leaning over so far they'd be pulling out their stakes, peas in bushel baskets waiting to be shelled, green beans almost darkening to that purple color the sky turns to when the light is too much and bruises it. Corn was gonna turn sour if I didn't pick it soon, the water dripping out of the kernels at a touch just like the milky water flowing outa my breasts. Vines followed their fruits to the ground, bees hummed, pigs as fat as they was ever gonna get and me pregnant as I'd ever be, ready to pop my skin like one of them tomatoes. Strawberries, blueberries, cucumbers for pickling, zucchini for succotash and bread, the whole garden coming due at once and me, standing alone, panic-stricken and hysterical, in the middle of it. What did I know about putting up a whole garden?

What did I do? Now some folks, if they don't know how to do something, they just don't do it. They stand there and worry 'til somebody comes along to do it for 'em. Not me. Do what you know, that's what I was taught. I thought: I know how to make jam and I know how to pickle. I thought about it for exactly three minutes, then started picking everything in sight. I got out the jars and set the water boiling. I suppose I thought I was gonna pickle or make jam out of it all. I run out of bushel baskets and I started using pans. I laid some old horse blankets on the ground and began piling vegetables onto 'em. Dot helped me. It was amazing how little time it took to break every stem and pile 'em up. It took ninety days for most of it to ripen, and in two hours Dot and I had the lawn carpeted with harvest. I fed Dot, put him down for a nap, then weaved out again like a drunken woman, my butchering knife in my hand, heading for the pig yard and the chicken coop.

I don't know what woulda happened that day if I hadn't, at that exact moment, heard a commotion, wheeled around, and saw a wagonload of women driving down my lane toward me, singing and calling out, "Mrs. Gall? Hi, neighbor! Nettie Gall!" And there I was, with Dot screaming to let him outa the house, the flies buzzing mad around what coulda been a picnic spread across my lawn if there wasn't so much of it, my whole garden thrown out onto blankets pell-mell, and my abundant craziness spread out around me, too: a knife in my hand, the juices of every fruit and vegetable I had picked that day staining my bare feet, my mouth, and my ragged dress. I took one look at that wagonload of farm women, screamed, and started running for the house.

It is to their credit that they have never brought up that incident to my face or to anyone else's and I trust they have never even discussed it among themselves. They didn't even come knocking at the door 'til one of 'em needed to borrow a canning spoon. They started fires out there, set my pots and water on them and sat on the ground like a flock of Canadian geese just landed and began jabbering away like 'em. It got so loud I had to look out. And there they was, shelling my peas, filling neat kettles and bowls quick and expert as it comes. It shamed me into coming out. They was doing all my work. So I rinsed my face, changed my dress, grabbed Dot, and went out to face the music.

It was high summer and from that day on, there was camps everywhere. Us women moved from one farm to another and back again, dragging our children, canning and drying, salting and making jam, slaughtering chickens and canning them, too. We didn't have freezers then. It was our job to make sure what we worked for all summer didn't go bad on the vine and would feed our families through the winter. I didn't know a thing about farming. Mrs. Larson and her sister Kate, Minnie and her married daughter from Pinola, Jonnie and Paula Jablonski—they taught me everything. How to put meat up by frying it down, layering it in a crock with lard. That summer, we put up grape juice and canned pears, peaches, even corn. We stewed tomatoes and canned tomatoes and made tomato juice and tomato sauces. We was young then, in our prime, hot, sweating women with our kids screaming around us, women squatting with our paring knives and our butcher knives, our kettles and our spoons. Everybody brought their set of jars and their favorite tools. We had such a good time, eating our fill of whatever harvest we was keeping, beginning as soon as the sun hit each other's kitchens or our men left for the fields. We'd laugh loud and gossip, talking about stuff would make a husband blush if he could hear us, holding up vegetables and fruits and comparing 'em to our men.

We held camp for two months, three months, digging potatoes and carrots and onions at the end, delivering apples to those who didn't have an orchard and making applesauce together. One of the last things to do was make the sausage. Blood sausages 'cause Minnie had slaughtered cows and had gallons of it, sweet and dark and thick as chocolate. You can't find blood like that anymore. It all tastes sour like it's been stagnating in the cow's veins. Probably the way they don't graze 'em anymore. We'd been putting off making 'em for weeks since it was so close to my time, but you can't put your life off forever. It was one of those cool fall days, perfect for sausage-making, when we knew it was the last day we was gonna be able to make 'em.

How did we know? We just did. The senses was stronger then, I think. I suppose 'cause we had to depend on 'em. Marie once told me she stopped off two days in Stüttgart on her way here and she still remembers every German word she heard. Now you don't have to depend on yourself for nothing. The world's explained on TV by the politicians. We get told what food to cook and what books to read. People asking the experts what kinda job to get or what their dreams mean. If there's a self left inside 'em, do ya think they'd know it? We have weathermen who don't take a peek outside. We had weathermen, too, but they was different. Like Art. He understood waves and winds. And birds, especially birds. I don't know what the farmers will do when the birds is all gone. Till says they're already out of crows in Hawaii. It was Art said he seen a hundred of 'em circling at twilight the night before, said we better do the slaughtering 'cause the weather was gonna change.

It was Minnie and her oldest daughter Laura helping me that day. We had all the sausages hanging from broomsticks, the ends balanced on the backs of two chairs. We was pushing out the ground pork from the end of the sausage-maker and into its skin. Have you ever seen it done? The meat comes pushing out into its sack, pushing its head into it, filling it up, hardening it. The more I looked, the more I felt my face getting warm and before ya know it, all three of us was stopped and staring at it like a parched land to rain. "Momma!" Laura squealed, "do ya know what that looks like?"

"Who taught you about rubbers?" Minnie said, acting the mother, but when she seen I was about to bust a gut to keep from laughing, she had to, too. It's a wonder we finished the rest of them sausages. We was still wiping away the tears when I felt the first pains that was Ivy coming into the world.

It was just like her to wait till we was almost done. No, I don't know what time she was born. She's always asking me that, too. Hard for her to believe that clocks, alarms or otherwise, wasn't a part of our lives. It was before suppertime for sure 'cause I remember worrying who else but me was gonna make it. The sun went down, the ladies went home, Lizzy and Joe appeared with the doctor, Mrs. Larson with a covered dish, all like in a dream, all without me. The only thing I recall distinctly is hearing how Dot had taken off into the woods at the first sign of my screaming.

Sure, I was scared, I tell my kids. Sure, I wondered if it was gonna be her this time or me, if Art would decide to save a boy to help him with the farming. It's true women think they're gonna die when they have a child and some of us cry out that we're gonna. It ain't symbolic, that's for sure, 'cause in those days, we seen our mothers and sisters, friends and cousins cry out one minute and be crying no more forever after that. Now they save the women, cut the baby out of her stomach if it won't come. It's still a horror. Coming in or going out of this world is a horrible thing on a body, a violent thing and bloody, whether you're the mother or the child. It ain't about gentle and it ain't about peace.

I was so damn tired of pushing and being scared I must've passed out on Ivy as soon as she slipped out between my legs. I awoke in a wash of blessings the next morning, as if the whole house had been cleansed by her arrival. I could smell it, fresh, I could feel it wrapped around me. I was lying upstairs, my breasts hanging over my belly, lying against it soft as the air around me. Lizzy was downstairs washing all my bedding, my new child was in my arms, and Art was smiling, I knew, out in those fields by himself. That morning I felt like never leaving my bed, like stopping right there in the changed quiet of what took place and just make it a shrine.

I peeled back the swaddling and spread her tiny legs. A girl. I had no idea. Some folks say they can tell, just by how they feel inside. Others say kin dreams the child and lets 'em know. If somebody dreamt her, they didn't tell me. And if they had, what would they tell me anyhow? Did they see pink or blue or did they see dresses? Is it like the difference between the feeling of willow by the river and birch deep in the woods? Is it sunlit versus dappled? Is it prairie versus creek bottom? Or is it like the difference between the lady finch and the male one, her hiding deeper in the shadowed, leafy parts, only talking about food and no grand advertisement? Or the red-headed and red-breasted crowing atop the weathervane? If so, I guess I shoulda noticed that my baby was gonna be a girl child 'cause Ivy hid so deep in the folds of me I swear I couldn't tell her from myself.

"Nettie? You awake?"

I opened my eyes and there was Till, smiling, holding a bouquet of bachelor buttons in one hand and opening the window with her other.

"There's so many spirits gathered round to welcome this child," she was saying. "How are you, Nettie? We've missed you at church." She came close and kissed me on my forehead.

"I'm good," I said, dreamy-eyed. "A girl," I said. The cold air felt good, whispering under the raised window, racing around the room and lifting the edges of things, the rugs, blankets, my hair, sending the cobwebs shimmering. Like Till was ushering in all those spirits she was talking about. She smiled. I noticed the first traces of that cobweb color in her hair, too. I was ashamed I hadn't thought of her for awhile. It seemed so right that she was there.

Till's spectacles was flashing the colors of the outside world to me as she stood by the window. When she turned in my direction, I could see Ivy reflected back, her tiny head buried in my breast. I turned her toward my face and, to my surprise, she was weeping, baby-size tears rolling down her eyes and her, calm as can be, suckling me. Weeping for joy or weeping for sorrow and not a whimper from her. It wasn't 'til later that I'd take it for granted. Ivy's eyes wept without her whenever she was around anybody that could talk to the dead. Every time Till would speak, Ivy would try lifting her head. I put my palm around her neck, pulled her from me and lifted her to see.

"She already sees me, Nettie," Till said. "Oh, she's a dear one, a special one, to see without her eyes."

"Do ya think we can keep her special?" I asked, amazing myself. I smiled, embarrassed, and said, "Her name's Ivy."

Till approached us. "As I place onto your heart these beautiful flowers, I name thee Ivy and consecrate thee to the care of the angel friends now and always." Till held the bouquet against Ivy until she made her baby moves to fling it off. "May the blessing of the Infinite Spirit rest upon this child and select for her a guardian angel through life. Bless this home and the parents and guide them as they care for and educate this child."

Till handed me a package. "I brought you something, too." Inside the box was a spice rack built of cedar and hand-painted with a string of leaves.

"Till, how did you know about my ivy wallpaper?"

She laughed. "I didn't, Nettie. You think I know everything."

"How's the church going? How's Mrs. Jones? Is her daughter still working at the mill? And Harold? Did he ever end up helping Stanley and Marie?"

Till consulted her spirits about everything in those days. I imagined her asking 'em when it was time to pick her nose. She'd cock her head, murmuring, "Mmmmm hmmmm," closing her eyes a bit and answering on a plane way above what you was asking about. Most folks is just making conversation, I'd tell her, but Till never talked light about life. She raised you up faster than most folks was prepared for. I guess that's why most of us loved Till and why some people hated her. Happy? Maybe she was happy but never like the weight of all she had learned wasn't right on her shoulders. One time I asked her, "Till, how come, after all your studying about the world and all your talk with God, you ain't happier?"

"Nettie, the spirits don't talk to me to make me happy. It's to help me to see beyond my own little world. So I can help people. The more I know of history, the more I know about the suffering of others. The more I know of God, the more I see pain in the world. I'm not studying to be happy. No, I'm studying how to heal the pain."

"How's the church going," I repeated.

"Everybody asks about you," she said. "We'd sure like to have you and Art with us."

"We'd like to be there, too, Till. It's so far from here to town and we just don't seem to have extra time like we used to." Ivy was staring at me from the mirror of Till's glasses again and I had an idea. "Still, maybe we would see ya more if you was to agree to be my daughter's godmother."

Till looked at me and at Ivy and back and forth. One of the few times I seen her listening to herself for an answer. "I'd be honored, Nettie," Till said.

"Ivy," I said, holding her up so Till could take her, "this here's your Aunt Till now."

Till held Ivy like a sister would, like it was a favor, like she'd be giving her back. "Looks like I'm responsible for your spiritual education," she said.

"Yeah. Tell her something about the world she's come into, Aunt Till."

Till thought a minute, raised her head and said seriously, "In women's freedom is the world's redemption."

I laughed. "That's a hell of a thing to say to a child who's but half a day old."

"Is that how old she is?" Till said, handing her back quickly. She sat on the edge of the bed, patting my leg. "Nettie, I've been thinking. How about we meet at your house once a week. Say Wednesday nights. Do you think Art would mind?"

"You mean have the church here at the farm?"

"Why not? I don't mind traveling. You're closer out here to Harold than I am. Mrs. Thomas and Mrs. Jones can split a taxi with me. You could invite your friends out here."

I must've frowned. I could just see Mrs. Larson and Minnie talking to ghosts. They'd think I was off my rocker for even mentioning it. "It's awful nice of you, Till, but don't you think most folks is more comfortable at your church?"

"To tell you the truth, you'd be helping me out. I've been renting some of the rooms out. I changed the big meeting room into a dining hall. It's been a little crowded for us to be meeting in my extra bedroom, though they all say they don't mind."

"You? Taking in boarders, Till? I didn't think you was a cook at all."

"I get by," she said.

"What about your studying?"

"I still make time for it. Besides, I have a friend who's moved in. She's helping me."

"She? Till, you're making it hard on yourself. No woman's got a chance of making it on her own. How are you paying bills? What are you eating on?"

"I told you, I'm getting by. I have the boarders now and I've been taking in some sewing."

"What about the money you used to make giving speeches?"

Till started picking at my blanket. "Used to be people

wanted to hear what I had to say. About their crops. About their families. About the country or the future. Others wanted to know what the spirit world was like, you know, what happens after death. Now all people are asking about is Germany and the war, whether we're gonna join it, whether their sons are going to it. And if they don't take to my answers, they don't invite me back. Seems like when a war's about to happen, what women have to say doesn't matter as much as before."

"You've been preaching against war?"

"It's not me, Nettie. You know that."

Seemed like the spirits was always encouraging Till to do what everybody else warned her against. "You can't blame the people. You forget. Most of us lost family in the last one," I said.

"All the more reason to be against another one."

"Till, why don't ya get yourself a man," I sighed. "Be easier on ya."

"I don't need a man, Nettie."

"The hell you don't! Listen, you may know more about the world of the dead than I do but you don't know beans about the world of the living. You sound just like my friend Marie, and look where that got her. Imagine, pulling a knife on a man and losing her job. Lucky she had a man in love with her to bail her out. Ain't there anybody you're interested in? You know people are gonna start talking about you."

"They talk about me already without it having anything to do with that." Till sighed. "The Ku Klux Klan's been grumbling about me having a mixed congregation."

"What do ya mean 'mixed'? Mixed black and white?"

"Mrs. Thomas. Mrs. Jones. All their friends who come to me for private consultations. They've put crosses out in front because of it and one of my windows got a rock thrown through it the other night."

"Why didn't you come to us with such troubles? It's just like you to do it all yourself."

"I am coming to you, Nettie."

"I'll ask Art tonight. Seems like we could start next week if you wanted to. After suppertime'd be best. Tell everybody, including Harold and Rosetta. I'll make the coffee and some kinda pie."

"Rich, no rich, poor, no poor, style, no style," Marie said, her lip curling, "smart, no smart. All gotta die soon or later."

It wasn't exactly the thing to say to a new mother, my baby in my arms. I gripped Ivy tighter than I was already, bit my lip, and whispered to Art, "I am sorry I came."

There was men lined up three deep around the bar and Stanley was rushing from one end to the other, filling orders. When he got a glimpse of me holding a baby, he dropped everything and came running over, clucking and cooing and motioning all his friends over. "Such beauty!" he said. "Such beauty!"

"Looks like I'm gonna have to drag Dot out of his first bar," Art said, winking.

Dot was staring at the stuffed owl Harold had given Stanley as a grand opening present. Art held him up to touch it and to see the glass eyes. Dot started to cry. "Did Marie kill one of our owls?"

"No, hon. That owl's been stuffed longer than you been living. Harold runned it over the day he was gonna open his own bar, in Pinola back in 1928. Said if it was a bad sign, he might as well hang it out for everybody to see. That way, they knew what they was getting into. Place is cursed, he'd tell his customers, but nobody ever paid him any mind."

"This ain't no place for kids, especially on a Saturday. We'll all come back together some other time," I said to Marie, knowing full well we wouldn't.

"No, please," Stanley was begging, "stay. Marie's going back to the kitchen right now to fix some sandwiches these men ordered. You go back with her, Nettie. She can use being around a woman."

"I'm taking Dot to the feed store with me," Art said. "I'll be back for you in about an hour."

I followed Marie obediently behind the bar though I couldn't tell whether she wanted me there or not. She wore a wool scarf wrapped round her head like she used to, the same old boots and that long, dreary skirt. She was quite the contrast to the blond calendar lady on the wall who was pushing her titties up with her hands. I guessed Marie woulda been asking for it, wearing her city-slicker clothes in a Polish workers' bar.

"Customer bring it," Marie said when she caught me looking at the calendar.

"Marie," a man shouted, "let me buy you a drink."

"Can't you see my friend visits? She is young lady. Mother." Marie pointed to my bundle.

"Quit making excuses," the man said. "I'll buy her one, too."

I shook my head, but Marie sighed and went to him, holding out her palm. "She no want drink. You pay first, I having."

He dropped the coins one by one into her palm, satisfied. Marie reached under the counter, bringing out a bottle of Polish vodka. She poured herself a healthy shot. "Nostrovia," she called out to everyone, throwing it down her throat.

"Nostrovia," the men at the bar answered, shaking their heads in wonder. "Stan, you got a woman who drinks like a lumberjack!" one said and the rest pounded the counter in agreement.

"Don't such sour face making," Marie said when we got to

the back rooms where she lived. "If I say no, I never show face as boss again. Good money they pay for me to drink."

"It's not good for you to drink vodka like that."

"Vodka?" Marie laughed. "Is special bottle. I drink whole fifth vodka, still be on feet. Nobody know is water, even Stanley."

I relaxed. "You don't drink at all?"

"Little beer, warm. Canadian Club maybe."

It was my turn to laugh. I missed her. Not that I hadn't thought about her. I kept track of her outa the corner of my mind, just like I did the moon for planting. Harold let us know they'd opened the bar, that they'd called it the Three Star Tavern and that it was doing well. Still, if it wasn't for Dot, I doubt whether I'd be paying Marie a visit.

See, it had taken a lot of prying to get Dot in the house after the doctor left. You can't blame him. Every time Dot seen a doctor walk in his house, they carried somebody of his family out in a casket not too much long after. Art brought him in when things had calmed down, in to see me and the new baby sleeping. In a way, Dot got to see Ivy before I did. There was a bit of blood behind her knee after Lizzy cleaned us up. "Did she fall?" Dot had asked. "Didn't Nettie catch her?" I guess Art had told him that age-old story about storks. Till says storks is extinct now. What are we gonna tell the kids now? There ain't a bird left round here big enough to carry a child 'cept a buzzard and you sure don't want to trust them with one.

I was back on my feet in a couple days. What with Ivy spending most of her time in the milky sleep between worlds, I made time for Dot. I called him in from play to tell him stories: George Washington and the cherry tree, Lincoln reading at night by his lamp, Paul Bunyan, and my favorite, Johnny Appleseed with his tin pan hat and a coffee sack around his middle, planting all our Indiana orchards just because he liked the way the blossoms snowed in April, like a worn-out feather pillow being shook over the land. That's one thing we needed here that the Indians didn't have yet. The Bible gave us apples and the Bible gave us Eve. I asked Till once if the Indians had a story where some woman ate corn or green beans when she wasn't supposed to. She said she didn't think so, leastways never heard of it. She said Indians thought food was here for people to eat it and so do I.

I messed the stories up a bit, of course. I always wondered where Johnny got the money for all them seedlings. He must've had money somewhere 'cause seedlings is expensive and I didn't believe that bunk about the seeds. Has any apple seed you ever planted sprung up outa the ground? 'Course, I didn't tell Dot that. I didn't want to be telling no story about a rich Johnny Appleseed. I told him that Johnny made his way west eating through people's orchards, trailing a Choctaw wife that left him to return to her own kind. Johnny was just like them birds and deer that go around shitting out seeds, planting a whole forest or meadow behind 'em without thinking about it.

"Ain't there any heros who is women?" Dot asked me once.

I thought and I thought and damn, if I could think of one female except for Babe, the blue ox. Betsy made the flag, but she didn't design it. She just sewed what she was told like me in the woolen mills. That's when I decided to tell Dot about Marie. "Marie is the bravest and biggest woman I know," I told him. "Six feet, six inches tall, a magic number, taller than Art, taller than Pa, with muscles the size of grapefruits. Marie left her family in a country so far from here you'd have to travel backward in time just to get to it. There people live in houses with roofs of sod. They grow all their vegetables up there, right on top. Rain doesn't have so far to travel that way. Marie was the fourteenth of twenty-seven sisters, a magic number, too. The sisters were like the rungs of a ladder. The oldest could almost reach heaven.

"The first half of her life, Marie lived as a man. She dressed like one, worked like one, went wherever she pleased, could twirl on one foot, round and round all night as the violins played. She grew like a man, eating the special turtle soup prepared by her grandmothers for the sons. She carried a knife in her boot, and once she went to war. She was afraid of nothing. Nothing. Not even the ocean and its waves. When she decided to come to America, they didn't have turtles. That's why she changed back into a woman."

"I didn't eat turtle soup," Dot said. "Will I turn into a woman?"

"You did eat them," I said, "when you were a baby."

"But what about now?"

"There ain't none of them big sea turtles left," I said. "It's changed everything. But don't worry. You ate enough."

Is it any wonder that he started begging me to take him to Marie?

The back room of the Three Star Tavern served as Marie and Stanley's kitchen, living room, bedroom, too, all crowded into an area smaller than out front where the men were drinking. Marie had started water a-boiling and began dropping sausages into it, cutting open hunks of sourdough bread, smearing mustard on 'em. "Four?" she yelled out to Stanley.

"Six," Stanley answered.

"Don't you even want to look at her?" I said, unfolding the blanket to show her Ivy's face.

Marie did come and look. "Art no mad about girl having?"

"Mad? Why would he be mad? We're lucky we're both alive. That should count for something. You did hear I almost died with the first one? I lost him, too."

"I hear," she said, walking away from me. "You just like me with first."

"What do you mean?"

"I make baby, too." Marie picked up the plates of food. When I grabbed her arm, she said, "I no much time having."

I took the plates from her and set them down. "Marie, what happened to your baby?"

"She two hours live. Doctor say my fault. I be built like man, not woman. See? No hips having. No room for baby way out making."

Ivy started screaming and you can guess how awful I felt, coming into Marie's bar, gloating about my healthy child. "I'm sorry, Marie. Really I am. I feel so bad for ya."

"Doctor say I no milk having anyway. Doctor, he take it. Say I no good as mother."

"What? What did he take?"

"He say no good children I make it. Kill me next time maybe. He want to take mother, take her out," she said, pointing to her groin. "I have to live. I have to."

"Are you saying you can't ever have kids? Oh, Lord." My heart sank. "How's Stanley taking it?"

"Stanley blame me. Blame doctor. Say in Europe doctor no take nothing. Now he never doctor going. Get weak and no work much anymore. Stanley stay in kitchen, stuff cabbage, soup making."

"Marie, if there's anything I can do…"

"Rich, no rich, poor, no poor," she shrugged, picking up the plates of sausage, "all gotta die soon or later."

Chapter Six

We shoulda noticed when the heavens first started backing away from us. The sky bruised, not giving a drop and the sun 'bout disappeared. Even the stars looked like there was a curtain going down between us. The neighbor kids think the stars are spectacular and, like I did, spend hours staring up at 'em with questions too big to be asked. But the stars they see don't thrill me like they used to and it's not from my memory that they're dulled. The night sky has lost its polish, dusting over like the grain on a nice piece of wood. Happened so gradually, nobody noticed it 'til they seen it reflected in their grandkids' eyes. It made 'em different. Some say made 'em hard. Maybe it was the foundries. Some say too many cars. All I know is, if I could raise my hand and wipe the sky clear like my daughter does with her shirt sleeve to the windshield of her car, I would and show them kids what they was missing.

Nineteen thirty-eight and the first of those late and heavy-hanging springs when the entire weight of the sky felt like it was resting on your forehead, grape-cool and damp and ripe for nothing but disease. The fogs grew like mold on the fields and thunderclouds slid across the ground, sponging it like a crew of women on their hands and knees. And still, no rain. Dot's breathing got so bad they sent him home from school more times than not, the poor thing stooped over like an old man from coughing and a curious blue like a mustache above his lip.

The cow died calving. It was luck to find a buyer for the pigs so we could get another.

Ivy was on my hip and waiting for the hour or two when the sun broke through. She quieted only when I could find a piece of it for her, some stray ball of sun unraveling in a corner upstairs or down. Ivy was a strange child from the start, less equipped for this world than Dot in her way. Not that she was ever sickly like him. She could holler like a bull and her cheeks was red like an iron stuck to 'em. They had the same kind of wanting in their eyes. Her first spring, and I could see it, a disappointment, as if she was expecting the air to come fresh, the clouds to bless us with rain. Always looking around for something and nothing coming. I often told Till it was her fault, spoiling Ivy with flowers when she wasn't here a full day. Made her think life was gonna come like that, in gifts and flowers.

Dot, on the other hand, wasn't waiting for a thing, though most folks would disagree, seeing how he suffered so. His allergies to grain, to animals, to dust. Imagine! Dot hated to get dirt on his hands, and us farmers. The way I see it, the farming side of the family came to an end in Dot, what with his stunted growth and his sensitivities to all that was good for us. Not to mention how we knew in our hearts Dot was never gonna have children. Ivy? She was a beginning. The world, if anything, wasn't ready for her. Dot gave us sorrow and Ivy gave us hope. Excuse me for laughing, but we did have high hopes, me and Till both, high hopes for Ivy and that world she was waiting for. We just wished it'd hurry. How was I to know I'd be so stuck in my old one it'd get harder and harder to cheer her on.

Ya know, every year has that running-out spell, when you're heavy with root crops and salt, before the first tips of wild asparagus. Marie says it's fasting time in Europe. Rosetta sells teas to thin your blood just like the rains is supposed to thin the streams and clean 'em. But that year, they didn't come. Guy who bought our pigs come back saying they came down with cholera. Within a month of taking 'em home, not a one had lived. Naturally, he wanted his money back. Instead of the lean, healthy season we was expecting, the creeks rain-swollen, wind and clouds moving, it was quiet. Like a hand being lowered over the mouth of the world. All the farmers felt it. And all the women worried.

Till says, "Worry is the moth that destroys the fabric of human endeavor." Says it just like that. "Its only antidote is optimism, constructive thinking and mental poise," she says. "If you can't do anything about it..." People tell me day in and day out like it's some disease I got and my fault I got it. I always wondered why it is people hate worry, swear they don't do it and, if they get caught doing it, call it by a different name: thinking or planning or nothing. Personally, I think worry's got a bad name 'cause it's women who do it, just like pity and guilt. To most of us women, worry's been around longer than most of our friends has. We grew up with it. It's who we told our secrets to, who we wasn't supposed to hang out with. And we still got to deny her. Folks are jealous, I think, because we tell it everything.

The only joy around that spring was in being back in Aunt Till's circle again. Oh, we was so glad to see each other! Everyone loved Till. It wasn't so much that she kept us in contact with our dead as it was how she kept us in contact with our living. She raised us up and made us proud to be together. Till was the leader, but she didn't act smart or holier than thou. She had a way of making us feel smart and holy as each other. And that there was a mighty smart and holy circle. It seemed wrong at first to be having religious service in my front parlor, kinda disrespectful what with the baby crying to be changed, the cobwebs and kid toys but Till insisted. If the true prophets in the Bible prophesied in the camps, not the tabernacles, why couldn't she?

Mrs. Thomas and Mrs. Jones dressed up like they was

church-going, even after I told 'em they needn't bother, and always wore their hats. They looked so pretty and took it so serious, I got to washing and bobby-pinning my hair before the meetings, though one time I forgot to take the pins out and Till had to remind me. She said all that metal was interfering with her reception. We called ourselves the Wednesday Group and it wasn't long before we was vying for the turn to bring pie or cake and was trying to outdo each other in the kitchen.

Everybody took to Till's new friend immediately. Fritzie came with Till to our first meeting and she never missed another. She was bright and sparkling as her black eyes was and she was the only one of us with nerve enough to tease Aunt Till, tickling her legs under the seance table, telling Till she wanted to bring back Belle Gunnes, a famous murderer who'd lured fourteen men to Town of Pines. And to our amazement, Till would take it, smiling uncertainly like she didn't understand the joke but happy, anyway, for the attention. And oh, would we laugh. Much as Fritzie was mischievous, she was kind, remembering to ask Art about the crops, calling every child, cat and chicken of mine by name. I was particularly fond of her, how she loved my peach cobbler, how she'd say, "This coffee tastes better than anything," so's not to favor anybody, winking at me and working on a second helping of my lemon pie.

Fritzie on Till's arm or Till on Fritzie's. They didn't look alike but they acted like spinster sisters, only they was gossiping about reincarnation instead of the neighbor's wife. Two skinny sisters, Till in her cardigans and dark shawls, Fritzie in red or pink or lavender or all three, her curls cut shorter than Marie's, her brows full and striped black and white like a caterpillar. Fritzie had an education, but she didn't lord it over us. We could understand her despite her big words, or thought we could, and she never told us otherwise. The only thing that wasn't absolutely perfect about the woman was the way she'd get protective of Till, leading her out for coffee after the seances, asking her to take it easy or call it off short. "No, it doesn't strain me," I'd hear Till complaining as they went out alone on the porch. "My trances strengthen me. I'm renewed after them." It made me kind of jealous, like Fritzie was trying to take Till away from us.

'Course, there was more than eating and gossiping. Aunt Till woulda never stood for that, though I can't say I woulda minded that much. It was my favorite part. We'd start out with a song, join hands, and it wouldn't be long before we'd hear something like a rock thrown against the house that told us the spirits were near. Ivy would begin her weeping and Dot would go running outside to catch whoever it was we set up to do it. Sometimes he'd hide ahead of time in the big oak. I guess he expected to see Harold or Art sneaking out there with a shoe. Regardless of what side of the house he positioned himself on, the knock would come from the opposite side. It about drove Dot crazy. He never did find a rock, though one time he found a batch of burnt rolls I threw out the window when Minnie and Laura came visiting without notice. Any one of 'em woulda broke glass for sure.

By summer, when the rains came, too late and steaming right back up to the sky with the heat, the thunder loud and crabby with waiting, the clouds upside down and bloated as a dead heifer in the field, the Wednesday Group had pretty much exhausted its departed. Every one of us had been in contact with every aunt, uncle, and fourth cousin who'd ever set one foot in the grave. And the dead, bored with us, too, kept retelling their stories, repeating old phrases and advice, like the senile do. When her great-aunt, who died in childbirth three years before Mrs. Jones was conceived, showed up, telling her how heaven smelled like sweet williams and the hands of infants, Till didn't need her second sense to know we was at the end of our ropes.

"Why in the hell are we wasting our time with this crap?" Rosetta said. "I got people coming to me with diseases I never heard of. I got every doctor in the county forcing me out of practice. I'm convinced the dead is with us. So what?"

I was so shocked I dropped hands on either side of me, breaking the circle. I was afraid to look at Till for fear she was offended. But she was smiling.

"That was never the point," she said.

"I don't mean to be ungrateful, but I can't see how learning about the life that's to be is helping anybody to live the life we got right here," Rosetta continued as if she hadn't heard.

"Don't pay attention to her, Till. She's foul today," Harold interrupted. He turned to Rosetta. "Till's been real good to us."

"Mmmmm," Mrs. Thomas murmured, shaking her head. "If them doctors is after you this week, Rosetta, they're gonna be after me the next. Just 'cause they made us midwives legal last year don't mean it won't be against the law next year."

"I got a right to be foul," Rosetta said, rising. "I studied all my life to know what I know. It's how I make my living. It's bad enough I can't find half the plants anymore. Goldenseal? Since folks learned they can get $1.50 a pound for it, it don't grow wild anymore nowhere but Appalachia. Ginseng? I gotta walk all the way to Kingsford Heights to find it. Half the sassafras in the county disappeared when they cleared them woods near the tracks for a tractor factory. They keep cutting the woods down, there ain't gonna be no healing left."

Since everybody was standing up, I went to light the lanterns. "Till, I don't understand," I said. "If talking to the dead ain't the main thing, how come we've spent so much time doing it?"

"Because most people have to be convinced before they accept the teachings of spirits, Nettie," she said kindly, then got that teacher face of hers on. "If we are densely ignorant and grossly material, we can't be open for spirit communication."

"We're convinced," Rosetta said. "Now what?"

"What do you want? They're all awaiting whatever you may ask."

It was as if the walls sucked in their breath, it was so still. Not a curtain or a foot stirred. What'd we wanna know? What'd we wanna know? I couldn't think of a damned thing. How to get a better yield from alfalfa or how to put darts or a zipper in. How we was gonna pay back the money we borrowed to pay for them pigs. But Till wasn't asking about that. She was fishing us for questions we had no business asking, holding open a door we'd just as soon pretend was a wall. Aunt Till might feel she had some special invite, but the rest of us, following her in, would get nailed for trespassing, sure as shooting, and we knew it. I was surprised any one of us had the nerve to speak, let alone it was my husband.

"I'd like to know how to heal my animals when they get sick. I lost a cow and a calf this spring. I'm gonna be paying years on them pigs that come down with the cholera."

If Till didn't scold him, I was gonna. You didn't ask God to pay your bills. You asked him for all those things you can't touch, like patience, like strength. And if we wasn't asking God, who was we asking?

Till only smiled. "Anybody else?"

"I'd like to get them damned doctors off my back," Rosetta said. She thought a minute and added, "And where the hell the woodbane's disappeared to."

Mrs. Thomas sighed. "We work so hard to keep things from unraveling. Is it true it'd be better if we just let 'em unravel?"

"Now you just stop that, honey," Mrs. Jones said. "Your husband's gonna pull through just fine." She turned to us. "She wants to know if there's anything else she should be doing."

I was getting nervous. "What I'd like to know is who's gonna want coffee and who wants ice cream with their pie," I said, clapping my hands together loudly.

"Nettie's right. It's getting late. We'll continue this next week," Till said, pausing and nodding as if the spirits had just thought of something to tell her. "I think we're on to something. The first thing we'll do is figure out what you know already."

And that's just what we did, though I was hoping she would forget. It was one thing for Jelly Beans to let me know I was pregnant. It was another to think I could do anything about it. Till didn't forget. We started the very next week, after the prayers and the singing. For some of us, it was like pulling teeth.

"Jack Tyler's wife is suing him for divorce," Harold told us. "He's been seeing that little waitress at the bowling alley."

"About healing," Aunt Till said. "Tell us what you know about that."

"Healing? You said we was gonna talk about what we know."

"You said you were tired of talking to your departed ones. Most of you have talents, know special things. Makes sense to talk about them."

"Till knows what she's doing," Fritzie butted in. "You trusted her before."

"For Christ's sake," Harold muttered. "I ain't got nothing to say then."

The rest of us exchanged glances. We all knew Harold had a piece of paper. With it, he could coax the fire out of any burn. We knew 'cause just last week, Minnie's daughter broke a jar of canned beef while she was tightening the lid of the Mason jar. When the scalding, greasy broth spilled over her arm and Minnie screamed, Fred threw a coat over Laura's shoulders and took his wife and mother-in-law to Harold. Minnie said she saw him take out a piece of paper and mumble something over and over and her daughter said she could feel the fire being pulled outa her arm. It healed over without so much as a scar. It was all over town by now.

"How about you, Rosetta?" Till asked.

Rosetta had her arms crossed in front of her and such a scowl on her face, like to stop you in your tracks. Harold couldn't resist teasing her. "What's the matter, Rose? Afraid somebody's gonna steal your secrets?"

"They ain't secrets. They're knowledge. What I know's been passed down from my great-grandmother, from aunts and cousins to me. Comes from years of watching where the deer go when they're bleeding, what the birds eat when they're poisoned. I ain't just giving it away."

"Why not?" Till asked.

"Because. It's the way I make my living. If everybody knew what I knew, nobody would be coming to me."

I couldn't help laughing. The likelihood of any of us ever finding, picking proper and drying, making tea or oil or a poultice, depending, out of any plant she might mention was ridiculous. Still, Rosetta was frowning. Just to aggravate her, Harold made believe he was taking out a pen and paper. "You first," he said to Rosetta, "I'm gonna take notes."

Rosetta glared.

"Okay, I'll start," Till sighed, looking around the room like she'd lost something. Her eyes landed on Ivy, who was grabbing and throwing whatever toys I'd put within her reach. As usual when Till was around, she was weeping. "Tears heal," Till said simply.

"I know something," Mrs. Thomas joined in. "Anything will heal itself if you let it alone, quit beating it. Same with me or you or nature."

"They shall lay hands on the sick and they shall recover," Art said, quiet and shy like he must've been when he was in school.

"Every spoken word's a charm," Mrs. Jones said. "Everything we say can bring us closer to or further from Thee."

"Rosetta?" Till urged. "It's back to you."

"Alright," Rosetta grumbled. "There's always the antidote next to the poison. Mud near the nettle to take away the sting. You just got to look around."

All eyes were on Harold. He shifted nervously in his seat. "I got two pieces of paper," he said, and we about busted our guts laughing. He didn't have a chance to finish.

It was my turn. What was I gonna say? I wasn't no healer like like Harold or Rosetta. I didn't have religion like Mrs. Thomas and Mrs. Jones. I was just a wife, a mother, and not even them very long. I turned to Art but he was no help. He just smiled like everybody else did, waiting for my answer. "I don't know," I began. "Healing, for me, don't have no knowledge to it, no one thing or another. If one of 'em's sick, I make something special in the kitchen, bread or pudding or I start the mending or the wash. I like 'em to smell good things and see good things and not worry that anything's out of kilter, that things ain't hopeless or too serious or..." I was flustered. I realized I was talking more than any of 'em and hadn't said a thing. "For me, I guess, healing is the step-by-step small things and the taking into my hands of time."

When I looked up, I seen everybody nodding to each other and beaming, like I'd just won a prize.

Through the years, damn near forty of 'em, there was nothing too big or too small for us to tell each other and it got easier and easier. Seemed like telling relieved us of a burden, gave us room to breathe, how I woke with the word "coltsfoot" on my tongue and made Dot a tea and he'd quit coughing awhile, how Rosetta said weeds pulled easier if you breathed out while you was doing it and they did. Till encouraged us to talk about what worked and what didn't and she wouldn't let us pin our successes or failures on anything but ourselves and the knowledges we were sharing with each other. "Thank God," Mrs. Thomas would say. "It's a miracle."

"You can thank whoever you want," Till would say, "but remember also that healing is a natural phenomenon, not a supernatural one. Just like being in contact with those who've passed on is."

Our personal dead still made appearances, especially when we had a new grief, but now a whole new slew of spirits came trampling through, ones we didn't know 'cept through Till introducing 'em to us. The higher beings, Till called them, though Harold insisted they was angels. "Angels, yes, but we must remember," Till said, "every spirit that visits us has lived here at one time before." I can't recall what names most of 'em went by, but I do know there was a lot of Indians. People make fun of the idea now, especially my grandkids. How am I to know why they always showed up? I figured it was 'cause we lived in Indiana, but Aunt Till said they appear in seances all the way in Europe. Till says they're just natural teachers. I don't know about that but they was always nice to me.

One time I asked Till what it was like to have the higher beings talking to her, whether they had deep voices or what language they spoke since I didn't think most of them old-time Indians knew English. She said it wasn't a voice. It was a weight like that of a bird on a limb, a touch that was female in its closeness to her.

Sometimes I worried how comfortable our meetings was for Harold and Art. Not only was they outnumbered, but the way we talked of recipes and plants, about death and sickness and how to remember the names of family, it was like what we women did all the time. Sometimes we plumb forgot Harold and Art was even there. But, over the years, I seen how our meetings did 'em good. Even they admitted it, how they enjoyed being able to talk about something besides work. Still, I'll never forget the time Mrs. Jones was telling us about her son.

"You know what he's really mad about? He's mad 'cause she's

had four daughters and no sons. It don't have nothing to do with how she can't cook or with the house being so dirty. She don't want to get pregnant no more and he wants the name to go on."

"A man's gotta think of his future," Art began. "Carrying on the family name."

"Art," she said with exasperation, "his name's Jones. Jones. There's enough of us in the world to keep that name going to Judgment Day."

And Art laughed. Said he never thought of that before. I was happy he was laughing. Till said not to worry. It didn't matter what sex we was, we're the opposite in the astral world. Men was women and women was men. So it was natural that we should understand each other. I wouldn't of believed her for a second if it wasn't for Art's hands.

I already told you about his hands, how he could lay 'em out side by side like two pieces of perfectly planed wood and they'd be level, how, at the end of the day, he'd remove each finger from the brown work-gloves and no man watching a striptease would be hotter than me. They were man's hands and they were woman's hands and they touched everything like they had eyes. Art's hands never moved faster than he was thinking and so they met whatever it was, tool or bread or skin, with precision. Art didn't talk much, it's true, to me or anybody else, not liking the company of women any more than the company of men. He'd sit in between, by himself, watching me. Art had the touch of a man butterflies landed on. I was the one fed the dogs, doctored 'em, and still they'd fight over who got to sleep on the floor at his feet. People he was scared of and I never seen him get near a sick one. Used to tick me off how he'd spend all night with a sick pig and sleep like a log through Ivy's fevers. Animals loved him. It was only natural that, when it came time, his gift would be for them.

Sure, I remember the first time it happened. Not that Art didn't already give us sign enough. They say his pa could see how a tree was stirring in the wind and tell ya every storm coming for three weeks ahead. Rain, snow, a low morning fog, a mild breeze, a tornado: Art loved each one like I do people and, like I do people, was good at guessing at each one's approach. When the sun rose. When it set. What stars came up where. Mrs. Jones had been studying 'em and knew how they affected us, but it was Art who could point to 'em and call 'em by name.

It was a cool spring night, before supper, while the mourning doves was complaining, that Art went into the barn to check on our new cow and found her with her calf dead beside her. We was devastated. It had taken us a year to save for her. There was no more money we could borrow. He couldn't eat that night and I couldn't either. We just sat, drinking our coffee, thinking about debt. When Art told me he was gonna check on the mother, I only nodded. "She's bleeding, ain't she?" I remember asking him. He didn't answer. It was no use to even think about calling a vet.

"She was still breathing when I left her."

"There ain't a damn thing you can do about it. You'll catch your death in this chill."

"Least I can give is comfort."

There was no sense arguing with him when he pressed his lips tight like that. "I'll make ya some hot coffee to take out then," I said.

He didn't come in and he didn't come in, and me sitting there all night with worry. I didn't think about going to bed without him, I guess. I was just blowing the lanterns out for the dawn when I heard the screen door slam and Art come in. "Ma, ma!" he was calling me. He never called me that.

"What's wrong?"

"She's gonna live." He collapsed into a chair and stared at me in wonder. "She was just about gone," he whispered, hoarse from the cold. His face was pale, tired, but his eyes was new and on fire like the sky at noon. His hands were on the table. There was blood on them.

"What?"

"Something told me I could stop the bleeding," he said, grabbing my sleeve. "When I put my hands on her, it stopped. Thank the Lord!"

"Till said it ain't the Lord."

"Who the hell is it then?"

"You."

"I don't know, Nettie. That scares me."

"Scares you? Ya got the gift. Nothing else. Just like I got a gift of cooking."

"What if people hear about it?"

"People are gonna hear about it. You don't open a door without expecting somebody to come through it, do ya? You think I slave over a stove for my health? It's 'cause I like to feed people and people is hungry. It's natural, like Till said."

The next morning that cow looked strong and she was putting out milk by the end of the week. I was so proud of him I was ready to shout it on the mountaintop. While Art was washing up, without turning to me, he said, "Nettie, I don't want ya telling the kids."

"Why not?"

"They're too young to understand," he said with a glance that warned me against discussion. That week he grew quieter and quieter, but losing a night of sleep'll do that to ya. I didn't pay much mind. I was holding my breath till Wednesday, and I was sure Art was, too. I pictured him early in from the fields, scrubbed up and waiting before the first person arrived, which was likely to be Harold since he liked to get in some gossip before his religion. Wednesday night, Art came in so late we didn't have time to eat supper and he barely got changed. By the time he came down, everybody was waiting and I couldn't contain myself any longer.

"Tell 'em. Tell 'em," I said to him, holding on to his arm.

"Hush, Nettie," Art said sharply.

My mouth must've dropped to the floor. Art never talked like that to me.

Everybody was looking at him. "It's nothing," he said, at Till's questioning glance.

Shamed of myself for opening my mouth and shamed now for not being able to close it, I looked at my feet and wiped my hands up and down my apron.

"What is it, Nettie?" Till coaxed.

Her kindness gave me courage and I stared at him, defiant as I could be. "Art saved our cow last week. Stopped it from bleeding to death." He was making me feel like I was tattling.

"I didn't stop it," he snapped.

That did it for me. "What the hell? You told me you did it. You said you put your own hands right on the wound and it healed. Right before your eyes, you said." I felt my face turning red and my hands were shaking. "I saw the blood," I said to the others.

"This ever happen to you before, Art?" Till asked.

"No," he said sullenly, knowing they'd believed me.

"It's nothing to be ashamed of. It's perfectly natural that you can do this," she said, speaking to him the way I do when the kids wake from a bad dream.

"It don't mean it's gonna happen all the time," Harold said.

"It ain't your fault if it don't work all the time neither," Rosetta said. "But you gotta try. It's your only obligation."

"Lord never gives us nothing we can't handle," Mrs. Thomas agreed.

"But it wasn't me that done it," Art said, uncomfortable. "I don't want people thinking I'm claiming some special powers."

"There's nothing special about healing," Till said. "Only human."

He never did say he was sorry about snapping at me in public and I never brought it up again, but a week later he mentioned that if I wanted to tell Minnie, maybe he could help out in emergencies when the livestock took sick. 'Course, that's if people couldn't get a vet in time or couldn't afford to. And I chuckled 'cause telling Minnie was telling everybody down the road.

"She's coming! She's coming!" Dot screamed, running into the kitchen where I was making Sunday dinner. I'd dropped two forks on the floor already that morning so's I wasn't surprised a bit that we was getting unexpected company. I wiped my hands and walked out to the porch. I didn't think to wake Art up. I liked to let him sleep all day on Sunday if he could. Dot pointed and I squinted up my eyes. Through the waves of heat rising from the white fields something dark and slow was moving toward our yard. Man or woman, I couldn't tell, and I remembered Harold saying if a ghost came in the day, it traded its white sheets for black. If I was a religious woman, I woulda crossed myself.

"Well, I'll be damned," I said when the figure opened the gate and I recognized Marie. It's a wonder I did. Her hair was tucked under a brown wool scarf so I could barely see her eyes and she was draped in the longest wool coat, down past her ankles. And here it was June! Funny as she looked, Marie was looking at my bare feet with scorn.

"I never be farmer again. Farmer no having money even shoes buying."

I laughed. "It's too hot for shoes, Marie. And you ain't got room to talk about nothing. You're gonna suffocate to death with that blanket wrapped around you."

"Somebody see I coming maybe."

"So what if somebody sees you. Is the law after you or something?" I joked.

Marie took the chair Dot offered her. "Are ya," he stuttered, "are ya running from the law, Marie?" His eyes were wide as quarters.

Marie only scowled.

"Go get her some coffee, would ya?" I asked him. "Why don't you take that scarf off? Did you walk all the way here?" When she didn't answer, I raised my voice. "Marie? What's wrong?"

"Shhh. Somebody hear you my name saying like that."

Dot came back with the coffee. He served it, then sat down on the porch steps, holding his knees, scrawny, needing a haircut, as excited as I'd seen him with firecrackers on the Fourth. I didn't have the heart to tell him that Marie was like the moon in her Polish folk tales. When she appeared, all good children were supposed to be in bed. She was still scowling at him. I couldn't send him off. "He's okay, Marie. He can keep a secret longer than the sky is wide."

Marie took a deep breath. "Can I hide in your barn?"

"Hide? What kind of trouble did you get yourself into?"

"I never go back. Never. I am America, no matter."

"Settle down now. Nobody's going nowhere."

"No cheat Death. Death find you. No matter, America, Europe. No run away Death."

"You're saying Death is after you?"

"What does he look like?"

"Dot, be quiet," I said, but Marie only nodded and pulled the scarf further over her eyes. "You're crazy," I continued, "if you think Death is looking for you like some man walking right into your home. That's a fairy tale."

"Two men. Dark suits wearing. Come into bar while I am in back cooking. Skinny. Mean face like this. Very skinny. I am in back when I hear my name. Name nobody know to call me all time I am in America. Name nobody, even Stanley, know."

"You mean to tell me Marie ain't your real name?"

"Not even Stanley knowing," she repeated, getting perturbed. "'No Katy here,' I hear Stanley say. 'I never hear of this woman. Who is she to us? Why you bother me and my wife?'" Marie looked straight at me. "Oh, I am so scared. I hear them call me."

"What did they want?"

"Hold something. Show to Stanley. He look, nod, maybe take and put in pocket. Maybe silver, gold give to Stanley."

"Did they find you?" Dot asked, unable to keep quiet.

"I hide in curtain. No find me."

"And they left?"

"Stanley say he not know where I go. Say they will come back for me. Maybe Poland take me."

"That don't sound like Death visiting. That sounds like Immigration," I said. "I thought you was legal. I thought I seen your name on them papers."

"Papers Marie belonging."

"If you ain't Marie, who the hell are you?"

Marie sighed. She knew this was gonna be the price of her lodging and she didn't like it. "I tell, you let me stay? No telling Art or Stanley?"

"Stanley doesn't know you left? When did the two men come?"

"Friday."

"What did you tell Stanley?"

"Stanley is sick. I say I know nothing. Must be big mistake men making."

I looked at Dot, who was on the edge of his seat, hoping I'd say yes. "Well, sure, but only 'til we get this thing straightened out."

"Who's Katy?" Dot asked. Now that he had a chance of getting in trouble for helping her, he felt he had a right to ask.

"I am Katy. Is long story telling."

We heard Art stirring from his nap, and me with not a damn thing ready for our dinner. I motioned to Dot to show Marie out to the hay barn, making him promise to be back in half an hour to eat. After dinner I sent him back out with enough food to feed an army, and before supper he brought her blankets, pillows, and hot tea.

"Dot sure is enjoying the weather," Art commented that evening when Dot came in after dark. Which meant he was glad Dot wasn't hanging onto my apron strings like he usually did when he wasn't at school. Which couldn't of made me happier but made Art angry for some reason, angry and shamed, especially when we had company.

That night, I could hardly wait till bedtime. I was sleeping apart from Art already in them days, in the big room with me and Ivy in one bed and Dot in the other. Unless Art called me to him which he did less and less. Used to upset me, but it was better this way. Art snored and I couldn't help but wake him up by pushing at him, trying to get him to turn over. And I could never get used to the idea of him wearing that long underwear to bed.

"Nettie," I heard Dot whisper as soon as Art was sawing wood.

"Shhh," I said.

"Can I stay home from school tomorrow? I can sneak her food and water and you can come out when Pa's gone to the fields and she'll tell us stories and we can all have some coffee."

"Dot," I said sternly, "this ain't some picnic for Marie. Can't you see she's worried about getting shipped back across the ocean?"

"The cook told on her, I bet," he whispered.

"Told on her for what?" I said. "The whole thing's confusing to me."

"Nettie, she told me the whole story. Want to hear?"

He said it so sweetly I couldn't help but open my covers for him. He crept outa his bed and snuggled close. "This story's long, like she said, but I made her tell it to me." I smiled and closed my eyes. Of all our family, Dot was the best storyteller. He could make a story outa a shoestring and a chance word. "Marie was born in a little village in Poland near the old capital of Kracow but far enough that she had to take a train to it. Her pa was a soldier and a fiddler at weddings. They were really poor. They ate..."

"Grass," I interrupted, tickling him. "I know this already. It has nothing to do with what's happening to her now. She's tricked you."

"No, listen," Dot insisted. "Listen, you'll see. They ate oats, rye, grasses they grew in the field. One day, a woman came to the town from America. She had tuberculosis and the doctors gave her one year to live. Unless she went back to the forests of Europe. Under the trees, they told her, her lungs would get healthy like a mushroom or a flower."

"Aunt Till said them woods used to be bigger than here," I said, half-dreaming.

"Because she didn't want to die, she went back to her country, leaving her husband to work in America until she got better. Her family still lived near the village Marie lived in. There, she got ready to move to the great pine trees in the south. When she heard how good Marie was with horses, she hired her to drive her to the neighboring towns to get supplies. Over time, they got to be friends. The woman told Marie how rich it was in America, how even the cats drank milk and the dogs ate meat. Marie told her how she was one of too many children and how bad she felt that she was getting old and just another mouth to feed. On the day the woman was leaving for the forest, she came to say good-bye to Marie and her family. 'Here, this is for Katy,' she said, plunking down a pile of papers on the table. Katy isn't the way you say it in Polish. It's what it means in English. I don't remember the Polish way," Dot said, hesitating to see if I was asleep.

"Go on," I murmured, caught in his story.

"The father lifted the first paper. He couldn't read. 'These are my papers to go to America,' she explained. 'Katy is young, strong. Why shouldn't she go back instead of me?' The mother looked at the father. The father looked at the mother. And Katy stood there waiting to see if they would really let her go to a place she'd been dreaming about ever since she heard the mud was so rich they made cakes out of it. 'I give her my name,' the woman said, 'Marie.' She picked up the pile of papers and held them out to Katy. 'Will you let her take them?' The mother and father nodded and Katy took them from her hands." Dot yawned and there was a long pause before he spoke again. "You know, Nettie, I asked her about the turtle soup, but she didn't remember it."

The next morning, I told Art we'd been half the night nursing Dot's coughing. Didn't he hear it? And I thought it best Dot didn't go to school besides it being the last week and grades in already and he probably wouldn't miss anything too important and I could use some help staking the beans, and Art looked at me sideways but didn't say anything. He left for his fields and I got my chores done, and then we hightailed it out to the barn.

"You mean I've been calling you Marie all these years and it ain't your real name at all?" I called up to her, still giddy with the memory of Dot and his storytelling me to sleep. I climbed the ladder like a schoolgirl and threw myself right down in the hay beside her. I was feeling devilish for lying, adventurous and free. Been a long time since I'd got outa the front yard during the day. "And you mean to tell me this was the first Stanley heard about it? When them Immigration men told him?" I slapped my knee three times and rolled over laughing. I was seeing Stanley's face. "I woulda paid to seen him when they told him he was married to Katy, not Marie. Oh, poor, poor Stanley."

"Is not poor Stanley. Is poor Marie. I never go back that country. I go back, I die there."

"Oh, Marie," I said, wiping away the tears.

"You laugh. There is war in Poland. German kill me I go back there maybe."

I stopped, suddenly realizing this wasn't any bedtime story. "Dot said you think it's the cook who turned you in."

"He probably find papers. Or wife talk too much. She loan me money for boat. She is friend of real Marie. She know whole story."

"Why would the cook do that?"

"He hates me. I no lift skirt like other women."

"But why now?"

"Maybe he jealous money I making."

"Marie, you've been in this country almost twenty years. That should count for something. Why are they looking for you now?"

"I tell you. Is war starting. German already go Poland. Maybe I am spy they think. Russia, German, who knows why? I am America. I love this country. I no talk to family. I no do anything."

I sat, thinking. "We need more brains than what we got here. Marie, come with me. We'll walk over to my friend Laura's. She's got a car. She'll take us where we need to go."

"Not to town. Stanley..."

"If he doesn't know you're with me, he's got shit for brains, excuse my French. Where else would you go?"

Laura was home. She had the car and she was more than willing to get out of the house on a mission. In half an hour, we was knocking at Till's red house. We must've looked a sight, me still in my apron, Ivy slung over my shoulder, asleep, Dot grown-up standing, holding my arm, and red-faced from trying not to cough, Laura puzzled, and Marie, who made the sign of the cross when we approached and would not take Till's offered hand.

"Nettie? What are you doing here?"

"We need some help, Till."

"Well, come in, come in. Where's Art?"

"Art don't need to know nothing about this."

"Well, of course, of course." I could tell she was flustered 'cause she kept repeating herself. She sat us around the table and served us all coffee, even Dot who stuck his tongue in it like it was ice cream. When she was finished, she seemed calmer and that made the rest of us feel better. "So?" she said.

"Immigration's after Marie," I explained.

"Immigration? Oh, dear, I don't know anything about that. I suppose we could ask the spirits."

"I was thinking more of Fritzie."

"Oh, Fritzie. Of course. Just a minute. Fritzie!" she called upstairs. Fritzie stuck her head out of Till's bedroom and I remember it striking me funny though I couldn't say why.

"Fritzie, this is Marie," Till said. "Marie's got a problem with United States Immigration."

Marie winced. She didn't like me telling her business to all these strangers, but what else could we do? Fritzie noticed and tried to reassure her. "I'm a lawyer. I might be able to help you where Nettie or Till couldn't."

Marie was even more uneasy. "No woman is lawyer, even in America."

"My father was a lawyer, so that helped," Fritzie said, laughing. "Now he's a judge. Maybe someday I will be, too."

"Tell her," I said, angry, to Marie. "Who else you got helping you?"

Marie told her story reluctantly and when she was finished,

even I was convinced it was a losing battle. She'd be hiding in our hay barn forever. Everyone was hanging their heads. All except Fritzie, who started asking questions. "What year did you get married? Is your husband a citizen? What year did he get his papers? What name is on the marriage license?"

Marie said she didn't know to most of 'em until Fritzie asked her, "Have you had any contact with the real Marie?"

"She's dead."

"Dead? You never told me that," Dot gasped.

"Did she die of tuberculosis in Poland?" Till asked.

"No. She go to woods like doctors say, every day walking, every day looking for her breath. Every day, seem to better making. One day, storm come. A tree, big evergreen fall on her. Kill her."

We stared at Marie in disbelief. "A tree fell on her?" Dot shrieked. "How do you know? You made that up."

"Mother write to Laura in Canada." Marie turned pale and bit her lip. "Marie give name away, try to cheat Death. Death look for her in America, no find her. But no cheat Death. Now, maybe Death be mad at me, help cheat it."

"Death ain't looking for you any more than the rest of us," I said.

"Let's go talk to Stanley. I think we might be able to get you out of this, and easier than you think," Fritzie smiled.

"How?" Marie said, not rising with the rest of us.

"Trust me," Fritzie said, winking at Till. "There's a law. If you were married when I think you were, you became a citizen just by marrying a citizen. If your husband was, you most likely are, too. By whatever name you were going under when you were married. Long as you're not wanted in Poland, there should be no trouble." She chuckled. "You sure that tree fell on her?"

Till followed Marie and Fritzie to the door. She straightened

Fritzie's hat and squeezed her hand. I remember thinking that someday I was gonna make Till proud of me like that.

"Like I said, we'll go talk to my father," Fritzie was telling Marie.

Marie stared at Fritzie like she was a god. "You just like man," she laughed. "You big brains having."

Chapter Seven

You know, men scare me. What with how unsure they are about what they're doing. Take that old fart on the phone the other day, acting rude when all I did was ask a simple question about my new washer. He argued, he complained, made me feel like I was asking the wrong question, like I was too stupid to know what I wanted. "I'll tell ya what I want," I shoulda told him, "I want to know why men invent things it takes fourteen different tools to fix and why I gotta say am not, are not, or is not when ain't takes the place of all three." I kept him on the line. He tried everything he could think of to get me to hang up on him, rather than admit he didn't know. Come to find out, he was just filling in. Finally admits it to me. Wouldn't know beans from Adam.

Marie says if it wasn't for men, we'd still be living in caves. Women never want to change anything, she says. Well, I say a cave is a hell of a lot better than some things. Ya don't have to worry about any babies sticking their fingers in outlets or swimming in raw sewage off the pier. Or take Uncle Odie's grandkids. Three outa nine of 'em got something wrong with their heads. We all joke about it and cry about it and watch 'em clap out of time when we sing at family reunions and the kids just keep getting older and simpler and ready to have their own children. Uncle Odie will swear it ain't got nothing to do with them living near that nuclear power plant. Least his kids didn't end up working in the lead mines like he did, he'll say. Art's the same way. He'll argue for days about something he ain't even sure of.

Me? I don't know something, I don't say nothing. I only swear to what's pressed in my hand and when I close it, I know its shape and size, whether it's a rhinestone button or a snake. I study what's in front of me but not like a scientist would. If something don't work for me, I don't stand there trying to make it like they do, seeding the clouds with silver iodide to make 'em give up their rain, hybriding seeds to grow into fruit without bumps and vegetables without scars, food for summer grown in winter and winter food in spring. If something happens to me once, it's enough for me to believe.

Till says it's the scientists and religion who have given her the most trouble. You see, them scientists think if something don't happen a number of times in the same way each time, it don't exist. If the dead talk, they should talk every Friday at three o'clock. Till says the dead went through quite a time being tested all over the world by the scientists, taking turns assuming shape and getting photographed and playing accordions and ringing bells. Silly things they soon got bored with. Scientists, they act like everybody's at their beck and call. When they lower their baton, bacteria and rats and spirits is supposed to dance. 'Course, every good medium knows things don't happen like that. So lots of 'em started ringing the bells themselves and figuring out new ways to entertain the scientists like having whole arms come out of their navels, dressing up like Benjamin Franklin, and blowing smoke from between their legs.

If only the things that happened regular were true, half of life would be a lie. I always told Till that's where her Spiritualism went wrong, trying to prove that spirits talking was a scientific phenomenon. So what if the dead exist? Most people figured that out a long time ago. Some folks call it history. Some folks call it dreams.

I guess that is where religion comes in. Art is always arguing with me about it. "Nettie, you're always telling me if ya see it, you'll believe it. If you gotta touch something to believe in it, what about love?" I tell him there is invisible things that can be touched and things you can't touch but you can see. Love or grief, they're more real than a quarter in my hand. Love or grief move through the room like the wind moves through willows near the river, changing faces of the air to light green, ruffling this and letting that lie still, waking things up or settling them, and I believe in the wind. But religion? What I ain't sure of, I don't talk about and I rarely try to bluff myself or take on faith somebody's secrets that ain't my own.

Art wanted to get the kids baptized. "They're gonna go to hell," he said.

"How do you know that?"

"It says so in the Bible."

"Show me."

"Now, you know I ain't sure where exactly, but it says so. Everybody knows it, Nettie."

"Well, I don't know it. Any god that'd send these sweet little things to hell can just forget about my vote."

"It pleaseth God..."

"Till said it pleaseth God to discover slave plots, to massacre Indians and to close Rosetta's herb business down. It seems like all kinds of things pleaseth God."

"Nettie, what has gotten into you? When did Till put that in your head?"

"She didn't. Ivy told me. Her Aunt Till's been giving her history lessons."

"History lessons? You told me it was Sunday School."

"Well, it is, sort of. It's on Sunday." I took hold of his hand. "Look, Art, neither one of us ever laid a hand on Dot or Ivy and in turn, they don't lay hands on each other. How am I gonna explain a god who's ready to throw 'em in a pit of fire on account of not having a little water sprinkled on 'em?"

"What are we gonna raise 'em on," Art said, "thin air?"

"When they've grown up, they can make up their own minds."

"That Till is just making it harder for Ivy to be in this world."

"Till don't believe in hell. She said the Indians around here didn't believe in it either."

"Indians? For Pete's sake!"

The more things got away from us, the more we tried to control 'em. Art got a radio, and every night he listened to the news and the weather. If they said it was gonna rain, he put on his raincoat. If they said it was gonna be hot, he'd take off his long underwear, never setting a foot outside to see for himself. Made me angry. Made me wanna throw that new radio, the Bible, and the thermometer out the window if it'd make him trust himself again. It was sad to see. He quit watching the silver birch on the horizon, reading the stems, the moisture landing in the morning, instead ready to try every new piece of frozen pie set in front of him. It made him quit looking. And when he quit looking, he quit pointing stuff out to me, and I quit looking in that way, too. He used to wear long johns six months outa the year and here he was, caught more times cold or hot or wet than not. "They're just gambling," I'd say about the weathermen. But Art would say, "No, Nettie, it's science."

Ya can't blame him. Everybody was wild about science or religion in them days, one or the other, the times being so uncertain. And he worked so hard and for so little. He needed to believe if he used a compass for his rows, if he went out and bought that new fertilizer, if he got his children baptized in a church, things would work out. It was guaranteed. We was believers in the straightest row, the cleanest fence, and every apple, plum, pumpkin, radish, and peach was supposed to look alike. Perfect. It ain't scientific to have big corn one year and small corn the next. Till said there used to be more than a hundred kinds of potatoes. Now we got red for frying and we got white for mashed.

Oh, we would argue, Art believing and me resisting. He was especially rigid about the two boys. Junior we called the first one, and Grange was second, both coming so fast upon one another I didn't get a chance to quit nursing. I guess we wasn't always arguing. They was corn-fed, red-faced, and loud as the sows and, I have to admit, after Ivy and Dot, they scared the piss outa me. Big children and hard labor. Till tried to warn me, said most women in the world don't eat much while they're pregnant, to keep the size down. I ain't most women. I live in America where every day somebody was reminding me I was eating for two. I gained sixty pounds with each of 'em and I never saw my body the same again.

Dot was by now fighting with Art all the time. He had changed some over the years, growing from a boy's body into the heavier weight of a man's, less thin, less cute, less pretty. Though he had the same long eyelashes cradling those baby blue eyes, he had a man's needs and, changing his sheets, I could smell 'em. And that eye of his that used to wander round the room while the other looked straight at ya? It wandered less, not stopping altogether but resting in the corner like an egg in the skillet will if the stove's not level. When he was young, I told him it was a marvel. Now the teachers called it lazy eye, like it was something to be ashamed of. Dot was bright, but high school wasn't easy for him. He hadn't grown outa the asthma like the doctor said he would. He did grow outa looking like he had it. He'd filled out and gained height with my cooking and my forcing. Not strong-looking but certainly not weak. If you didn't know his history, you'd think he was a sissy, how his face got red running across the street or how he never tried out for sports. And the terror of not being able to breathe marked him, sure as shooting.

I felt for him always, but Art was angry. That Dot was going to school instead of being in the fields. That he'd come home eager to explain something he'd learned and Art would argue with him if it was something we didn't know. Which was a lot of things since neither of us had been to high school before. It wasn't Dot's fault. He wasn't gloating. I could tell he was proud of what he was learning about the world. That we was supposed to come from monkeys. That the French thought God was dead. Art would call him sassy and smart ass and stomp out when Dot used a word he didn't understand. "What good are those fancy words if you ain't gonna use 'em to help your people at home?"

"Maybe I'll be a writer. Maybe I'll write about you."

"Why? So you can show everybody how ignorant your kin is?"

Dot began to avoid Till and it was a long time since he'd participated in our seances. I suspect it was 'cause of Ivy. Till just wasn't interested in him. Ivy was her prize. Ivy was her godchild, you remember. Even Art had halfway given her up to Till. When Dot was younger, he worshipped the ground Till walked on, following her around like a puppy begging for a bone. He woulda thrived on the kind of lessons Till lavished on Ivy. He loved books. Ivy didn't. He'd listen intently to anybody, where in school Ivy just squirmed. "Dot talks to ghosts," I'd tell Till. "He hears voices more'n his sister does."

"I believe that, Nettie."

"Couldn't ya work with him, too? You said yourself he was sensitive."

"I can't take on everybody. You know that."

"But couldn't ya take turns?"

She frowned. "I'm working with Ivy now."

It was then I started agreeing with Art that maybe Till had something peculiar against men. Maybe you can understand it. I could almost understand it myself. With the war, they was different. Stirred up. It was awful hard to not be mad at 'em, how they followed the news of it like it was a baseball game, how they never complained about the rationing. We'd wring our hands, we'd plead and just wish we knew enough about the world to do something about it, that if it was me and Minnie and Laura and Gin up there, we'd figure it out and calm it down, just like we did the fights between our husbands and sons. Till was the only one of us who had the nerve to say it in public. 'Course, it wasn't her. It was the spirits.

She was her sweet, modest self until she went into one of her trances: "Roosevelt cares as much for the Jewish people as he does for the Negro in his own country. It's a war about money to make money. If it was a people's war like they say it is, all the people would be fighting it, not just the poor." Seemed like it was the only thing the Ku Klux Klan and Till ever agreed on. "Where do you think Hitler got the idea for those concentration camps? America used them to imprison the Indians, then used them in the Philippines."

Unfortunately for Till, folks in Town of Pines didn't care what happened to the Jews or the Indians or the Negro. They cared about paying their rent and feeding their children. They had a President they paid to care and to make decisions and who was telling 'em that before long, what happened at Pearl Harbor would happen to Town of Pines. Ya didn't question it. In them days, questioning your President was second to questioning God. Got so the only people that would invite Till to trance speak was the Negro churches and they had their own problems what with half their congregation off to fight the war.

The Wednesday Group quit meeting regular. Mrs. Jones and

Mrs. Thomas was spread thin with the new work opened up for women, relief work, and their own church. Harold was getting older and didn't wanna go out when the weather was apt to change. Personally, I think he suffered a stroke somewhere along the line 'cause he'd picked up a mean streak he liked to use against Rosetta and women in general, calling Till and Fritzie spinsters and did they think they was too good for any men. He was always starting something, taking sides with Art against me for baptizing the two boys, bringing up the war news just to make all of us nervous.

"How come you ain't joined up?" Harold asked Dot one Wednesday night when he was on his way out the back door.

"He ain't old enough, you know that," I answered.

"Lots of boys younger'n him is lying about their age. He ain't any good on the farm. Might as well fight for his country."

"Dot wants to go to college," I said.

Harold snickered. "Where's he gonna get money for college?"

"He could get a scholarship, couldn't you, Dot?"

"Nobody who ain't helping with the war effort is gonna get a free education, that's for sure."

I stared at Art angrily. To think he'd side like that against his own kind. "You don't know that," I said. "You don't know nothing about it."

Dot had one eye trained on me and one trained on Harold. I couldn't tell which one of us he was angrier with. "Nettie, please drop it."

"Maybe the army'd do him some good, Art," Harold went on. "Get his mind off them books and that gang he's been chumming around with." He smiled at Dot. "The only book worth reading is the Bible."

"What gang?" I said. "The drama club? The library club?"

"If I woulda known he was a member of clubs...No wonder he don't have time to help out around here," Art said.

"Can I be excused," Dot said, inching towards the door.

"What's this Drama Club? You think a farmer's son is gonna go to Hollywood?"

"Hollywood, hell," Harold laughed. "That'd be a good place for him. It's full of drunks and queers and rich people who don't lift a finger."

So I wasn't the only one who'd noticed liquor on Dot's breath. I heard the screen door slam and knew he was gone. "Why are you being so mean to him? All of you?" I shouted, running into Till on my way out the door after him.

I found him in the sheep barn. It wasn't really a sheep barn. We stored corn there after harvest, but none of the barns was called by their right name. The horse barn was for the cows and the cow barn was for the pigs. We called 'em what Mrs. Rose called 'em 'cause it seemed to upset her less. Dot taught Ivy to read in the sheep barn and to cipher, well before her second year in the public school. He didn't hear me open the gate and come in 'til I knelt down next to him. He had his limbs tucked underneath him in that way I knew so well, the one where he is searching deep for his breath. "Don't cry," I said, stroking his hair. "You're just gonna make yourself sick."

"I'm not crying."

"Shhh, I want to tell ya a story."

"I'm too old for stories."

"Nobody's too old for stories. Listen, I've been thinking about this. You remember them tiny birds you and me and Ivy seen that time we was walking clear back in the woods? That time we had to chase her? They was the tiniest green things and they had the prettiest voices. What did you tell Ivy they was saying?"

"I don't remember."

"You do, too. Very Old, Very Old," I said, mimicking the sound, "or something like that."

Dot dried his eyes and smiled reluctantly. "No, Nettie. It was Vir-e-o. Vireo. That's their name. They were saying their name."

"The name some scientist called 'em? How would they know that?"

"No, I learned it in biology. They got their name by what they sing. In Latin it means: I am green."

"You're ruining my story. Anyway, I was thinking about them singing, way back there in the trees where we never get to hear 'em, singing Very Old, Very Old, and not giving a hoot if anybody hears 'em or not. Anybody except them other things that live way back there with 'em. What good are they doing, I caught myself thinking, just like Harold says about the crows. Then it came into my head that maybe without 'em, everything would fall apart."

"Yeah, so?"

"Art just wants ya to be like us, that's all. He can't see any sense of it otherwise."

"Ivy don't have to work in the fields."

I thought a minute. "Some things is easier for a girl. Some things is harder."

"Like finding a place in the world."

"What'd ya mean? You have a place. Just like them birds do. It just ain't so clearly given. It's hiding behind all them tree trunks."

"That doesn't help."

"What about college?"

"Who are you kidding? The farthest I'll ever get is electrician's school, like he wants me to. Art's right. They're never gonna send a farmer's boy to college."

"You just finish high school. The rest will come later."

"Nettie, I'm gonna join the army."

"What?" I threw down his hand so hard it hit the floor.

"What? Don't you listen to Harold one iota. He's had a stroke and he's full of shit."

"You don't think I haven't thought about it? Harold just said it out loud. What kind of future do I have? If I come back, I'll have some money to go to school and I'll have been across the ocean like Marie. If I don't come back, what'll I have to lose? Art'll be proud, my country'll be proud, and Ivy won't have to keep explaining her brother to everybody in school."

I was crying and shaking him by the shoulders. "You ain't gonna do this to me! You ain't gonna do this to me! You damn men, you're trying to kill me with grief! What am I gonna do with you gone? What am I gonna do if you don't come back? All you ever think about is yourselves."

"If God wills it, I'll be back. If not, I'll be going home."

"Home? This is your home and the only home you know of. There ain't no other home if you never been there."

"But what about what Aunt Till says? All those talks you had with your ma and pa and Jelly Beans?"

"You think that makes death any more bearable? You think just because I have five minutes with 'em, maybe see their faces in Till's if I squint just right, that it's the same as holding 'em? Same as watching 'em eat? Same as having 'em with me?"

"Nettie, calm down. I probably won't ever be sent to the fighting."

"I'm going with you to the enlisting office. I'm gonna tell 'em how you're too young, that you can't breathe regular. They won't take you like that. And we can tell Art you tried and I wouldn't let you."

"Nettie, don't do this to me. I'm gonna come back fine. I promise. I had a dream about it. You were sending me things, food and letters. And there was a medal."

"You're trying to kill me."

"What else can I do?" He grabbed my hand and it seemed

like both eyes for the first time was looking straight into mine. If there was something to say, I woulda said it.

The next night at supper, Dot announced he was leaving for boot camp. "I need your signature on this form. Says I'm eighteen years of age."

Art lowered his fork to the table and it seemed like it was hours he sat chewing and looking at Dot. I watched many things cross over his face and some of 'em I was proud of and some I wasn't. I held my breath. Neither one of 'em would look at me. Then Art stood up and shook Dot's hand.

Suddenly I was so tired, the tears running down my face, tired at how quick they all line up to get themselves killed, how somehow it was me, how I couldn't make it worth staying, even with my cooking and fine sex, my housekeeping and music, even with giving 'em children or wearing flowered dresses or combing my hair. They line up in an instant and wait for their names to be called. And they knew it. They still wouldn't look at me. In three days, Dot would be gone. Art would quit bugging me about the baptisms.

"Aunt Till says I'm gonna marry somebody tall, dark and handsome. He's gonna be driving a new red convertible and we're gonna have three children, two girls and a boy." Ivy was posing in front of the mirror, lifting her hair above her neck and letting it fall to her shoulders. "Can I put on some lipstick? Please? I'll scrub my face good before Dad comes home."

I dug in my purse and handed it over. She pursed her lips and painted 'em in perfect. Where'd she learn that, I wondered. Not from me. I put on rouge and lipstick if I was going shopping or to a funeral. "Do you think I'm pretty?" she asked.

She was ten. She still had freckles and she still sat on our laps. Her hair hadn't been cut yet and Art let her ride with him on the tractor around the fields. But he didn't know what I knew. That Ivy wanted one thing in life. She wanted to be beautiful. Beautiful. I'd never thought about it growing up. Girls like me was pretty or we wasn't. But beautiful? Movie stars were beautiful. They got paid for it. We had enough to do. I could see it in the way Ivy was already fretting about her clothes, and how once she'd pretended not to be with me at the grocery store when she'd seen some of her friends. Her big, guileless laugh was getting quieter the more she listened to the women on the radio, and sometimes I saw her cover her mouth while she did it, just like Laura down the road had started to do. I guess you could say she was like other girls of the time, but to me it was new and just one more thing that was odd about Ivy.

Already Ivy had begun to hear voices and would shock total strangers by reading whatever was in their minds. I seen the sick, wide awake with fever, close their eyes when she walked in and fall asleep. And the retarded grandsons of Uncle Odie's took one look at her and adored her. Sometimes, sitting by herself, chairs would move or windows open, and once she showed us how she could blow out a candle from across the living room.

"These tricks will just get you in trouble," Art would scold.

Ivy spent every Sunday afternoon with Fritzie and her Aunt Till. They'd take her for sodas at the soda fountain or sometimes on the new bus that went up and down the one main street in Town of Pines. Or to the library, which Ivy hated. She didn't like to read, which bothered Aunt Till to no end. "How do you expect to become an intelligent adult if you don't read? In books are the answers to life's questions."

"The spirits will tell me anything I need to know. Isn't that right, Aunt Till? Isn't that how you know what to say in your trances?"

Till was pushing for us to let Ivy be her student, said she

could tell by her frequent tantrums that she'd make a good medium.

"Not till she's sixteen," Art would say. "That ain't no kind of life for a child."

Till had a good story about a ten-year-old medium who was hired by President Lincoln. She was at his side when he was gonna sign the Emancipation Proclamation to free the slaves. I guess he wasn't so sure about it till he looked down at her and saw her smile. "I guess the Ku Klux Klan are right," Till smiled. "Even then, the Spiritualists were in cahoots with the Negro."

This didn't help to sway Art. I mostly agreed with him. Still, there were things that made me feel like siding with Till. Ivy was a child of frequent fevers and headaches and long sleeps. She'd come out of 'em old-looking, wrinkled and so solemn, and it would take her days before she talked and walked like a child again. She was the kind of person who couldn't remember if something really happened or if she dreamt it and once I saw her talking and gesturing to nobody at the end of her bed. I have to admit, I didn't know what to do with her.

Till and Fritzie enjoyed taking her and I let them because she enjoyed them, too. Deep down, though, I knew they were teaching her to leave me. Wasn't their fault. Wasn't intentional. They figured they was teaching her courage, which they was. I'd take Ivy for a walk in the woods and she'd be pushing past the rock pile where I usually stopped and would plead with me to go on, even when I said I was scared, that I'd never done it. She'd talk me into buying fabric when I knew it was too expensive and she made me try to drive once by laughing at my lack of interest until I drove her and me smack into the silo. Oh, Art had a fit! We laughed and laughed, but most times she was dragging me behind her, angry at my fear. There was Till on one side urging and there was the me side holding back. No wonder she didn't have no choice but to play one of us off on the other.

"Till says on our honeymoon, we'll go to Niagara Falls," Ivy said, handing me back my lipstick.

"How does Till know that?" I said, getting out my mending. "Will you thread this for me, hon?"

I watched her run the white thread through her lips, dying it scarlet. "Grandma Louise told her."

The mending dropped to my lap. "Did you have a seance with your Aunt Till?"

"Yes, but..."

"Who was at this seance?"

"Just me and Aunt Till and Aunt Fritzie." Ivy looked confused. "We were just playing. It was just a game."

"You know I'm gonna have to tell your pa."

Art came home from town itching for a fight and I admit, I had second thoughts about telling him. "The government expects the farmer to feed the whole country for nothing just 'cause it's wartime. We got less than we got last year for all them soybeans, oats and corn. And prices rising? Who do ya think is making all that money? The government and the rich? Who is governing who?"

"Art, we got a little problem here."

"We sure do have a problem. Like what is Mrs. Rose gonna say when I offer her less than last year? She's gonna say if things don't improve, she might just take that offer from National Foods. They're buying up everybody else round here."

"Ivy tells me she's been having seances with Till and Fritzie. I thought you might want to know since we have expressed..."

"If I've told you once, I've told you a thousand times," Art exploded at me.

"It ain't my fault, Art. I told Till, just like you said. I know as much about it as you do."

"And you don't care. You'll leave your daughter to do who

knows what in the company of two middle-aged women who—Ivy, leave the room."

"Fritzie and Till are our friends. We've known 'em forever. They were probably playing a game. A fortune-telling game is what Ivy called it. I only told you because you'd find out anyway."

"Nettie, I can't believe you are this stupid. She is not to go with those two again unless one of us is chaperoning."

"Chaperoning? What for? Two women and a little girl?"

"How do you think it came to be that neither one of 'em is married? Harold told me just the other day about a medium and her assistant who performed seances nude. What if they were doing something like that with Ivy?"

"Art, you are making this up to have something to fight about."

"You ask your friend Till about it. Things started making sense to me. It's as clear as the nose on my face."

"Clear? What's clear?"

"Nettie, you are as thick as they come. Just mind my words. Ivy ain't to go out of this house with Fritzie or Till unless one of us is with her."

The next Wednesday Group, Art said he had to work late at the neighbor's baling. Soon as she came, I cornered Till in the kitchen. "What's this about women having seances in the nude? You better not a brought my Ivy to one of 'em."

"What on earth are you talking about?"

"Harold said there was two women performing seances in the nude. They took photographs of the spirits coming outa one of 'em's nipples and Harold seen 'em."

The last thing I expected Till to do was laugh, but laugh she did. "I wondered where some of my history books disappeared to. I must have loaned them to Harold so long ago I don't remember."

"History books?"

"Sure, books about the history of Spiritualism. Leave it to Harold to find the few pages that have anything remotely to do with sex."

"Then it's true?"

"He must be talking about Juliette Bisson and Eva C. Eva C. was famous. Sometimes she and her assistant, Juliette, would hold private seances for each other, and sometimes, they would be nude."

"That's the most scandalous thing I've ever heard of. Where do they live? And why on earth would they take pictures and show Harold?"

"They didn't show Harold unless they came to him in his own seance. They've been dead at least thirty years and they lived in France." Till smiled. "If you are really curious, I could pay a call to Harold Hullinger this week. I'll bring the books to show you when I come to pick up Ivy on Sunday."

"I got a better idea. Art's gonna be still baling next weekend. Why don't you come to Sunday dinner? Just you and Ivy and me and the boys?"

The next Sunday, Till arrived with two heavy, worn books under her arm. She leafed through one until she came to a photograph of a small, boyish-looking woman with short hair and small breasts like a man. "That's Eva. She's the medium. That's plasma draped across her chest. That was in the days of emanations."

"Looks like that nightie I shredded in the wringer washer last week."

She flipped to a different page. "Look at this. Many mediums of the time believed that spirits issued from and returned through the vagina."

"Oh, my God! Close that book!"

"Juliette once saw an orchid land on Eva's breast, travel

down her side until Eva spread her legs and it disappeared inside her."

"An orchid?"

"A spirit orchid. Then a head came out. A spirit head."

"She looks like a man."

Till grinned. "Many female mediums look like men. Or the men look like women. They say the most famous of them all, Madame Blavatsky, was rude and big and had all the mannerisms of a man, but everybody was charmed by her."

"You don't look like a man. And Ivy sure don't."

"Ivy's confused. We had a little seance here the other day to reassure her. Just on the porch here. Bet you didn't even know it."

"Confused about what?" I said.

"You know, adolescent doubts. She somehow has the idea she's not going to have a normal life like other women."

"You know, what you told her about the handsome man and the convertible did seem to cheer her for days." I suddenly found myself laughing. "To think Art was afraid you and Fritzie was doing the same thing as that Juliette and Eva. Can you imagine? You and Fritzie in the nude together?"

Till was awfully silent. "I'm sorry he feels that way."

"Oh, don't be offended. You know how he is. He'll forget about it once he sees you and I tell him it don't have nothing to do with you and Fritzie." I was really laughing. "Where would you get an orchid in Town of Pines anyhow? You'd have to ship all the way to Chicago for it."

"I told you it wasn't a real orchid."

"Oh, Till, come on. I've heard of some of your tricks at least. The lifting tables?"

"I thought you believed."

"I do believe. It's just that Harold said..."

"Harold, hell!" She brought her fist down on the kitchen

table and, as if in slow motion, every glass I'd set began a crack from its lip deep into its center and one of 'em split exactly in two. I was speechless, more from hearing Till cuss than the breaking of my glasses. "Excuse my French," she said.

Her eyes were twinkling. I couldn't help but smile myself. "Harold told Art you and Fritzie was like man and wife. What a load of baloney."

Till paled like an egg white on the pan. "Harold is sticking his nose where it doesn't belong."

"Everybody knows that. There ain't no truth to half he says."

"People listen."

"People like to be amused. Me included. You take life too serious."

"I don't think it's amusing." Where Till's face was wide open a minute before, now it was thin and I could hear the doors closing like a street in summer when a skunk is coming through. "I love Fritzie. I won't have it made into a subject for dirty gossip."

"I love Fritzie, too. So what? Lots of women live together. Spinsters. Old maids. That don't mean nothing." I winked. "If it wasn't for my Art, I'd do the same."

"That's not what Harold meant."

"You ain't got nothing to worry about what ain't true."

"It is true."

"No, it ain't."

"Yes, it is."

I wasn't backing down. "No."

She sighed. "Alright."

"It's a lie?"

"It's a lie," Till said.

I smiled and took her hand. It was ice cold. "Let me handle Art. Maybe you should stay away from Ivy for a few weeks."

"Maybe I should talk to Art myself."

"Damn it, Till, listen to me."

"But we're old friends."

"He's already got a corncob stuck up his butt about Ivy and you having seances."

"Ivy has been at seances since she was able to crawl."

"He don't want her to end up a medium, Till."

"Like me, you mean."

"He's concerned about it being too hard on her. He don't want his daughter charging money for magic tricks. You said yourself all people want to see now is fake flowers and live doves. He don't want his daughter ending up a circus act."

"I am not a circus act."

"That's not what he means. She's just a child."

"She's got talent, Nettie."

"Let her decide when she's old enough."

"If we wait, she'll be married and have children before she's out of her teens."

"Like me, ya mean?"

"Nettie, don't stand in her way."

"She's our daughter, Till. Not yours."

The sun was high as it gets, July, the light traveling so fast it closes off the blue behind it so that everything you look at shines right at ya and you can't get close, just stand back and admire. We was moving fast, too. I'd made pies and canned peaches, had two loads of wash on the line. All the dishes done from seven hungry hired hands at dinner. Art would come home for supper and be back on his tractor 'til it was pitch dark. We had to move fast. We was in debt up to our elbows with the tractor and the balers, the mower and threshing machine. Didn't even have time for a garden. It didn't pay to raise food for people anymore. Only feed for pigs and cows would pay off all them machines.

I missed Dot more than ever. He was always more of a help

than Ivy, who was so dreamy. He was dreamy, too, but more like me, dreaming of what was in his hands. For two years, I'd sent off a box to him a week, full of cookies and raisins, sugar and coffee. Ivy would make drawings of herself in the corn, reaching to show how tall she was, or she would draw the empty garden. He'd send back letters full of love for me and Art and enclose a separate sheet of paper on which he'd write poems. I didn't understand 'em much. Maybe Art woulda if I woulda shown him. As it was, I burned 'em. There was nothing wrong with 'em but some part of me suspected that writing poems was a harm and would just cause trouble.

"How come Aunt Till doesn't come over anymore?"

Ivy and me was upstairs, changing the sheets and putting on fresh ones. "She's busy, I suppose."

Ivy had opened every window until the sheets was billowing out of our hands. "Mmmm, they smell so good," she said. Without Till around so much, Ivy and I got along better. I wasn't always saying no and Ivy sank back into the boundaries I'd set for us. After a day with Till, Ivy would come back with all kinds of ideas in her head, asking me did I ever want to go to college and did I ever want to go traveling like Fritzie and Till. Sure, I do, I'd say, but not without Art. I'll never go anywhere without my husband. I wanted for Ivy what I had. I was happy with it and I thought she should be, too.

"Pretty soon it'll be fall and we'll be changing these back to flannel."

"Till said I can be anything in the world I want to be."

"She did, huh?"

"She said I can go anywhere I want to go, too. She said if I can see it, it can happen."

"Honey, sometimes it works out that way and sometimes it don't. Your Aunt Till gets your hopes up, and then I'm the one that dries your tears."

"I can see myself a nurse. In white with a pointed hat. My hair is long and pinned up and I have white shoes and a white slip and white..."

"You might change your mind by the time you grow up."

"No, I won't."

"You have to go to school to be a nurse. You say already how sick you are of going to school."

"I won't change my mind! I won't!" She threw the pillowcase onto the bed and ran downstairs.

"Don't slam that door!" I called. It slammed. Then all I could hear was the fan down in the kitchen.

Upstairs, it was dark and breezy and warm with all the windows Ivy left open. How good it felt to have the floors swept and new sheets and finally this breeze, even if Ivy was mad at me. Maybe later it'd rain, since they'd left off seeding the clouds for the summer. That's what I'd do if I was the rain, wait 'til they quit pestering me. I moved to a window. From it, I could see as far as I wanted to and what I couldn't see, I could hear: Art's tractor and the green sigh of the wheat falling under the blade, my sheets snapping on the line, and Ivy sniffling, heading for the sheep barn. I listened closer. I remember thinking I should check on Grange and Junior, who was down for their naps.

The big oak spreading wide as a barn and the butterflies down in my sweet peas and the flies sticking to the screen and the blue and white lilacs, so old and big they was trees and you could crawl up in 'em. This was enough to take in. I never wanted to get higher than that window and I haven't, not in any building or in a plane. I could see my whole family from that window, before they started moving places I don't know nothing about and nobody can tell me, places with names that sound funny, to work in factories or mines or plants like Uncle Odie's kids and look what happened to them. In those days, I could see everybody, except for Dot. Where was he?

I'd been standing at a window just the other day with my sister, Lizzy, upstairs in the house we was raised in. We never expected the view to change. Sure, more houses, less trees. But things had started changing so fast out Lizzy's window what with the highway and smokestacks and cafes. Why, the corn field was paved over faster than you can whistle Dixie. "Ugly, ain't it?" Lizzy had said.

I looked out over my forest and fields like I was a grand duchess. Here it was still like it used to be, with clothes snapping and babies sleeping and women staring out the window to a world we like to look at. Hell, nobody asks ya. Nobody came to my sister Lizzy's door and said, "Would you rather look out your window at a corn field or a parking lot, have lamplight or that nuclear power plant, have Fishtrap Lake or the landfill?" And that's just how they do it. They don't ask us. They change the view out our windows and then convince us it's what we wanted.

And then, there was Ivy, running toward the house again, smiling, a bouquet of lilacs for me in her hands.

Suddenly something dark and round flew toward the glass in front of me and I heard a loud thump. I jumped back, then opened the window to yell at Ivy. "Don't you dare throw anything at this window, missy."

"I didn't." She pointed to the ground. There was a bird lying in the dirt, its wings spread in a fan around it. It was flapping and trying to lift its head in that broken neck dance I'd seen the chickens do. I ran down, but by the time I got there it was dead and Ivy was sobbing. I took the flowers from her hands.

"Poor thing," I said, not knowing what else to say.

"What'd it do that for?"

"Thought it was air, I guess. Must've seemed pretty sure of it."

"It's my fault. I opened the windows."

"It ain't either. It woulda ran into glass, closed or open. See where it hit the top part?"

Ivy was inconsolable, so without a word I went inside for an old shoe box. She lined it with grass and dandelions and the blue and lavender sweet peas while I scooped up the body with a newspaper. The head fell first into the box. Ivy wanted to kiss it, but I wouldn't let her. Art said birds carried lice and we shouldn't ever touch 'em. Once we'd taped the lid shut, I let her kiss the box and we carried it to the lilac grove to bury it, both of us crying so unreasonably hard that our eyes was puffy all through supper. Art was so tired, he didn't notice.

"It's Dot, isn't it?" Ivy said the next morning. "He's dead."

Chapter Eight

Birds come to tell ya, also bees. If a cow moos after midnight or a white dove circles the house three times. If you carry a shovel backward through the house, dream of a white horse or muddy water. If you see fire in the distance or a sick person plowing: somebody is gonna die. Used to be people picked out their own clothes for the funeral, ahead of time bought the coffin boards and wine. Now nobody wants to talk about it, their own death or anybody else's, and nobody sees it coming, as if pretending's the ritual we've been looking for, the one that puts an end to it. I guess I'm different. After Dot died, I didn't need no signs nor signals. I could see it coming in every person's face, how someday it'd be Art, someday it'd be Ivy, Grange, or Junior. I guess you could say I developed an eye for it. I even started noticing how many baby birds fell from their nests onto the pavement in the spring.

Some folks say it don't really happen, say they can feel their dead around 'em, still with 'em. "He walks with me," they say or "she's watching over me every minute." Some people don't feel 'em but they dream 'em, how their pa held their hands. Art had a dream where he was riding a train with Dot and the train stopped. It's not what you think. Dot didn't get off, Art did. The glory train, I once heard Mrs. Jones call it. "Bound for glory and all aboard," she said. Ivy, poor child, 'stead of dreaming or feeling 'em, she sees 'em. Sees 'em on the side of the road a-waving and the family driving past too fast to see. Sees 'em in crowds, a-whispering and nudging and pointing the way and, if somebody's sick, how they breathe slow with 'em. Sees 'em approaching with gifts and bouquets. Used to be I couldn't believe a word Ivy said, not 'cause she was lying but because the lines between dead and alive, between waking and sleeping that we got down pat by ten, wasn't clear for her yet. As she got older, she learned what to say and what not to, though she never did learn completely what not to see. "Ivy," Till would tell her, "don't open the doors to just anyone." But Ivy opened hers wide as the world she was new in and she wasn't gonna deny a thing. I'm glad we was poor. The rich was starting to get names and cures for people like Ivy by then. Seemed like the whole world was getting names and cures for everything.

After the war, factories was streaming into Town of Pines from Chicago, Detroit, building closer and closer to the center of town 'til the foundries was flickering in the windows at night and Lizzy could no longer hang out her wash for fear of bringing it in dirtier than when she hung it. The garbage started drifting onto our farm from town, tin cans in the drainage ditches, papers caught in the barbed wire and so many piles of broken glass I feared to let the boys go barefoot. Even the sunsets was changing from the pale rose and lilac, violet and lavender—colors me and Lizzy used to name after flowers—to brash oranges, greens and reds that appeared west over the steel mills and in our clothes, our papers and in our food. The corn seeds came, dyed a bright pink. Art said it was so the rats wouldn't eat 'em.

We quit going to town much but for groceries. We couldn't find nothing that was there before and we didn't recognize half the faces. New faces without family moving into our old neighborhoods like they owned 'em. Faces that stared back with suspicion, grimy with soot and sweat and nobody to go home to. After the war, the electricity became cheap and the factories stayed open round the clock. Lizzy's husband worked the graveyard shift. She said they never saw each other. Bethlehem Steel, National Can, New York Blower, and all the new plastics fac-tories smelling worse than steel ever did. U.S. Plastics, American Plastics, Victory Plastics and the poor lined up to work in 'em, making parts to wholes they'd never see, parts for jets to take the rich on vacation or our boys to war, plastic packages for our food so we'd have to pay more for it. The train tracks crisscrossed the streets and we had to wait at least once going from one side of town to the other. Their whistles moaned all night, and every year one of our young men was killed trying to beat the trains at the crossing.

Everybody had a car by then, even the poorest, even if they couldn't afford the gasoline. They built a highway next to our farm—straight from mud to four lanes of pavement was how fast things was changing. Eisenhower said the new highways was for national defense, but what with all the grumbling about frozen wages and high prices after the war, and how all the police in town got new patrol cars, I got to wondering who was protecting who from who. People started appearing quite regular at our door, peddlers and people running out of gas. We posted a sign. Art said he wasn't gonna keep petroleum but for his tractors. Still, folks came, knocking after midnight, folks without relation who'd just as soon rob us as pay us. And they got mad if we said no. Joe Ault went to do his milking one night and found a man in his barn holding a siphoning hose. A farmer in Three Oaks who refused to sell gas woke the next night to find his barn on fire. And we all heard about Widow Larson, who let a man in to use her phone and the next thing she knew, he's knocking her on the ground and raping her. And her a seventy-four-year-old woman! Widow Larson's never been the same.

Art said I should quit sitting by myself on the porch at night and I shouldn't feed the tramps neither, which I didn't, all but the scrawniest-looking ones. It was against my nature to turn people away hungry. I'd watch 'em leave and look at my full cupboards and my new freezer full of strawberries and roasts and I wouldn't be able to cook good for days. I felt stingy with myself and my family. Art got a gun. He said it was to teach the boys to hunt rabbits in the woods, though in years past I remember watching him feed 'em.

On the border between Pole Town and where the Negroes was moving in, far enough away from the courthouse to make the older families hesitate and to keep away the law, smack in the middle of a row of factories, Stanley and Marie's Three Star Tavern was booming. Marie and Stanley kept it open from dawn till two the next morning, trading shifts so one or the other could sleep. The Negroes didn't like drinking with all the new hillbillies brought up from the South so they bought their liquor from the package liquor store Marie had the foresight to open. Already she'd saved enough money to buy their first car. It wasn't a Cadillac yet, but Marie always kept it shining.

It was Harold who told us about Stanley. That his insides was always hurting and that he'd grip his side and turn pale if he moved too quick. On bad days, he laid on their couch in the back room; on good, he watched Marie work from a stool at the bar. He was weak. Harold had heard Marie tell him so. "I never be sick day in my life," she'd say, loud enough for anyone to hear her, including Stanley. Slugging shots that by this time was half water and half gin, waiting on twenty men at once and loving it, laughing and flirting: Marie could do it every day of the year and she was proud she could. She had money, her own business. She made her own hours and got paid for all of 'em. Fritzie had helped her get a driver's license, and from then on she never walked. America had won the war. Marie flew an American flag outside her bar and if any of the old men wanted to talk about their lives in Poland, she scolded them.

"War is over. America is our country now. Forget Poland."

"But, Marie, don't you worry about your family? If they made it through?"

"What good is to know?" she'd say. "Poland is Russia's now."

"Don't you wonder? Don't you write?"

"Laura write. She no letter get since 1942. Look, I am America. I write, what is America think of me? Think I am Communism maybe."

"There's a woman I know," Harold heard one of the old men say. "She calls herself a seer. If you can give her something, a letter, a photo, a piece of cloth they wore, she can look for you. See over the ocean. See if they're alive, what they're doing."

Marie hesitated. "You do this thing?"

"For my sister in Warsaw," the man nodded. "The seer couldn't find her."

"No one is left in Warsaw," Marie said.

"Sometimes they're not dead, they're drunk. The seer says she can't get through to them if they've been drinking." The man chuckled. "With my sister, it might take us years of trying."

The more Harold went to the Three Star Tavern, the worse he'd talk about Marie. And the madder she made him, the more he'd go back. "Stanley's so sick he can hardly get outa bed and will she take him to a doctor?"

"Since when did you believe in doctors, Harold?" I said.

He frowned at me but went on. "Says she's too busy with the bar."

"Stanley's feared doctors always," I told him. "He wouldn't go if she asked him to."

"What she's busy with is men. Has two, three, four different ones in a night, dancing with one right after the other, whoever'll ask her, whether they's married or not and right there in the bar in front of Stanley. Him just sitting there, too sick to fight 'em off and she knows it."

"So what if she dances? You said yourself Stanley is right there."

"Folks say on Sundays she's up and down LaCroix County, hitting the bars. Last week, she was with Harry Chalmers, brother of the guy who owns the tractor factory. What do ya think she sees in him? His good looks? He's over sixty and has a wife and three grandchildren. She goes with him to Phil's Supper Club without either of their spouses along. While poor Stanley's waiting at home for his supper."

"That's where you got your story wrong," I said. "If they had to depend on Marie's cooking, they'd of starved a long time ago."

What Harold was saying didn't shock me. Talk followed Marie, an old dog, and she was never one to shoo it away. Fact is, I think she fed it, found it helped her business. First, it was why she came by herself with no husband following that peaked our curiosity. Then it was how Fritzie introduced her to trousers and her legs never saw the light of day again. Folks weren't happy with that neither. I coulda cared less about any of that crap Harold told me about Marie. Stanley being sick was another matter. The next Sunday, after breakfast, I got it in my mind to pay them a visit.

"Ivy, put on your good dress. You and me is gonna visit an old friend of mine."

"I'm supposed to go with Aunt Till on Sundays," she complained. "You promised I could. I haven't seen her for three weeks."

"You heard what your mother said," Art said, not surprisingly. Since Ivy'd turned sixteen, he was even less approving of her time with Till. Said it put ideas in her head that was bound for disappointment, created strife where before there was none. Love Till as I did, I had to agree. Two years from graduating and

Ivy was coming home from her afternoons with Fritzie and Till with plans to go to college.

"We don't have money to send you to college, honey," I'd say.

"Till says there's ways I can go for free. She says she can help me."

"And how are you gonna support yourself once you get there?"

"There's dormitories. They feed you. It's the same university Till went to in Chicago."

"I ain't about to let any child of mine leave home to live in a big city like Chicago."

"You never said that to Dot. You wanted him to go to college. Besides, lots of girls live in big cities."

"Well, mine don't. What do you need to go to school to be a medium for anyhow? Till said herself you was born to it."

"Till says I'm gonna need a good education if I'm a medium or not. She says the world's changing and I should change with it."

"And what if the world ain't changing for the good?"

Ivy gave me a long, hard look. "What can I do about that?"

"Don't change with it."

Ivy sighed. "Mom, you just want me to be like you. You want me to give up all my dreams to the first man who says he loves me."

"Give up? Give up? Ivy, I don't know who's been talking to you. You ain't giving up nothing by loving. Loving is what makes you strong, not weak. It makes you more, not less. If it's really love."

She was quiet awhile. "What if nobody loves me?"

I smiled. "I love you."

She slammed her fist down on the table. "I mean what if I don't meet somebody I love as much as you love Pa? That doesn't have to be the end of the world."

"You'll meet somebody. Just give it time."

"Mom," Ivy said, raising her voice, "what if I don't? All I know is poisonings and healings and people scared until almost too late to show anybody their goiters and the rocks growing inside 'em. People with grief gnawing at them so bad they'll believe anything a sixteen-year-old girl will tell 'em. I'll end up a spinster like Till. I want to have a normal life."

"Till would call her life normal."

"Do you think it's normal? Talking to ghosts and dressing like a man and always worrying about money? No wonder she's going to have to spend her whole life with Fritzie. And she doesn't even care. All she cares about is learning."

"Have you told your Aunt Till you don't want to be a medium?"

"I am a medium. It's not that I don't want to be a medium."

"You just don't want to be like her. And you don't want to be like me. So, what is it exactly you do want?"

Ivy sank down in the chair with a groan. "You've got it all mixed up. That's not what I was saying at all."

Till was having her own troubles with Ivy. Not that Ivy had lost her talent. Since she'd turned sixteen and Till had started letting her lead services at the church, Ivy'd become a favorite of many in the congregation. She'd just glance at a person and she could tell ya how many of their loved ones had passed away. She said she saw it in their eyes, the dead swimming in 'em. All she had to do was hold somebody's hands and the spirits would start lifting out of 'em like smoke out of a snuffed candle, spiraling up toward the sky like the sweet peas in my garden do. Ivy'd follow 'em with her eyes, tilting her head out the window, and just by the way the clouds was moving, she could name their dead one by one. "Henry has just come," she'd say, "and he's bringing you such beautiful flowers."

"She thinks that's all there is to it," Till complained. "Just open yourself up and there they are, stampeding the gate, fighting to get through first."

"She's young, Till," I'd say, "give her time."

"She's lazy. She believes anything anybody tells her. I give her theology books. I give her history books. I tell her I want her more than anything to learn how to think for herself. What she swears to one day, she forgets the next. If I told her to jump off a high building, I think she'd do it."

"She trusts you, Till, that's all."

"That's just it. I want her to trust herself, not me. Otherwise, they'll walk all over her."

"The spirits?"

"Everybody."

Art dropped Ivy and me off in front of the Three Star Tavern that Sunday and, contrary to what Harold said, we found Marie at home. "Is something wrong?" she asked when she opened the door. "Your husband is sick?"

"No, but I heard yours was." I pointed to Art, waiting in the car. "Art's taking the boys to a ball game. He'll be back for us in a couple hours. You remember Ivy, don't ya? She's grown up since you last seen her."

Marie looked Ivy up and down. "You tall like father," she said, then winked at me, "but you have big bucket like mother."

"What are you hurting her feelings for, Marie? Look, you made her cry. You ain't exactly sitting on skin and bones."

Marie laughed, patting her rump. She wore the pants Harold had told us about, plain gray flannel with a zipper up the front like a man's. They made her look stouter than she was already. She wore a thin line of red lipstick and I noticed she had started dying her hair, a no-account brown that covered up all her gold and red shades and made her seem older. "She ain't pretty," Harold had said. "Ya wonder what all the men sees in her."

If I didn't know her better, I'd of thought she wasn't glad to see us. Ivy and me sat for half an hour on two bar stools Marie pulled into the kitchen while our hostess talked about how much money she was making. She didn't so much as offer us a cup of coffee, let alone something to eat. That got my goat. I woulda left in five minutes if it wasn't for Stanley. "Where's Stanley?" I said when I could get a word in edgewise.

"Stanley no feel so good. You want to see him? I see if he's awake."

We followed Marie behind a wall she'd built and plastered herself, dividing the bar kitchen from the rest of their lives. Marie had sheets over all her furniture and she didn't remove 'em for us to sit down. I motioned to Ivy and we went to get our bar stools and join Stanley by the couch. He looked gray and too sick to sit up. "Marie, why didn't you tell me we had company? I'm sorry, I must have dozed off," he said to us. "This must be Ivy. Oh, has she grown up beautiful! Marie, did you offer them coffee? A shot? Have you ladies eaten?" He was digging in his pants pockets beneath the blankets. "Here," he said, offering us fistfuls of lemon drops.

"Thank you," Ivy said, smiling sweetly. "We don't need coffee."

"Harold Hullinger comes by the bar once or twice a week to see us, but he says you don't have those circles as much as you used to. He doesn't think much of Till, but I always liked her. Do you see her?"

"Sure, I see her," I said. "She's Ivy's godmother. And no, we don't have the circles much. It was too hard on everybody to get out to the farm. You know, once we all got cars, we realized how far it was from one place to another." From the corner of my eye, I could see Ivy looking at me, hopeful. "Ivy's been studying with her Aunt Till, though. She's gonna be a medium herself." She blushed and nodded, happy I'd told him.

"Young man hear you talk to dead, you never date having," said Marie.

Ivy glanced at me, unsure whether Marie was kidding or not. "I'm studying to be a Spiritualist minister. And a healer."

"No woman is minister this country. Is it, Stanley? Lawyer, yes. This I learn from Fritzie."

"Maybe you could ask Till to say a prayer for me," Stanley said to Ivy. "Maybe you would, too?"

"That is old country," Marie interrupted. "America no believe farmer religion. No believe hocus-pocus."

"Of course I will," Ivy said. "If it's okay, I can even ask my Aunt Till to come see you. She could heal you, I bet. Make you feel better."

"No," Marie said. "I no like that woman. Fritzie is smart. Very smart. She teach me how to license take it. She give me pants. But that other, she stick nose where no belonging. I never look her in eye and I never be sick day in my life."

"You're lucky you ain't been sick, that's all," I said. "Till's good. She's just like a doctor in her way. She ain't up to any black magic. If she was, would I trust her with my daughter?"

"I no trust her with my daughter." Marie narrowed her eyes. "Harold say she witch practice. Say she no money having. Why is Fritzie pay everything? She is young woman still, very smart. No look for man but stay inside with witch?"

"Marie, you don't know your ass from a hole in the ground. Fritzie is living in Till's house. Till inherited that house from her folks."

Marie nodded her head, but I could tell she didn't believe me. "Fritzie's father is judge. Lots of money making. Fritzie be rich woman when father die."

I rolled my eyes at Stanley. "What about you? Have you been to a regular doctor?"

"Stanley say if he go doctor this country, he never come home," Marie said.

"What if a doctor came here?"

"Stanley say doctor is same here as in old country. Doctor see where Death stand. If at foot of bed, no matter what he do, patient live. If Death stand at head of bed, doctor say nothing to be done, patient die. Old story Stanley tell. Doctor, no doctor. No matter. Death stand here, there. You live, no live."

Stanley laughed. "Nettie, I don't need a doctor. Some days are just better than others. Being around this lovely young lady has made me feel stronger today."

"We'll be sure to do all we can to help you," Ivy said.

"Stanley, you're welcome out to our place anytime. I sure miss seeing you, and Marie, too." I heard Art pulling up with the boys. "We got to go now, but we'll talk to Till for ya. I'd get myself to a real doctor, too. Can't hurt. No reason you shouldn't try everything."

Ivy'd been sharing my bed since the boys got older and Art made me give 'em her room. I thought she'd never forgive me for it. It was my fault, she thought, and to an extent it was, asking her to come back to her ma's bed just when she was feeling grown. But I could see Art's point. It could be four years before Ivy left home. The boys would be fourteen by then and sleeping with their mother. So we got two twin beds and they took over the big room and Ivy and I moved into the small. She laid clear over on the edge of the bed each night and would swat my hands and feet if they brushed up against hers. She never wanted to talk in bed neither. That's why I was surprised when she nudged me awake the night we came back from Marie's.

"Why are all those men in love with Marie?" she asked.

"Who told you men was in love with Marie?"

"I heard Harold talking to you. She's ugly. She shaves her chin, did you notice that?"

"I wouldn't say she was ugly."

"Why does she do that? Shave her chin, I mean. It looks hideous. And did you see that scar next to her mouth? She probably cut it with a razor. It's disgusting. It makes her look mean." Ivy sat up in bed.

Marie didn't look mean to me. Not mean like the men in her bar with their broken noses and close calls to the eyes. "It's just a little nick. It happened a long time ago."

"Why do men think she's so pretty?" Ivy repeated.

"I don't think they see her as exactly pretty," I said, thinking: not pretty like Ivy's friends wanted to be pretty with their made-up eyes staring up at men like men was gonna save 'em from something, like if they stayed looking like little girls with pink and bows and waists the size of a ten-year-old, the men'd treat 'em gentler. You could tell where they got their ideas. The magazines published the hip, waist, and breast sizes of every woman whose picture was in 'em, the smaller the better 'cept when it came to the tits. Ivy leafed through those magazines for hours and when she was finished, she'd be mad at me and planning another diet. "Pretty ain't everything," I said.

"It's rotten how she dates other men when she's married," Ivy said.

"Listen, young lady, what Marie and her husband do is their own business, not ours. You pay no mind to what Harold says."

"You don't go out with other men. You don't go anywhere without Dad."

"I would if I wanted to. I just don't want to."

Ivy backed down under the blankets again. "I'm not gonna be like that. I'm gonna go around the world and meet all kinds of people and I'm gonna fall in love a hundred times before I get married."

"So what's the difference between you and Marie? She does exactly what she wants to, too."

There was a silence. "Marie is ugly," Ivy said, "and mean."

The next morning, Ivy decided she was gonna save Stanley. From what, I'm not sure. His illness, you would suppose, but I suspected it was from Marie. Whatever it was, Ivy put her dozen eggs into it. My ma always warned me to keep at least one egg for myself and I was constantly repeating her advice to Ivy. Most folks don't want your whole basket, my ma'd say. There was no telling Ivy that. She decided it was her calling. I gotta admit it tickled me to see her so sure of herself again. Like there was some voice inside her that finally hit the high C. And sure enough, it wasn't two weeks after our visit, two weeks of Ivy praying and studying and calling to Till, that Stanley came driving up the road to see us. His Sunday visits became a habit for the next year and a half.

None of us could complain. Me and Art liked Stanley fine. And Ivy? Stanley and her would sit in the kitchen after dinner, drinking coffee and eating whatever special I'd made for dessert. At last there was something about me that wasn't a tragedy to her life, and she became almost sweet to me. "Ma, would ya make that coffee cake of your mother's this Sunday?" she'd say. She started missing service with Till on Sundays, but she made it every Wednesday night to the healing circles and she poured over the Spiritualist manuals that was collecting dust before. Ivy stayed up reading and lighting candles in the kitchen 'til almost daybreak and there was nothing Art could say about it 'cause her grades was better than ever.

The books taught her that, with healing, suggestion is everything and the more she suggested, the more Stanley believed. "Don't ever say you don't feel good, even to yourself," she'd say. In six months, Stanley was near looking like the same man I met twenty-five years before with coins and hard candy in his pockets for the boys and in his hands, a box of chocolates for Ivy or dollar bills for her clothes shopping. Only his hair, white, and his face, red from walking the short distance from the car, let on he was suffering from anything but too many good meals.

For the most part, we let Ivy and Stanley alone. After dinner, the boys'd go to their chores and Art and I'd go out to the porch. Sitting there, it seemed like the first time we'd sat together like that for thirty years. There was a happiness there for me that year, not fighting about Dot or Ivy or the boys, Art beside me in the shade of the porch like the shade of a tree and the breezes blowing round my bare legs. Next to Art, who was so proud of me, how I raised all them kids and how my cooking was the talk for miles around. 'Cause he was proud of me, I was proud of me. I didn't have no shame about being good in the kitchen like some do now. Cooking was as important as planting then and to hell with the housekeeping. I have always been more interested in talk of crops, animals, and weather. It drove Ivy nuts, but then she wasn't the only one. Her and the damned TV was always on my case. Smudges, stains, smells, and streaks was my downfall. Lucky Art didn't care about 'em neither, the sparkles, gleams, and the spanking cleans.

To love, honor, and to obey. That was our vows and we kept 'em, though I have to qualify that by saying that love and honor is a different and simpler thing for a man. There was Art, smoking and looking out to his fields and he was thinking about them fields and I was thinking about him. Did he ever look back from them fields and think about me? I doubt it. Art loved me, don't get me wrong, but sometimes, sitting next to him like that, I'd think how I'd spent half my life with a man I couldn't tell if he was happy with me. Marie or Till? We always knew who was in favor and who wasn't. We always knew what the other was feeling. Art? I'd bend over backwards for him forty times a day and do ya think he ever asked himself if I wanted to do it? I never asked myself. Nowadays, my granddaughter tells me, they changed the wedding vows for women. We no longer have to promise to obey. If ya ask me, it don't matter. Women is funny. For most of us, more than some ceremony has got to change.

Most of us but Marie, and it seemed everybody hated her for it. Most of all the women. Stanley never talked about her, but Harold came even more frequently with the news. How a man's wife caught him with his arm around Marie and ripped his sleeve off and how Marie had slapped her. How Marie had a new mink-trimmed coat last winter that Stanley didn't buy for her, and how one day she showed up with diamonds in her ears. Despite the hysterectomy, there was rumors Rosetta had sold Marie herbs more than once to get rid of babies. And all them expensive dinners out, Harold said, was making Marie fat. There was so many stories over the next year that when I saw her pull up with Stanley one day, unexpected, I expected to see a monster. It was the same old Marie, only younger-looking, happier, wearing her fur-trimmed coat and walking with the health and the strut of a woman who's had plenty of sex and is proud of it. Stanley got out of the car to open her door. He seemed to be moving slower.

"Marie? This is a surprise!" I said, hurrying to greet her.

I seen Ivy peeking around the back door. She was wearing a dress she'd made from money she got from Stanley. She was biting her nails. Next to Marie, Ivy looked like she was in grade school. I felt Marie noticing how I didn't dress up for Sunday dinner. I wiped my hands on my apron and untied it from behind.

"Dinner's just about ready," I said, motioning her in. "Ivy," I called, "call Junior and Grange. Tell 'em to wash. We got company."

The table was spread with my homemade bread and pies, fresh corn and string beans, fried chicken, so there was no room to lay an elbow. "So this is how my husband so fat getting," Marie said.

I thought I was used to Marie, but my kitchen suddenly seemed small with her in it. Smaller than when I had twelve field hands after the baling, smaller than with three kids, Stanley, Art, and me eating in it the past year. Junior came in and offered to take Marie's coat. She shook her head like she thought he was gonna make off with it and he backed away. I unwrapped the bottle of cream sherry she'd brought us. Though we never drank, I poured each of us a small shot.

We was all still standing, even the boys, who was staring at Marie in awe. "I no believe you but my Stanley is much better," Marie said, turning to Ivy. "I come to thank you."

Ivy tried to catch Stanley's eye. It was obvious she wasn't flattered. "I thought you went out on Sundays," she said to Marie.

You can imagine how quiet that room got. I held my breath. I could tell by Art's face that Ivy was gonna get a talking-to later. Stanley's eyes avoided everyone's. Marie surprised us. "Is true. I am busy today. No dinner stay for. I come back for Stanley later. Three hours maybe?"

"Three hours will be fine, Marie," Stanley said, taking his seat at the table as if nothing had happened. I waved stupidly as Marie walked out the door.

I looked at Art. It was impossible to tell what he was thinking. What would he do, I wondered. What would I do if he got sick so young in life? I didn't need to ask myself. I knew I would stay home and take care of him. "Let's sit down and eat before it gets cold," I said as the sound of Marie's tires skidded on our gravel road.

When we finished dinner, seemed like everybody but me and Stanley had something important to do. He sat there in silence while I stacked the dishes at the sink.

"She's good to me, Nettie," he said finally.

"I know."

"I love her. I always will."

I wiped my hands. "She ain't sleeping with any of them hound dogs, is she?"

Stanley sighed. "She's still young, Nettie."

"Well," I sputtered. "Well."

"Why shouldn't Marie enjoy herself? I can't keep up with her. Marie likes to go out, to dance, to have a good time. She deserves to. Look how hard she works all week. What should she do, pretend she's weak and sick like me?"

Of course she should, I almost said. I loved Art so much that if he was sick, I would be soon. Art didn't have a pain I didn't feel. Marie was different. I could hear Harold saying, "She asks for too much. She thinks just 'cause she has money she has the right to act like a man." Who was Harold to say Marie asked for too much, Marie who worked six days a week, eighteen hours a day? Who had a sick husband, no children, and a houseful of drunks every night? Who didn't have a wife who excused her so she could go on week-long fishing trips or day-long trances? Who was Harold to say, when sex came at the drop of his drawers for him whether his wife was sick or not? "I don't know," I told Stanley.

"I'm not well, Nettie. I'm getting better, Lord knows. I can't satisfy Marie, though. I never could."

I took a deep breath. "You know my daughter's in love with you."

Stanley's eyes twinkled. "She's just a girl."

"She's a grown woman. Next year, she's out of high school. I haven't heard of one boy asking her for a date since you've been coming on Sundays. It ain't right."

"She's a sweet girl. You must know how I adore her," Stanley smiled. "You can't say it hasn't been good for her, too. She believes in herself now. We're friends. She has someone to talk to."

I felt my temperature rising. I thought of Ivy giving up her Sunday preaching at her Aunt Till's, giving up her evenings with friends. Ivy telling boys she was busy on the weekends. Ivy giving, giving, giving and for what? 'Cause this man had convinced her he needed her. What right did Stanley have to convince her of that? "I worry about what's gonna happen to her. I don't want you breaking her heart."

"You don't have to worry about me. Ivy will meet some nice man soon."

"What if she ain't looking? Already she's talking to Till about putting off her schooling for a year so she can stay and make sure you're completely better."

"I thought you didn't want her to go to college."

"I don't."

"Well?"

"I do, I mean. I changed my mind."

"Nettie, what do you want me to do, tell her I don't want to see her anymore? You know as well as I do how hurt she'd be."

"Tell her you and Marie is getting along better. Tell her now that you're feeling better, you're needed around the house. Tell her she should use her gifts for healing on somebody else for awhile. Shit, I don't care what you tell her."

"I can't do that, Nettie."

I clenched my teeth, waiting for whatever it was I was gonna have to say. "Well, if you can't, I can," I said, fuming. "As of next week, I ain't cooking Sunday dinner for you no more."

The next Sunday, just as we was about to sit down to dinner, the phone rang. "Ivy, you want to get that?" I said, casual-like. I hadn't told anybody what I'd said to Stanley the week before so I could count on surprised faces. I settled back into my own innocence and waited for whatever Stanley was gonna tell her.

Ivy came back in the kitchen, pale as a sheet. "Mom, it's Marie. Something's wrong."

I put my arm around her. What a chicken way out, I was thinking, using Marie. "Stanley's not feeling so good today?" I guessed.

"He can't breathe. He's got pains in his chest, bad pains. I told Marie we'd be right there."

"We can't be right there. Your pa's over at Pa Bartz's all day, you know that. He's helping with a sick calf."

"Grange knows how to drive."

"We ain't gonna take the car without asking your pa."

"Grange!" Ivy was shouting. "Grange, go start up the car. We gotta go to town on an emergency."

"Wait a minute. I'll call the Bartz's. It shouldn't take more than an hour to track him down and get him back here."

"We don't have an hour. We can't wait."

I looked at Ivy and I could tell this was serious. I was scared to death, but we did it, me, Ivy, and Grange, leaving Junior behind to explain to Art how the car wasn't stolen. I got madder and more scared the closer we got to Marie's and it seemed like it was taking Grange forever. "Drive faster," I whispered. "We gotta get this car back in an hour."

When we got to the tavern, Ivy went running to the back door. When no one answered, she rushed in. There was Stanley on the floor, clutching his chest and moaning, his eyes rolling back in his head. "Did you call an ambulance?" I shouted at Marie, who was standing over him, knowing she wouldn't have. I was dialing like a madwoman, ordering Ivy not to move him, Grange to cover him up.

"When they come, you gotta go with him, Marie. We'll stay here and wait."

Marie was gripping her arms, still staring at her husband on the floor. "No," she said, so low I could barely hear her.

"What'd ya mean 'no?' He's your husband." Marie smelled strong of perfume and booze and she had on her high heels. I imagined she was on her way out before this happened. "Here comes the ambulance," I said. From the color of Stanley's face, I doubted he was gonna make the ride.

The ambulance crew put Stanley on a stretcher and wheeled him into the van. Then they paused, looking back at all of us standing there in the parking lot. "Anybody coming?" one said.

Marie shook her head. "I can't," she said to me.

I sighed and crawled in the back next to Stanley, who was breathing with effort. Without thinking, I yelled, "Ivy, you come with me."

We wasn't a mile out of Marie and Stanley's driveway when Stanley gasped and stiffened. A minute later he gurgled as the last of the air escaped his chest. Ivy looked at me, horrified. "What's wrong with him?" she screamed.

"He's dead."

"His eyes," she said, pointing at poor Stanley, "they're still open!"

When the taxi brought us back to the tavern, Marie was sitting with Grange on the stoop. "Where is he?" she demanded. "Where you take my husband?"

"He's at the hospital," Ivy said, looking Marie straight in the eye.

"Is he alright?" Marie said, grabbing her car keys.

"He's dead, Marie. He died on the way," I told her, taking her hand.

"Is not true? He was fine when he left."

"He is too dead," Ivy said angrily. "I saw it happen. He died in pain with his eyes open wide. They wouldn't take him at the hospital morgue unless they were sure he was dead. I watched the coroner poke his finger into his eyeballs to make sure."

Marie moved to slap her.

"You should've been there," Ivy said, grabbing Marie's wrist, "not me."

Grange opened the door. "Come on, Ma, Ivy. We better get the car home. Do ya want to come with us, Marie?"

Marie shook her head, then turned to go in her house.

"You gonna go to the hospital?" I called after her. She didn't answer. "I'll phone ya later. Soon as I find Art, we'll be back."

It wasn't 'til we was out of Town of Pines, heading home, that Ivy began to cry. "Why didn't you tell me it was gonna be like that? Him struggling? It was awful. Why'd you make me go with you?"

I put my arms around her and let her cry. "I wish I could save you from that, darling. I wish I could but I can't."

"He was doing fine. He was doing fine with me. You saw it yourself."

"It was a heart attack. He's been sick for a long time. The medics suspect diabetes. It ain't your doing."

"It was my doing. I was wrong, wasn't I?"

"You couldn't know he was that sick. What is right is that you loved him."

Ivy disentangled herself from my arms. "I did know. I saw it, like Marie said it would happen. I saw it the first day when he was on the couch and we came to visit. Only it wasn't Death standing at the head of his bed like she said. It was spirits, old people and children, young men and women with boots on like Marie wears and bright scarves and aprons and they were all smiling at him like they had loved him once and reaching out their hands to touch his hair and his hands."

"Did you tell Stanley that?"

"No, I saw it and I just didn't believe it."

"You didn't want to believe it."

"I thought I could pray hard enough. I thought I could love hard enough and they would all go away."

"Ivy, I wanted you to go with me because someday you're gonna have to do it alone." I tried to put my arm around her again, but she moved away.

"I shoulda told him, that's what you're saying."

"No, I'm not. Stanley probably knew himself anyway. Besides," I smiled, "hope is never a mistake."

"Why didn't you tell me it was gonna be like this?" she repeated.

Six months later, Ivy met a man at the soda shop who was just back from the Korean War, a man with a red convertible and no belief in God or religion and who laughed when she told him people could talk to the dead. In a year, she was married to him.

Chapter Nine

Any farmer could tell ya the year that started the winds moving. We didn't need the papers to know something was wrong. We could feel it in the quiet between gusts that swept up the stubble in the cleared October fields. We could hear it in the way the skies sifted down from the cities, a hollow sound like company coming late to a party and calling—calling and calling to find everybody has gone home. Not one woman or dog walked the dirt roads anymore and the oaks that used to waltz out to greet me, whispering and a-waving in their cured, country time as I walked with Art's lunch to the fields, now the oaks ignored me. We noticed, without reading the papers, how still the woods was getting, how few birds was coming back and just the common ones, the starlings and crows, a few robins and barn swallows. The crops gave themselves up to the gypsy moths without a struggle and rain had to be more and more coaxed from the sky. It was the first year we learned of limits: on deer, quail, squirrel and rabbit, and on bluegill, lake perch, catfish, any fish you could think of. I'd never heard of anybody catching too much fish in Town of Pines. Least not any of my relatives.

When they started leaving us, we knew we was in trouble. When they disappeared, so did our way of telling. Telling when to plant and telling weather, telling change coming and telling cures. Used to be we watched what leaves the dogs ate when they was poisoned and put the storm windows up when spiders clamored round the door. People think I'm talking in jingle-jangle, in sign for this or stands for that, but it ain't so. I'm talking direct about my world. Take the weather, for instance. Used to be weather was a local matter. The Big Lakes controlled it and the robins and woodchuck let us know. Sure, we was governed by the worldwide things. We knew that if the moon was full near midnight, the next week's weather would be fair. The nearer to noon, the fouler the weather. But for the most part, how much trees we planted was how much rain we was gonna get to water 'em and the more we built fires, the hotter the summers was. Whatever the birds and bees was doing across the Pacific, the Atlantic, or even in the county next door just wasn't any of our business.

Talking to the birds, the trees, to the air or water for that matter, wasn't no supernatural thing like talking to ghosts or God was. It was natural and everybody did it, whether anybody was watching you or not. They didn't talk back in English, but you watched for awhile, listened for awhile, and there was your help or your answer. Plain as day. Nowadays, all that's natural is human. "The great shady orchards are a thing of the past," I read in the Farmer's Almanac the other day. "The modern orchardist wants a tree pruned enough for a crow to fly through and no higher than may be reached by a modern sprayer or duster." No wonder the young folks is so lonely. The walls is closing in on 'em until all they got is subways of humans, and airports of humans, and highways of humans all going and going and half of nature closed off to 'em. Not even a window to let a little bird song in.

It's not that we didn't listen to the humans. We talked to the Farm Bureau and the experts at the Grange. We used the things they told us to, the DDT for the gypsy moths, the rain-seeding planes and Christ, more and more fertilizer each year and none of that comes cheap. Seemed like the more we spent on bigger

yields, the more we owed at the end of the year. If it wasn't happening to everybody, Art said, he'd think he'd lost his luck at
farming. Minnie and Jack sold out in 1950. Laura's husband took
a job in a foundry and moved the family to Tennessee. I ain't a
believer in luck or God, but I had the feeling something was
abandoning us.

Junior was studying to be an electrician. Grange was a
dreamer, like his ma, and had already started to drink. They
both complained pitifully whenever Art wanted 'em to do anything, baling or sowing or just bagging the beans. They acted like
we'd shamed 'em when we asked their friends to help. "They're
busy this weekend," they'd say and I'd know they never asked.
Neither one of 'em was entertaining a thought of being a farmer
past leaving high school and Junior, especially, was full of advice.
"You should get out while ya can," I heard him telling Art one
night on the porch. "It ain't worth your time unless you got capital for new equipment. You're competing with machines." I know
it hurt Art, but I could see him listening, plotting how to borrow
more money for a new tractor or them automated milking
machines. Grange was different but had the same story. "Ma,
nobody's ever made money off a farm he didn't own. Look at you
two. You've worked your fingers to the bone and what've you got?
I don't know what you ever hoped to accomplish."

"Hope to accomplish? We did accomplish. We accomplished
you and your brother and sister, not to mention my mother's son.
We accomplished food on the table and a marriage alive for
almost thirty years. See if you can do better."

"There ain't no money in farming," they'd say.

Ivy was pregnant and, bless her, coming every Saturday to see
us, though half the time, I swear, I wasn't so glad to see her, what
with her recipes from frozen boxes and mixes for gravy. Recipes
outa the married-women magazines and nothing from scratch.
Recipes that created more garbage than food and tasted like the

packages they came wrapped in. "Here, Ma, try this," she'd say. "You don't have to make mashed potatoes the old way. Nobody does that anymore and besides, this is cheaper than real potatoes." Coming into my kitchen with her store-bought clothes, telling me what to scrub my floors with, coming with her laundry and no husband and her nose stuck up in the air. It seemed like they wasn't getting along too good 'cause he never came to visit with her and she looked scared at her watch if she ever stayed more than three hours. She did have us for Sunday dinner once. We crowded into her dining room off the kitchen that sat exactly four and we ate instant and mixed everything and meat without any fat to it. Roy, her husband, sat, scowling at her and calling me "Ma," and Art "Art," and complaining 'cause the roast was falling off the bone.

I guess you could say I was lonely. You might even think I was unhappy. But on good days, when I could forget that the blue mist in the air was the dust from the drying-out fields, exhaust from the traffic and the smoke stacks of town or from the soft purple rot of apples a week of wind had knocked down too early from them overly pruned branches Junior had talked Art into, it was the land of my childhood again and it was beautiful. I'd take the long ways through the fields, walking miles outa my way, all by myself, and sometimes Art'd be starving for his sandwiches and still he never said nothing. He'd seen me on my bad days, pacing and pacing my empty house, overcooking for eight at every meal, adopting everybody's problems just to have something to take care of and still not caring much for nothing.

It was Indian summer. When I was a kid, I loved the stories of it, how the smoke in the fall air was smoke from their camp-fires and if ya listened careful to the air that dropped heavy as deer hooves as soon as the wind quit lifting it, you could hear their drums. How the old grasses died and blew down, leaving in the flattened fields their feathers, arrowheads, and hide scrapers for us kids to find, the wind blowing away everything that happened after them. Here in Indiana, people don't like thinking about Indians, but that year I got to thinking about 'em without even trying. That's why I decided to call Till.

"Why Indians?" I asked her.

"Nettie, is that you?" She was surprised as I was to be on the other end of the line. In those days, we only phoned each other in emergencies. This time, I hadn't called Till for a year.

"Nothing's wrong," I explained. "I can't believe it's been so long since I heard your voice."

"I thought that was you. How are you, dear?"

I'll never forget the sound of that "dear." I hadn't known how much I'd missed her. "Till, I was just thinking. Didn't you say you had two Indians come to you?"

"Oh, I suppose I must have told you at one time or another. Indian spirits, of course. Why?"

"I was just thinking. Do you think all these bombs stirred 'em up?"

"What bombs?"

"Them bombs in the Pacific. Fifty-six of 'em in all and all last year. They say they could be affecting the weather."

"Where did you hear about the bombs?"

"I read about 'em in the Farmer's Almanac," I said proudly. "Don't you know about 'em? They were testing 'em in the Pacific Ocean. In 1954."

"Well, I don't know." There was a pause in which I was scared she was thinking I was loony. I should have known Till would take me serious. "I haven't been thinking about bombs," she said. "I'm sorry."

"The government says they won't know for ten to twenty years about the weather but the Almanac knows. They say each one of 'em was the strength of a good-sized hurricane. They think that could keep the rain a-falling or cause this drought."

"Honey, what have you been doing with your days? Have the boys left home yet?"

"I still feed 'em, if that's what you mean. Junior just gradu-ated. Grange has a year to go." I chuckled. "Are you trying to tell me I got too much time for thinking on my hands?"

"No, Nettie, of course not. It's just that I'm not much good on the telephone and hearing your voice makes me want to see you in person. Is there any chance of you coming back to church now that the children are gone? Everybody misses you."

"I'd love to, Till, but Art's working by himself a lot and I never learned to drive."

"Never mind, I'll come to see you. I've been thinking too much myself and with Fritzie in court most every day, I'm a bit lonely. Those beautiful oak woods on the edge of your place—are they still there?"

"Sure, they're there, though Grange told me they built a golf course on the other side of 'em."

"I'd like to take a walk in them."

"Walk in 'em?" I felt puzzled. "Well, it is getting on mush-room season."

"I'll bring my basket and be over tomorrow."

"Nettie, what do bombs and Indians have to do with each other?" Till asked the next day as we was heading behind my chicken coop toward the woods. "I'm not sure I understood what you were asking yesterday."

She was leading the way despite the fact that it was my trees and, as far as I knew, she'd never been in 'em. She looked outa place outside with her long, dark skirts, her glasses and graying hair, like a deacon at a baseball game, but in her smile was enough blues and pinks and yellows to put a month of Sundays at the other churches to shame. "Till, there's a gate down here," I said as she straddled the fence.

"I know. There's just something about climbing fences that makes me feel young again." She jumped down, catching the hem of her skirt on the top board.

"If I remember correctly, you never climbed fences as a girl. You always had your nose in a book."

"Is that true?"

"You were a serious child when I met ya."

"It must be this weather. I don't think I've been walking since the day I came out to see Ivy when she was born. Dot and I had a real sweet walk that day." She turned around and gazed back toward the farm. "Where's your pigs? I didn't see them out."

"Got rid of the pigs. It was an insult what people were offering for 'em."

"You have cows?"

"We have to. We make a lot of money off the milking. Art still does it by hand, though."

"By hand's the best way."

"Yeah, but it sure ain't the fastest. And fast counts nowadays." I stopped. I seen something moving against the bank of golden dogwood fencing in the older trees ahead. "Look who's come to usher us in." I pointed to the red fox staring, stock-still, at the forest edge. Not a horsefly stirred.

"Funny how a quiet animal can remind you to be quiet," Till whispered.

Despite all them dried leaves on the ground and the fact we was staring at it, the fox was there and then it was gone, and we didn't see no coming or going. Till took my arm and we continued walking.

"I was just wondering if all them bombs was stirring up the dead. The dead Indians, that is."

As we walked, Till watched me outa the corner of her eye in

that special way she had, watching like that fox watched me, not seeing what you and I see when we look at somebody, their clothes, their eyes, the scared or at ease of 'em, watching where their hands go, to their collar or their heart, seeing where their eyes light and where they touch you. The fox was seeing something altogether different and so was Till. I don't know what it was, but I stood still, like I did with the fox, and let her.

"Why?" she said finally. "You've been seeing something?"

"No, I haven't. I don't see things like you and Ivy do and you know it. I just been thinking. I get out here alone in the middle of one of these yellow fields with the land slipping off the edge for miles on every side and Art like an army ant on one of them edges. Art on his plow and I can't even hear his motor, as if my life is misplaced and I'm really over there almost slipping off the horizon with him and the part that's in the middle of the field is just listening, not me. And what does it hear, this big ear that isn't myself? Singing. Some low words that could get mixed up and go right back into the wind if I let 'em, or into the sound of the trees murmuring at the edges like dark armies marching in line on the rim, or get lost in the sound of his tractor suddenly coming in loud and clear and just as suddenly leaving. But it is words other than I am thinking 'em and I don't know why I think they are Indian 'cept they belong to the land here and not to me and it is as if a group of people is singing, it doesn't come from one direction and we don't all sing together round here unless we're in a seance or the church." My hand flew to my mouth. "I am sorry, Till. I guess I haven't talked to somebody about this kinda stuff since Dot left."

"You could talk to that boy about anything, couldn't you?"

"I sure do miss him."

Till walked with her head bowed. "In my experience, there seem to be three kinds of spirits. One is the kind who hang on because they miss this plane, the food or the sex, an open window, a certain color, maybe the touch of a hand. Any point of contact will do for them. Two's the kind we're attached to out of love. Two's all our relation, our family. Three's the kind the Indians are, I suppose. The developed and higher spirits who come to teach us. Their prophecies bear this out."

"What would a dead Indian have to say to me?"

"You forget that they had an Eden once, too." She paused. "They're not all dead, you know."

"So the dead ones were just waiting for the Spiritualists to show up?"

"Long before the Fox sisters heard the spirits tapping in New York, convincing the American public the dead could communicate with us, the Indian spirits were coming to people. The Shakers saw spirits and went into trances, and once a tribe that had died off way before Columbus walked right into their meeting, saying, 'Don't be afraid. We share the same mother.'"

"Now, what is that supposed to mean?"

"I'm sure it meant a different thing to the Indians than the Shakers. The Shakers believed God had a female partner, whom they called Holy Mother Wisdom. They also noticed that, in the traditional Christian Trinity, the daughter was missing. So they replaced her. They say the Second Coming has already happened when their leader, Ann Lee, appeared."

"I knew a lady was a Shaker friend of my ma's, lived down near Busro. She didn't want to hear nothing about sex. She was a hard woman for Ma to take places."

"It's true. Celibacy was part of their teachings."

I was starting to get an idea. "Is not having sex part of Spiritualism, too?"

"No, it is not a tenet of Spiritualism." She smiled like she knew what I was thinking. "I'm happy, honey. Fritzie and I are happy."

"Fritzie ain't what I'm talking about. It's only natural, no matter what them Shakers say."

Till paused. "Do you think, with all we've been through together, that your love for your husband is more natural than your love for me?"

"I'm talking about something different."

"Are you? You're talking about love. Love isn't unnatural, period, Nettie, and you know it. We were put on this earth to do it." She sighed. "Do you really think what you have with Art is so much better?"

"Well, I..." I couldn't think of what to say. "Don't ya ever want to have children?"

"It's a little late to be asking me that," Till said. "Really, Nettie, I thought about it, especially after you had Ivy. I loved that girl from the start."

"Till, I'm sorry about what happened with Ivy. All that time you spent training her, I mean."

Till grabbed my hand and squeezed it. "Nothing is ever lost."

We was far enough in the forest that the highway sounds, then the planes, and gradually our own voices were muffled by the thoughts of the big trees. I'd been noticing, while Till and me was talking, how the quieted birds got used to us and had resumed the songs they reserved for afternoon, not the flamboyant songs they share with us at dawn and sunset but the ones they reserve for each other. The leaves had resumed their falling and there was so much shuffling back and forth on top of 'em that it made me feel as if all the missing deer and green and quail, even them buffalo they named things after, was still here. It made me feel that if I kept walking, we'd come across my ma's chair and my ma sitting in it mending while she rocked, and Dot reading behind the trees or ready to play his tricks on us. We could tell, just by the sound of things, where the center of the woods was and, in our walks over the next few years, we usually stopped there, setting out our secrets like jewels in the dazzling green and yellow shade. We had to come clean with each other. It was impossible to lie in there.

Till came at least once a week and sometimes more. We probably made quite a sight in them days of nobody walking nowhere, the days in between walking 'cause you had to and the days when people jogged, those years when everybody lived in their cars. Me with breasts to my thighs, in a farm dress and apron and the tennis shoes Ivy bought me 'cause she said I'd get flat feet from going barefoot. Till, skinny and straight-backed as my kitchen chairs, carrying a pair of binoculars she kept trying to make me look through. "I like seeing things the way they are," I'd keep telling her. "Besides, them things make me feel like I'm spying on the animals." We went in the afternoons, in summer and in winter unless the ground got so heavy with snow we couldn't push open the back door.

"Look at this woods," I said one day. "It's like us. It's poor. The rich come in, stealing its best years, taking its water, trees, and game, leaving it to fend for itself with a highway on one side and a golf course breathing down its neck on the other."

"I don't know," Till said. "It seems pretty wealthy to me. Inside. Just like it is with us."

All those years of farming, thirty years of watching weather and worrying, of raising children, of cookings and cleanings and all the feeling that comes with all the people, and I had never had a chance or a thought to go where Till was leading me. Many an afternoon feeling sorry for myself, looking out the window, and the woods right there, under my nose. Till says this: "You turn off the lights; the shadows in the room are still there. I come out to visit you and stay until dark and there's the stars. It's all still here but we have to leave our houses, our rooms. It's the same with all you think you're losing, Nettie. You just can't be guaranteed to find it in the same place as before."

We would stand in the middle of the grove of maples, surrounded by the buzz of the world, and sooner or later, no matter
what was troubling us, I'd start noticing the blue between limbs,
a sky blue like a birthday cake it was so pretty, a child's blue like
when I was one and went on adventures of my own. I felt young
and brave in them woods with Till. I understood why Art didn't
want to come in 'til late. "Till," I said, "I hope this place lasts
forever."

Till sighed, just a moment but long enough for me to see I'd
said something wrong. "Not mountains, not forests, not even the
Big Lakes are here forever."

"Not even the sky?" I joked. "Till, I was just kidding."

"Maybe the sky," she said, and I was relieved to see her smile
again.

"Nettie, what was you to say if we got out," he said, and I felt
like my world was crumbling.

I knew he'd gone to town to settle with Mrs. Rose. Every
year, he was coming home from their meetings more discour-
aged. "Mrs. Rose was hard on ya today?"

"She's talking about selling again. American Grain Company
from Chicago. Same place that bought out Jack and Minnie."

"Damn that woman! Can't she see you're working your
fingers to the bone? I guess not, since she never had to lift a one
of her own."

"Now, Nettie. Look at all the years we've lived here. They've
been happy ones, productive ones. It's been a good life."

"She always was a hateful witch."

"It ain't her fault, Nettie. It's the times. She was offered so
much five years ago that if she didn't like us so much, she coulda
sold it and not worried about a penny the rest of her life. Just the
other day, they doubled it."

"Doubled it?" I sank in my chair.

"This farm is worth more than everything we own, we owe, and our life-long labor combined."

"If she sells it, won't the new owners let us farm it? We've been good, showed a profit. Even Mrs. Rose would vouch for us."

"Nettie, you don't understand. There won't be anybody living here. Farmers ain't gonna be living on the land like they used to. They're gonna live in town and get paid by the hour. They're gonna plant it and mow it down in shifts, just like the mining and lumber companies."

"They ain't gonna cut down them trees!"

"I ain't talking about trees," Art snapped, and I seen, for all his defending, how he had never expected this.

"What'll we do if we quit farming?" I asked him. "I can't go back to the mill. The mill ain't even here no more. They moved it to Mississippi where they don't have to pay for heat."

Art was silent. His hands was in his lap, holding each other, his thumbs rubbing up and down their insides. One hand pretty and precise, the other strong enough to pull the starter on the tractor. One holding the handle of the shovel and one directing it. Brown, farming, healing hands that had touched every part of me and still, wouldn't think to reach over, in their fear at being useless now. I remember thinking that if them hands is useless, there ain't no use for beauty in this world.

"We'll still be farming," Art said finally. "I'll go to work for Old Man Bartz. He says he can always use me. And no matter how many folks take their animals to the vet, just as many will still be calling on me."

"You know what Aunt Till says about charging for healing."

"I ain't talking about charging, Nettie. I'm talking about work."

I slammed my fist down on the armchair. "I am just getting used to this place. I'm not gonna pick up and leave it."

"We've been here twenty-five years. Twenty-five good years."

"I don't give a damn how many years. I want to raise my grandchildren on this farm. There's things I gotta teach 'em."

At a time when I felt like most of what I had come to call life was leaving, Little Roy was born, tainted by the falling of fifty-six atom bombs, a sickly child into a sickly world, ten years before that river in Cleveland got so disgusted with itself it set itself on fire. Did she replace the loss? Redeem it? Did she move into my view like a switch of channels on the television? Was it true, like Till insisted, that "whenever you are overcome with grief, look around and there is surely something being born"? No, I'll tell ya. A baby ain't an eclipse of the sun or your memory. What it does take is your attention. Like this one did, carrying Dot's long lashes and my ma's smile, and carrying so much of Art in her hands that all she had to do was brush her fingers against you and you was better. Least *I* was.

My first granddaughter was born in a hospital with Ivy pumped so full of drugs she missed her child coming out completely and kept pushing. They said the nurses had to hold her head up to look. They took the baby away so fast that when she woke up, Ivy asked the nurse if she'd had a girl or a boy. An hour after she was born, me and Art stood on the other side of the glass. Little Roy was the shade of a faded pair of overalls, breathless and blue, looking not quite sure if she got off at the right stop.

"Her name's Jennifer," Ivy said later from her hospital bed.

"We don't have no Jennifers in this family. Is that Roy's mother's name?" I asked.

"Roy and I picked it out of a book of names. We both think it's pretty."

"It ain't nobody's name?"

"I told you, no. We wanted something different."

I looked at Art, but he just shrugged.

"Jennifer Roy."

"Roy's a boy's name," I said.

"I know Roy's a boy's name. Don't you think I know that, Ma?" she said, then turned her head to Art. "Roy was disappointed we didn't have a boy. Guess he thinks he doesn't know how to raise her."

"What's wrong with my ma's name? What about your name? My name?"

"You're making Ivy upset," Art interrupted. "Jennifer Roy's a pretty name, Ivy."

"It isn't my husband's fault. Will you tell her that?" Ivy was saying, almost in tears. "It's just that..."

"Just what, honey?" Art said.

"Just that I wanted something nobody else had. Some name no dead person had."

Ivy wasn't home from the hospital more'n two hours when she called me to come and baby-sit. I didn't blink an eye and I didn't thereafter. Art drove me five days a week at 6:00 a.m. and come to get me at 2:00 when Ivy got off work. "I ain't no wet nurse," I kidded her the first day, but Ivy threw me the formula and left for her waitress job. So Little Roy, with her wheezing, her beauty, and her absolute refusal to digest the world, brought me to town.

"What'd ya think, Till?" I said the next time I seen her. "She's got her mother's gullibility and her father's skepticism. Do ya think she'll do alright in this world?"

"Sounds like she's made for it," Till said, smiling. "Have you any pictures of her?"

"Ivy's been meaning to bring her to ya. She's just busier than a cat in heat with her new job and this mothering. She's been meaning to bring her to Sunday service."

"I'm sure she'll get around to it," Till said, but I was hurt for her.

"You came right over when Ivy was born. You didn't need no invitation," I said.

"It's different now," she said, and I knew it was.

One morning, while Ivy was running around trying to iron Roy's shirt with one hand and zip up her waitress uniform with the other, Roy late and a-huffing and puffing and looking for his car keys, I had my chance. "This baby's mouth is almost swollen shut. No wonder she's howling like she is. Have you taken her to a doctor yet?"

"I thought you called the doctor, Ivy," Roy accused.

Ivy stopped what she was doing and put both hands in the air. "It's my fault. I got busy with something else. Do you think it's worse than yesterday, Mom?"

"It's a case of thrush if I ever seen one, poor child."

"I gotta be at work in ten minutes. I've been late three times this month. They said they might put me on probation." Ivy looked wild back and forth from me to Roy like she was caught in a trap.

"How about if I call Grange today," I couldn't help saying, "and take her over to your Aunt Till's? She hasn't had a chance to see the baby."

"I couldn't. I'd feel funny going back to ask her a favor. I haven't seen her since I got married, since Stanley's funeral. I'd feel..."

"Till loves you, honey."

Roy was half out the door when he heard that. He turned around. "You're not taking my daughter to that lesbian and that's that."

Ivy and I stood with our mouths dropped open, so shocked

we couldn't even look at each other. A what? I'd never heard that word out loud before and now that I did, I couldn't reconcile it with my friend Till. There must've been the wrath of them Furies in our eyes 'cause Roy was already defending himself. "Everybody knows about her and Fritzie Smith. Queer as they come. It isn't any secret."

I started quietly packing up my belongings, packing up the peach pie I'd just baked that morning for their supper, and was resolving to call Grange and ask him to pick me back up. I was resolving to hold my peace and leave just when Ivy blew up.

"You don't know anything about who my Aunt Till is or what she does. And unless you plan on taking the day off work to take your daughter to the doctor downtown and pay for it out of your own pocket instead of taking it out of that loose change you call grocery money like you usually do when some unforeseen catastrophe comes up and then gripe to me about the fatty piece of meat on your plate that night at supper, then you don't have a goddamn thing to say about my mother taking my daughter to get cured by my Aunt Till!"

Roy backed outa the door, then slammed it. He had to. There was nothing else but slink for him.

"You better call her," I said. "She ain't gonna believe I didn't sneak the child over there while you was at work."

"I bet it isn't easy coming up with cures for all her ailments," I said. "Ivy tells me she's been bringing Little Roy to ya every month or so."

"The cures are all the same," Till said. "You know it isn't me that comes up with 'em."

"She's sicker than any child I ever had."

"The child's got a lot going for her. I've never been at a loss for advice about what to do. The spirits line up to take turns healing her. All I do is hold out my hands."

"Ivy was ashamed of herself she didn't take her to ya sooner. The voices was telling her to but she didn't listen."

"I wonder where Ivy got her healthy dose of skepticism?" Till said, and winked.

"Well, spirits ain't the answer to everything, that's for sure."

"No, they're not."

"'Course they're not," I said, but Till had a faraway look in her eye that made me wonder if we was talking about the same thing.

"Sometimes they stand so quiet and far away, watching me with sad faces. Perhaps they are on orders not to interfere. Who knows? Lately, more and more people who come to me this happens to. Lately, many times, no healing comes."

She was making me nervous. "Till, I wasn't gonna mention this, but I need to talk to somebody. Yesterday, two men drove up to the house in a shiny blue car, uninvited. They said they were from the government and wanted to do a routine check of our milking operation. I said we never had a check before, least not from strangers. They said this was random. They were doing it up and down the county and we just happened to be chosen. I kept telling 'em to wait till Art came in from the fields for supper, but they said they was in a hurry and wouldn't let up 'til I showed 'em the cows and the separators and the bottling machines."

"It's probably routine, like they said," Till yawned.

"Well, I would think so, too, if this hadn't gotten me so worked up. Look, for some reason, neither of the boys was home. Junior's planning on getting married this year. Grange is talking about traveling. It would make them both feel a hell of a lot better if we was settled in some nice neighborhood of old people in town, within walking distance of a supermarket and with a schoolyard out my front window for me to watch the kids. Heaven for their aging parents, they'd figure. Then they wouldn't have to worry about helping Art and me out or leaving us alone and we wouldn't be throwing good money out the window or onto the ground, which is what they say we is."

"They worry about you. That's only natural."

"Don't you be telling me what's natural, Till. They worry they might have to support us when we get older."

"I'm sure they only want what's best for you."

"The hell they do! The best for me's this farm and Art planting, that poultice patch in my kitchen garden and the walk out to the lilac grove and the smell of field corn splitting open its seams in the heat. Best for me is the life I got."

"I'm sure your suspicions are unfounded. They know how much you love this place."

"Then why are they trying to get me kicked off of it? Don't think I didn't see Junior hang up real quick when I walked in the room the other day or that the milk pans I would swear I sterilized the night before was lying coated with milk when I walked in with them men. Or that the window I only open when cleaning in the springtime was wide open and the milk shed was full of flies. And don't think I didn't notice how them officials had the figures all ready, how much it was gonna cost to get new milking machines and how understanding and how nice. I never hear voices like you and Ivy do, but I'll tell ya, as I was walking around, I heard some and what they was telling me ain't nothing to be proud of."

"Nettie, look at you. Don't get yourself so upset."

My hands had started to shake and so I wrung 'em. "Till, I can't live if I have to give up this life."

She grabbed hold of my shoulders. "Yes, you can."

If Till wouldn't of been there, I don't know how I coulda done it, though for once, in all our years of farming, we wasn't short of help. The boys was better than usual, got their buddies and their girlfriends to come. By the end of the week, we had saddles hanging from the trees from the days we had horses, the plow and rake and wagons lined up in the pasture with the tractor and combine, the car engines and tires in the barn. Mrs. Rose even tottered out, two days before the auction, not to help but to see we didn't put nothing up for sale that wasn't ours. There was milking tools and welding tools, carpentry tools and mechanics tools. We were selling the hives and we were selling the cows. We weren't selling hardly nothing from the house. We was going to town to be house people.

Over three hundred people must've come through that weekend and I wanted to cook for all of 'em, but everybody told me that wasn't the way. So I sat back and all my old friends brought pans of fried chicken and potato salad and we had picnics going all up and down the farmyard, on the porch and in the way. Though I didn't feel much like eating, I talked to anybody that walked in my kitchen to say they was sorry we was leaving but it was time and we'd be better off. Ivy brought the kids, three of 'em by then, and they had a hell of a time, playing and laughing and not having a clue what was going on. Till stood beside me through it all, pointing that out to me. "The kids have no idea what they're losing," she said. "Don't you think we could exchange a little of our worldly wisdom for that?"

Art was busy for the last time with the men, testing joints and testing ropes and talking about the life of each tool like they was his children. I couldn't look at him, my thin man of the fields who couldn't think of anything to say without relating it to the weather. What were we gonna do? I looked at all our belongings spread on the yards, everything we thought we couldn't live without, everything we'd given up so much for, given up having a vacation together, given up buying a piece of clothing new or sewn for ya, given up movies in town and dentists and doctors for, all for sale now. If we couldn't live without 'em before, how was we gonna live?

Till stood by me under the elm by the back door. "Fritzie's coming to see you today," she said, just when I felt like I couldn't last another hour. "And another surprise. Your friend Marie is bringing her."

"Fritzie's coming? Oh, Lord, I haven't seen her for so long. And Marie? This is a surprise! Why is Marie bringing her? Since when couldn't Fritzie bring herself? She was the first woman in Town of Pines to drive that I knew of."

"Not quite the first." Till laughed to see me so cheered. "Fritzie's been ill, Nettie. She hasn't wanted me to tell you. I'm just telling you now so you'll expect it. She looks a little different than when you last saw her."

"'Course she does. We all do."

"Nettie, she's been very ill." Just as Till said it, a baby blue Cadillac pulled into the lane, honking children outa the way and driving right up onto the front lawn when there was plenty of parking by the barn.

"Who the hell is that, thinking they can pull up onto my grass?" I said, walking toward it.

Marie stepped outa the driver's seat and waved. "So sorry you lose farm, friend, but this happen in Europe long time ago. I could tell you stories. Fertilizer, machine, pretty soon everybody get eviction. No work keeping up with."

"Well, you did get that car? My, my, isn't it a beauty. What'd ya get yourself a rich husband and not tell anybody about it?"

"Why should I marry again? Stanley was good man. Stanley was kind to me. I get marry again, I might end up with monkey."

I laughed and followed her around to the other side of the car, anxious to greet my old friend. What I saw I was not prepared for. Marie helped Fritzie from the car, holding on to one arm and Till holding the other. Fritzie must've weighed ninety pounds and her skin was the color of ashes. "Sure is good to see you, Fritzie," I managed to say.

"It is not and you know it," she said. "Oh, Nettie, you're sweet, but I know I look like hell."

Till and I walked behind as Marie led Fritzie onto my porch. "Cancer," Till whispered.

"Cancer," I repeated under my breath. "Why didn't you tell me? All this time you listening to my problems like they was important. I feel terrible."

"Don't feel terrible, please. I didn't tell you because she didn't want me to. She saw how happy your friendship was making me, how my days with you made it possible for me to be cheerful with her. She encouraged me to continue. 'Aren't you going walking with Nettie today?' she'd say and there was no talking her out of it. Forgive me, but if I had told you, you wouldn't have helped me."

"She ain't gonna get better," I observed.

"No, she's dying."

After I settled Fritzie in my rocker on the porch and brought everybody coffee and pie, I sat down. Fritzie grabbed my hand. "I'm sorry about your farm, Nettie."

"It ain't the worst thing. We'll manage. I'm sorry you're so sick."

"Fritzie is not so sick. Be better soon, just hard spot hit," Marie said.

Fritzie smiled at her friend and shook her head. "What will you do now?"

"Junior's found us a two-bedroom house close to Ivy. We're on the same side of town as you, Marie. We're gonna be neighbors at last."

"Do you like it? Is it comfortable?" Fritzie asked.

I shifted in my chair. "To tell ya the truth, I haven't seen it."

"She refuses to," Till said. "She's so stubborn she's going to make them drag her there."

I'd felt the tears a-building, but Till teasing me was all I needed. I couldn't hold 'em back. "I guess it never occurred to me we wasn't gonna die here. I've even seen it, how Art would get sick and I'd tend him in this front room, how I'd die upstairs under my quilts soon after he did. How maybe it would be August and Ivy'd come and pick my sunflowers. Everything in me was moving in that direction, all my thoughts and body moving toward the day I would be put down in the Wanatah Cemetery next to my mother with Art beside me."

They all sat there quiet until I dried my eyes. "Honey, you can't be buried next to your mother. You're married," Fritzie, ever the lawyer, said.

"Marry rhyme with bury," Marie nodded. "Polish, English, no matter."

"I guess I never thought about it," I said, embarrassed. "What about you and Till?" I forced myself to say.

"We've made arrangements," Fritzie answered. "Though we're daughters forever, our wills specify that we'll be buried together. Outside the family plots."

We was all looking at each other. "Are you in much pain?" I asked.

"Honey," Fritzie said, smiling, "no matter what anybody tells you, we all love things the way they are. None of us wants to die."

Chapter Ten

Rosy finch in the blue spruce, how I love to watch 'em, scrambling over each other to get down to that pie-tin of stale bread scraps Grange put out for me on the lawn. Oh, there's a blackbird. Get away! Get away! If I swat the screen like this, he knows I mean business. The finch'll be back. See. Look at that one. Beautiful? Like it fell face first into a pot of my cherry soup. Art says there's so many finch here 'cause they haunt the valleys that used to be covered with pine. A certain pine bird they are, and now they're like me, circling what they once knew as if one day they'll wake up and it'll all be back. Like me, they return and return to what grieves 'em.

"To hear you tell it," Little Roy says, "all life is is one big lamentation. All life is is preventing death, sadness, and disease, as if it's a tug of war with you on one side and the forces against you on the other. What do you think would happen if you let go of your end?"

"I ain't ever letting go of my end," I say. "If you ain't troubled about nothing, you don't care about nothing."

"Not me," she argues. "I'm gonna enjoy life. I don't see why women have to be the ones worrying all the time. Why can't men?"

"It don't have nothing to do with men," I tell her, "nothing." I pointed out the window. "It's like these finches. They could fly off and find some other place that's better. But they stay here, close to whatever meant home to 'em. And full of grief, they live on."

Little Roy's afraid I'm going senile. That's why I can sit for hours with no TV on, staring out the window at the kids riding their bikes, at my neighbors coming and going, at the spruce swaying in our gray, foundry air. I'm not senile, I tell her. I'm finally slowed down enough to see. Slowed the way them scientists slow the song of birds down so they can hear the fourteen notes they are singing in between the two we hear. Slowed down the way air slows in heat 'til we can see it rising off the road. "Get up and do something," Little Roy scolds me. "You're gonna get stuck in that chair." But I've done enough.

It's true that I can't remember who's living and who's not. Minnie, Harold, Dot, my ma. I forget sometimes, get about ready to pen a letter when I think, are they or aren't they? Nowadays, I gotta make myself cross their names outa my book or I will write to 'em. My granddaughter thinks it's important that I remember. She thinks it's important who died and when. She don't realize my memory is doing something different now, is re-forming itself like them birds on my electric wires. One day it's a row of finches, next it's a month of crows. We spend hours this way when she comes to visit, hours that I'd rather be playing cards or when I'd rather ask about her life if I just knew the right questions. But I don't. I'm seeing outa the ass-end of fifty years between us.

Half the time I think she's asking 'cause she thinks I've rounded the corner and ain't looking back. "Wait," she calls, "what are the names of your seven sisters? What did your ma make for Easter dinner? What did Rosetta prescribe for cramps?" I tell her about my sisters, about Easter and Rosetta, but no matter how much I tell her, it's still telling, not living, and Rosetta is a life, not a story, is almost a century of plants disappearing and she was friends with every one of 'em. On the news the other night, they said they found history caught in the layers of ice in Antarctica. Take a cross section of Rosetta's bone when she dies, take a leg bone and cut it crossways—there's history, if you could read it, better'n a tree and its rings 'cause Rosetta has tried every plant and tree she has prescribed.

"She used whiskey for cramps," I tell my granddaughter, "like I did."

Little Roy ain't little anymore, is already in college, but she asks more questions than a four-year-old. Why this and why not that and when did this happen. She says she wants to write a book about me. I can't think of anybody wanting to read a book with no plot but living, no adventure past growing food and cooking it, building a home and keeping it warm, overcoming grief, burying the dead, keeping a family together. And friends. "Friends was my adventure," I tell her.

Little Roy is in my life to rile me. The other day, she asked me if the three of us was lesbians. "Hold your horses, missy," I said. "I've been married to Art half a century and we didn't get three children by using the same drinking glass." She said I'm like a lesbian 'cause all my life I've loved the company of women, because my strongest feelings are directed to Marie and Till. I love Marie and Till, it's true, but I ain't a lesbian no matter what my granddaughter says. Marie and Till is outa love, not sex, is outa companionship. And what is better than companionship, she asks me. Family, I say. Till and Marie aren't your family? More than Lizzy? More than your son Junior, who you haven't seen for four years, not even at Christmas? she asks.

"You're just trying to confuse me," I say.

"What about Fritzie and Till?"

"What about 'em?"

"They were together long as you and Grandpa. I bet the majority of their life together wasn't about sex. Was yours and Grandpa's?"

"Can we talk about something else?"

"Tell me," she said, "a story about Marie and Till and you."

I groaned. "After I'm dead, you'll be telling everybody how I kept repeating the same stories over and over just like all the old people."

"Tell me," she said, "one I haven't heard yet. But make sure Marie's in it."

People have always wanted to hear about Marie and who can blame 'em? If I wasn't in touch with her, I woulda hunted down the stories myself. Which woulda been no great effort. Stanley's death had not diminished the number of 'em. Or the feelings they inspired. True to her word, Marie never married again, though not for lack of offers. Rumor had it the diamond rings slipped on and off her fingers like, if you'll pardon the expression, a whore's drawers. Harold thinks she took the train to Chicago to pawn 'em 'cause they were never on her finger more than two weeks. Folks were saying she was the modern-day Belle Gunness, Town of Pine's claim to fame, who lured men and their riches from as far away as South Dakota, then chopped them up and buried them in her backyard. That was in the 1800s. There was a resemblance, seeing as Belle was also over six feet tall and weighed two hundred pounds. And Marie did seem to be getting wealthier every day. Rumor had it she was saving up for a move to Florida. She was already on her second Cadillac and was the first woman I knew to fly alone on a jet when she visited her sister Laura in Toronto. But the men she lured was still alive, much to the disappointment of their wives, and they apparently didn't mind if they never saw their silk dresses and pearls on Marie more than two or three times. This was not rumor: every Sunday, Marie loaded ailing Fritzie into her car and took her and Till for a long ride.

I know 'cause they must've asked me to go with 'em a thousand times. I wouldn't on account of Art. I never wanted to go anywhere without him. "Does he go places without you?" my granddaughter asks. Well, of course he does, but that's different. It was working. During those first years in town, he left every morning to drive to Old Man Bartz's and spend the day working for him in his fields. Them first years, his cap line didn't fade and he didn't have to get used to nothing. Sometimes, especially in late summer, I'd go with him, help Mrs. Bartz cook dinner for 'em all and play with her grandchildren. That got old real fast, being in somebody else's kitchen and waiting all morning just so we could do the dinner dishes.

Town for me was hard. I guess I'd never counted how many times a day I went outside on the farm, to call somebody or feed something or shake something out, where I'd feel the hundred different temperatures that rain can be on my bare arms, catch the sun on the tomato plants or a patch of alfalfa. Now that we was in town, I was scared to go out. The newspapers came right to the door, counting for me how many murders, how many got robbed. When Art was gone all day, I didn't know what to do with myself. I baked cookies for all the neighbors and started reading gothic romances. Until one day, I woke up and felt like if I didn't get outa the house, I was gonna die.

It was one of them hot Indiana summer days when ya got to have a fan in every window and still your legs stick together when you walk. I was pacing the hall when a bucket of apples going bad in the pantry caught my eye. Shit, I said to myself. I might as well do something with 'em. Else I might walk out that door and who knows what would happen to me. I spent the entire morning talking myself into it, how I'd make an apple pie for us and one for Ivy, and that way she'd have to come and get it and maybe bring the kids to visit. After all, I hardly saw them kids since they started school. She could bring 'em and maybe they'd stay for supper and Art'd be glad to see 'em and I'd frost one of them pies for him. I must've got the kitchen up over two hundred degrees. When I was finished, I was soaked to the skin, it was three hours later, and I was beginning to calm down.

Ivy said she was on a diet, and besides, sugar wasn't good for the kids' teeth.

Art called and said don't bother about supper, he was gonna be working late.

I was just about to make bird feed outa them pies when I heard a knock. "Yoo hoo, Nettie? Anybody home?" Till came in before I could answer. "Lord, it's hot in here. What are you doing, baking in such weather?"

I scowled. "You ain't gonna start in on me," I was thinking.

Till saw the two pies on the cooling rack. "Oh, how beautiful they turned out! They must be three inches thick. Nettie, you are a wonder!"

I smiled. "It sure is good to see you."

"I can't stay. Fritzie and Marie are waiting in the car. It's so hot we're taking our drive today instead of Sunday. Marie's friend Harold is watching the bar."

"Harold?" I laughed. "Must be hot as hell for Fritzie in the car."

"Marie's got air-conditioning. We're going to Michigan. To the beach. I talked Marie into stopping just in case you'll change your ways and join us."

I looked at the pies. "If I came, would you want to take a pie and have a picnic?" It had taken me exactly two seconds to decide.

"Wonderful! Fritzie loves your baking. I can't wait to see her face when she sees you're coming."

Marie drove like a maniac, screaming at the other drivers, aiming at every car and pedestrian in sight. "You slow down or you can just take me right back home," I said. Once she pulled out onto the freeway, she slowed down, leaning back in her seat and talking nonstop to Fritzie, who sat next to her, something about taxes and banking and liquor licenses. Me and Till sat in the back, playing gin rummy and looking out the windows. "We sure seem to be going a long way," I said.

"We're going to the Big Lakes," Fritzie called back happily.

"The Big Lakes?" I'd never been on a road trip in my life and here I was traveling to the last place I ever wanted to go.

"Fritzie's parents used to have a summer cabin up here," Till said, patting my hand. After an hour or so, we stopped at a cafe and went in, Till carrying my apple pie and Fritzie walking by herself with her cane. Till whispered to the waitress and soon, four dessert plates, a knife to cut the pie, and four cups of coffee appeared.

"Cream," Marie said to the waitress. "Is no cream this restaurant?"

We'd spent years around tables like that with each other, the bread-baking tables, the card tables, the kitchen tables, with dough dusted in flour, the heavy, greasy cards, the knives and spoons in our hands, and I don't think we'd ever been happier than we were that day, sitting in a cafe in Michigan or Indiana—who knows where we were? I sure didn't. Fritzie looked good. Even if all her hair was falling out by the fistful so she had to wear that big hat, even in the restaurant. Fritzie, like Till said she would be, was happy and I was, too. The waitress served the pie onto our plates, left and came back with a container of vanilla ice cream. "On the house," she said, "but only if I can have a piece, too. That is by far the most beautiful apple pie I have ever seen. Did one of you make it?"

"Marie, I didn't know you drank cream in your coffee," I said, watching her pour six or seven of them little plastic creamers into her cup.

"Real cream," Marie answered. "Is free."

"Marie's so cheap she never buys a bag of sugar or salt. She steals it from restaurants," Fritzie said, laughing. "When you go to her house, all the condiments come in little packets."

"Is free. I no steal it," Marie said. "Why else it be on table if not come with coffee?"

"She figures it's cheaper to drive a dying lawyer around every Sunday than pay for a healthy one. What she spends in gas she makes up in free advice."

Marie frowned.

"Fritzie, that's not funny," Till scolded.

"I'm sorry," Fritzie said, "but it seems strange to keep pretending we're going to be able to go on like this, having outings every Sunday, driving to the beaches." She smiled at me. "You don't know how much this means to me that you came today."

"The doctor said..." Till began.

"The doctor said I could continue the chemotherapy or I could quit now. Either way, my chances are the same. The cancer's too far gone."

I glanced at Till. Her face was like a sheet of glass. I couldn't read it, just flashes of many things passing. "Whatever you want, Fritzie."

"It's painful, Till, and it's not working. Nettie," she said. I was startled to hear my name. "I want to ask you something. I want to die at home. It's going to be hard, especially on Till. Will you promise me she won't have to do that alone?"

We were all staring at our plates. I felt sick. "Of course," I whispered.

"Well, then," Fritzie said, as if we'd been talking about the weather, "let's go to the Lakes. I'm so excited. I haven't been to this beach since I was a teenager. You get so busy, don't you? It's not far. We're almost there." She stood and balanced herself with her cane. She was almost out the door before we could come to our senses. Marie ran to open the door for her. She turned on the air conditioner and we drove.

"Where's the Lakes?" I said when we finally pulled into the sandy parking lot.

Marie turned off the motor. She looked at Fritzie.

"It's right on the other side of these sand dunes. See the trail?"

"I thought we was gonna look at the Lakes from the car," I said. I heard something through the car window, a rumbling that got inside my ears like the sound of wind blowing in 'em only there was no wind. It scared me. "I'll stay here with Fritzie and wait for ya."

"Don't be silly. Fritzie's coming. It's good for her to get some fresh air. We walk real slow, don't we, Fritzie?"

"What's that noise?" I said.

"That's the sound of the waves. Haven't you ever been here before?"

"Nobody said nothing to me about waves."

"It's a big lake, one of the biggest in the world. A fifth of the fresh water on earth is in these Lakes. Of course there would be waves." Till saw that she hadn't convinced me to come. "Come on, the waves can't reach you."

She was tying a large straw hat onto Fritzie's head. Outside, in the parking lot, Fritzie wasn't the same friend who was in the cafe or in the car, my friend, smart as a whip, talkative and happy, advising Marie on her taxes and negotiating her own death. Out in that parking lot, hours from home, under the glare of a hot sun moving toward evening and sirens from the nearest town, none of us seemed right to be there, small in the light, a small family with that beating sky without so much as a cloud. I didn't like it a bit, the four of us old women, one carried by the others, Fritzie frail, Marie without English, Till worried, and me overweight and never without my husband in my life 'cept at the grocery store and here I was in a parking lot in the middle of nowhere full of beer bottles and cigarette wrappers and so little a breeze that they stayed in their places. There was a string of beech trees above, on top of the dunes. They didn't stir.

"Strange how there are no cars here. I thought on a hot day like this, the beach would be full," Fritzie said.

"You sure right direction got it?" Marie said, holding her keys.

"Of course I'm sure. You saw the signs."

"Maybe is too hot to swim? Is too hot, too cold, body no like it."

"Maybe we shouldn't go," I said. "Maybe something's wrong."

It was so hot, so still. The roaring in my ears was coming from somewhere inside me as if I was a woods, full of trees, and there was a big storm coming. I tried one last time. "Don't you think the heat's too hard on Fritzie?"

"This is small ocean," Marie said. "I am not afraid any ocean." She stomped off in the direction of the trail. Till and me followed, holding up Fritzie between us. Once we were out of the parking lot, we felt better, though the sand was blinding us, sand paler than wheat and shifting under our feet so I feared we was gonna drop her. Sand shining so that we came in and outa focus with the heat rising and not even any birds was flying from the bunches of grass. It was taking us a long time to go a short way. Fritzie was starting to tire, I could feel it, the way she let herself lean heavier on my arm. I was watching her face for signs of quitting when her eyes lifted and she exclaimed, "Oh, there it is!"

Ahead of us lay one rolling field of huge water, a blue so deep I didn't think it could be something to drink and nothing interfering with it, no end in sight, to the left or the right or in front of me, the sky almost white next to it. Acres of water, too dangerous to think about. Till said more ships was lost in it than in any sea. And the roar. Even the trains that shook my house nights wasn't that loud. We had quiet fields and quiet birds, not these damn sea gulls and the sound of water that opened its mouth so wide it could swallow the jets and trains and sirens and, pretty soon, your hold on life. It was the biggest thing I'd ever seen and I probably coulda stood there for the rest of my days staring at it and not seen the whole thing.

"Isn't that something?" I whispered.

And then we smelled it. If there woulda been any wind that day, we woulda known it a long time before we got to that rise above the beach, woulda got a hint of it in the parking lot. Instead, the breezes we were waiting for, that lifted our dresses, that we drove so far for—hell, it took me my whole life to get there—brought it to us. The smell that makes me start looking behind the stove for something the cat dragged in only more so, only from the sea, without a fire. All the dead in the world piled together couldn't smell worse than that beach smelled that day, like the smell of something rotten in the heart.

"What is it?" Till said, getting out her binoculars. There was a dark band between the waves and the dry sand. I could see it then. A dark ribbon laid out from one end of the beach to the other. I squinted.

"What is it, garbage?"

"No, not garbage." Till sighed and put her binoculars back into their case. "No wonder there's nobody on this beach. That's dead fish down there. Millions of them."

"What is this? This is America lake. Big. Healthy. What is wrong these fish?"

Till turned around to go back to the car.

"No, please," Fritzie said, grabbing her arm. "I'd like to walk down there."

What could we say to stop her? So we helped her down the trail to the beach where we let go of her arms and she walked ahead alone, poking at them with her cane. The three of us stood watching as she moved among the silver bodies piled and drying, flashing like knives, swept up onto the sand. The sea gulls were thick within them, picking at them so that Marie finally shook herself loose and ran after Fritzie, kicking them from her legs. All the fish eyes was wide open. It was a much bigger band of them than it'd seemed from above.

"Even the lakes are dying," Fritzie said when Marie led her back to us.

"Stink like Devil," Marie said.

Till kept Fritzie at home, like she'd promised, bathing her, dressing her, one skinny woman lifting another. Me and Art came almost every day with covered dishes for their suppers, pies, and my homemade bread. "Get some sleep," I'd tell Till. "We'll sit with her." Rosetta came with a charm to ease the pain and lobelia tea to drown it and Harold came to measure for the coffin. Till said Rosetta came daily, hanging rosemary in the corners of the room, opening the windows. I hadn't seen her for so long, I got to wondering if Rosetta was another one of those I'd forgotten was alive or dead. Since she never seemed to come when I did, I still wasn't sure. One day, Till said, she came with a new vine she'd found growing in her garden, one she'd never seen before. "This one must be for you," she told Fritzie. "This one I ain't telling the doctors about. They already called the cops about my oriental poppies." Mrs. Thomas and Mrs. Jones came with food from their church people and when I came in one afternoon, they was both on their knees on either side of Fritzie's bed, praying for her. While they was there we sang, holding hands like we used to, Till, Mrs. Thomas, Mrs. Jones, Art, and me taking turns lifting Fritzie's hands.

There was an art to it and we had learned it. To wait without wishing for a beginning or an end. To look her in the face, to say goodbye with that. It's not a list we could write, we just knew it. We watched for what was needed. Between us all, the candles were lit at night instead of the lamps, flowers were in place, Fritz-ie's hair combed and her face washed. Harold started coming with whiskey from Marie's bar. "This'll put hair back on your head," he'd joke to Fritzie, but I don't think she heard him. Like I said, Rosetta opened the windows.

We all admired how calm Till was, floating through the house that week, meeting us at the door almost before I knocked, always remembering to thank us for the food or the flowers, making some special mention of 'em. "Death is not a cause for sorrow," she'd say. "Fritzie is going to join her loved ones in the Spirit World." Sometimes Fritzie was moaning or sometimes Till had dark circles under her eyes when she met us and she would whisper, "She hasn't slept all night," and still Till stayed sweet as always.

Some of us had advice. "This woman should be in hospital," Marie scolded.

"The doctor's been here. There's nothing to be done," Till said, smiling and patting Marie's arm. "Nothing we can't do here."

Some of us had warnings. "Just remember that death gathers up everything in its wake. If you're anywhere near it, if you can smell it in the air, you're just like a horse smelling fire. It's gonna make you a little crazy," Mrs. Jones said.

One day, I came and I stayed. Till didn't need to ask me. Fritzie waited till midnight, when I was sleeping upstairs and Till was dozing by her side, to stop her heart.

"Nettie? Oh, God! Quick! Nettie!"

I'd never heard Till scream before and I woke with a start.

"Hurry, Nettie! Call an ambulance!"

I was crying and running down them steps and tripping over my nightgown and screaming back what's wrong, I'll be right there, maybe we should call Art, and it was dawning on me real quick what Till was deciding to do and not do and that I was not prepared to do anything about it. When I reached the bedside, Fritzie's breath was smaller than a candle flame and she was gasping. "I can't wake her," Till said.

Till's face was wild, her hair falling round it, her eyes desperate. She was holding Fritzie's face in her hands. "Fritzie, what can I do? What can I get you, honey?" I called the ambulance. We waited. When they came, they threw Fritzie on the floor and began pumping her heart with their fists. "Wait," Till said, but it was already too late to stop them. Even I was terrified.

When they admitted her into the emergency room, Fritzie's eyes rolled back in her head and she stopped breathing. We watched as the nurses sent it through her nose from a machine. That was all we got to see 'cause they wheeled her into the intensive care with Till screaming behind 'em. "No code. No extra measures. She doesn't want anything done to prolong her life."

A nurse stopped her at the door. "Are you her sister?"

"No, I'm her best friend."

"Who's the next of kin?"

"She doesn't have one. She just has me."

The nurse frowned.

"Okay," Till said. "Some cousin she hasn't seen in twenty years. He lives in Elkhart."

"What's his name?" the nurse asked, her pencil ready. "Who are you?" she repeated.

Till and me sat outside the intensive care while the hours passed and the nurses went in and out of the elevators, asking us did we want them to call a cab or our husbands and we said no, we didn't want to wake 'em, we wanted to see our friend Fritzie. When the doctors leave, they said, we can let you in for ten minutes. Is she your relative or friend, they asked us. Yes, we said, but we still had to wait while the doctors was doing who knew what to call her back to life. I knew she didn't want to come.

"This is worse than watching it. Not knowing what's happening, what they're doing to her," Till said. "Not watching her die is worse than watching her."

I reached over to pat her hand, but she was staring straight ahead.

"I lost my faith back there," she was saying. "I hope she'll forgive me. I just couldn't let her die."

I sighed and leaned back in my chair. "It don't matter what you believe about dying. You ain't never gonna be able to rejoice in it."

"Maybe you should call Art and have him come and get you. I'll call you if I need you."

"What should I call him for? He can't do nothing. I'm sure he knows where I am."

All night in that hospital light that is like a fever we waited, parts of Fritzie appearing to me like Art's beard after a shave, sharp and spotty and tormenting me, her love and her names for me, the favorite foods of hers I used to cook. "Who's in charge of this now?" I asked Till. "The doctors or the spirits?"

Once a nurse felt sorry for us and let us peek in. We inched toward the bed she pointed to like we was moving to the edge of a cliff, nervous and out of place in that room of white and no windows and be careful and the masks. We could barely see Fritzie through 'em. Where are you, I thought, while what I took to be her fingers pushed at the blankets as if they, not the electric currents the doctors had sent through her body, was anchoring her the way swimming in wet clothes does. We couldn't stay long. Just long enough to catch the fright in her unseeing eyes as if she was realizing it, too. What she had planned wasn't gonna happen. There wasn't gonna be quiet or music or fresh air or goodbyes. There wasn't even gonna be an end 'til they took that mask and them tubes from her.

"Have you gotten in touch with her nephew?" Till asked the nurse who led us out.

"We're still trying," she said gently and pressed Till's arm.

"If we'd gotten it in writing. If I'd known I was gonna panic."

"Don't worry," the nurse said. "I don't think it'll be long."

"If her heart stops again?"

"We'll have to do what we can." She paused. "Only more slowly."

Just when we'd fallen back into our seats, exhausted, the elevator door opened and Ivy rushed to our sides. "There you are!" She bent to kiss me. "I'm so sorry, Aunt Till. Can we see her?"

At the sight of Ivy, Till burst into tears. "Oh, Ivy, it's so awful. Her dying alone in there like that. It's exactly what she made me promise wouldn't happen."

"There, there," Ivy said, taking a seat next to Till.

"Who called you? I'm sorry, I should've. I wasn't thinking."

"Nobody called. I woke Roy up and made him drive me down here."

"Where is he?"

"Oh, Mom, you know how he feels about hospitals. They scare the living daylights out of him." She turned to Till, taking her hands into her lap. "Of course she's not alone. You're with her."

"But if I could talk to her. Be next to her. I'm afraid she's going to die alone."

"Aunt Till, I'm ashamed of you," Ivy said, dropping Till's hands and looking stern into her eyes. "You are next to her. Say something."

"I..." Till started to say, then closed her lips.

"Talk to her," Ivy demanded.

Till closed her eyes, bowed her head, and grew quiet. I swear, I could almost feel, sitting next to her, her soul lean out to one side, slip and pour through the air like sugar into ice tea, and then dissolve. She was gone a long time. When she came back, Ivy said, smiling shyly, "Could we sing her a song? How about 'In the Garden'?"

"Oh," Till laughed a little. "Fritzie would hate that. You know how she never did like hymns."

"What did she like?"

"What she really loved was Nettie's singing. 'Roll Out the Barrel.' 'You Are My Sunshine.'"

"Would you sing, Mom?"

I looked around. All the nurses was drinking coffee in the office and gossiping. I began:

> You are my sunshine,
> my only sunshine.
> You make me happy
> when skies are gray.
>
> You'll never know, dear,
> how much I love you.
> Please don't take
> my sunshine away.

My voice echoed down the hospital corridors, embarrassing me. I looked at Ivy. "That probably killed a few of 'em off."

Ivy laughed. "I sing that song to Little Roy. She loves it."

"You're a good girl, Ivy," Till said.

Ivy blushed. "Remember that time you gave that trance speech at the VFW, Aunt Till, and we almost got run out of town?"

"*I* remember that," I chuckled. "Jesus, you shoulda known they wouldn't take to anti-war talk. Couldn't ya screen those spirits of yours?"

"Fritzie said she often wondered if my own spirit was speaking louder than the rest of them."

I noticed Ivy had grown quiet, was holding her hands over her eyes. "What is it?" I asked. "Don't ya feel good? You got a headache, don't ya? You ain't been eating right, I can tell. I bet you didn't eat supper again last night, did ya?"

"Shhh. She's gone, Ma," Ivy said. "Didn't you feel it? Fritzie's dead."

The nurses wheeled Fritzie out of the intensive care and into a regular hospital room, rearranged her on the bed with her mouth cleaned out, the tubes and masks disconnected, and her eyes finally closed. Then they let us in to see her. So much had happened to her since we let them take her dying from us and you could tell. She looked different, like she'd been almost there and then snatched back by the scruff of her neck and set down in a hospital in Town of Pines, half there, half here, her face still baffled. Permanently baffled. Till walked to the bed and kissed Fritzie's forehead.

"You are welcome to stay here with her as long as you like," a nurse said. "Can we get you some coffee?"

"I'm not staying, thank you. I've already called my driver. If you would so kind as to help me put her on a stretcher so I can take her to the parking lot, I would appreciate it."

My mouth fell open just a shade less wide than the nurse's. I admired how quick she regained her composure. "Absolutely not," she said.

"She's not leaving my side again until she's buried in the ground," Till said firmly.

"Now, Till," I interrupted.

"Don't you try to stop me now, Nettie," she said, biting her lip so hard it was bringing tears to her eyes.

The nurse looked at Ivy. Ivy shrugged.

"It's understandable that you don't want to leave your friend," she said. "You're upset."

Till was pulling the sheets off Fritzie and folding them. "You're not going to make me carry her downstairs by myself, are you?"

The nurse left the room in a huff. By the time she reappeared with two security guards, followed by an official-looking man in a suit, Till had Fritzie's clothes out of the closet and had started dressing her in them. Just when I thought sure the police would come, the crowd at the door made way and there was Marie, dressed in the first skirt I'd seen on her in years, red lipstick and heels high enough to make her tower over everyone. Marie kept her eyes off the hospital bed where Fritzie lay. "Car is downstairs," Marie said. "You got somebody Fritzie help in back seat?"

"See?" the nurse said to the hospital bigwig.

"I'm afraid that isn't possible," he said.

"My friend Fritzie is lawyer. She is smart woman, maybe more smart than you," Marie said, taking an important-looking envelope out of her purse.

"You found it!" Ivy said, crossing the room to grab it. "This is Fritzie's will. In it she states that she wants no funeral parlor, no embalmer. She wants to be laid out at home until she's buried in the church graveyard at Wanatah."

"My graveyard?" I said. "I mean, my ma and pa's?"

"But," the hospital bigwig said, "it's against the law. We will not release a corpse to someone to drive it across town."

"Then I'll carry her," Till said, tight-lipped.

I've been watching that blue spruce since we moved here, its black needles with the blue sky mixed in between the branches.

It's the only thing lets me know if a storm's approaching or calm. That blue spruce, it's my company. I am studying it to see how it is that it survives. Grange wants to cut it down, says it sheds too many needles and makes it hard for him to mow the lawn. Yesterday the men came back who want to put in new curbs and gutters and say it's in the way. Add to that my neighbor who thinks it's gonna fall on his house. I like to think it's been here forever, one of them million trees that stretched from one end of the eyesight to the other, full of shade and birds and people who didn't spend all day long in rooms, when rain came regular. Like a garden of Eden, Till said. If that tree can remember all that with cement poured up to its ankles and most of its kind gone, and still be good to me, welcome my eyes and wave, I can survive being alone and cooped up in this house, too.

"When it came time for Art to go to the hospital," I said to Little Roy, craning my neck to see the top limbs, "I sent Ivy. She's good at it now, what with Stanley and Fritzie and Roy's ma and pa. She was right there for all of 'em. I knew I could trust Ivy to do my part."

"What are you talking about, Grandma? Grandpa's just taking his walk," Little Roy snapped at me. "You're getting everything mixed up again."

Little Roy hates herself when she loses her patience with me. She thinks, 'cause I'm old, she should show me some respect, and she should. She bit her nails, stalked off to the living room, then came back and sat down next to me at the table. "Did Marie really put Fritzie's body in her Cadillac?"

"Hell, yes, she did. Or rather, we did. What'd ya think, I got that mixed up, too?"

Little Roy thought a minute. "Grandma, why do you think we're here? I mean, why do you think we were born?"

"You are getting too old to be asking so damn many questions." I pushed a plate of chocolate chip cookies toward her.

"I must gain ten pounds every time I come to visit you," she said, picking up two. She's the only one I can get to eat my cooking anymore. Everybody's either too busy or say they're too fat. I don't know what folks eat anymore. Grass, I guess. What Marie moved to this country to avoid.

"Have another one. They won't hurt ya." I'm lucky Little Roy comes as often as she does. Art quit talking to me a year ago with his stroke and only raises outa his chair when I call supper's ready or time for dinner. He can't work anymore. He can barely make it around the block. Which I wish he couldn't do. I worry to death when he's out there. "How long's he been gone?" I asked her.

"To love, to study nature, to help others," Little Roy was reciting, "to minister to children and to enjoy each other's minds. That's what Till says we're here for. It's right here in this Spiritualist manual she gave me..." she said, leafing through it, "...somewhere."

"What'd your Aunt Till say when you went for the reading? What'd she say about Grange? Did she say whether she knew if Junior was working?"

"I didn't ask about Grange and I didn't ask about Junior. I don't care about them. If they want a reading, let them go to her themselves." She glanced at me to see if she'd hurt my feelings again. "You're always asking about your sons. You never ask about Ivy."

"You shouldn't call her Ivy. She's your ma," I said. "You kids go off to college and look what you learn."

"Why don't you worry about her?" she repeated.

"I used to. But she's a good girl, your mother. I don't need to worry about her like I do the boys."

"Aunt Till says I'm not ever going to have children."

"No children? Don't believe a word of it."

"What's wrong with not having children? There's enough children in the world. I want to be like her. Psychic."

"Her sidekick?"

"Psychic. P-s-y-c-h-i-c. I want to talk to the spirits. I want to heal people."

"Well, it sure ain't a way to make a living. Ask Till."

"I already have a way of making a living. I told you. I'm going to be a writer. But I want to know what to do with all these shadows passing in front of my eyes, people bringing bouquets of flowers and strangers I don't know in dreams. Sometimes I stand at my window in the sun and I feel myself surrounded. I want to know by what and what they need to tell me, whether it's spirits or God or just the leaves of the maple."

"Till say you got a talent for it? You know, your mom had a real talent for it. Till was training her to be a medium."

"Really? Mom? Well, what happened? Did she do it? Why'd she stop?"

"Oh, she got married and started having you kids and it was a long way to Till's place from the farm and we couldn't afford taxis for our kids in them days, but I don't think she ever really stopped."

Little Roy groaned. She hates it when I mash together all of what happened in ten years into one sentence. She feels it's her duty to sort it out for me. "When was she doing seances with Till?"

"Well, let's see. Before or after her marriage?"

"What year?"

"Aunt Till thought she was pretty good at it, thought she should, you know, develop it."

Little Roy sighed. "I wonder if I could be a medium?"

"You could ask your Aunt Till. She'll be honest with ya. But ya know, I think folks is just born to it. Ivy was."

"Is that how she knows everything I'm going to do before I do it?"

"No, that's being a mother."

"What would you say if we had a seance right here? You and Grandpa and Aunt Till and me?"

"You can get that idea out of your head right now. Till's old. She don't come outa the house much anymore. And I don't know what your grandfather would think. You know how he is with company. It distresses him that he can't hear."

"We could visit her there. You and I. I could drive you. We could do it on Wednesday when she has her regular meetings. Would you go with me, please?"

"You know I ain't leaving your grandpa alone."

"Please? We'll only be gone a few hours and Mom'll come and watch him. She said she would. I already asked her. Till would be so glad to see you."

"Her name's Aunt Till, damn it."

Little Roy winked. "Aunt Till said she'd make the coffee if you'd bring one of your pies."

Little Roy picked me up the next Wednesday evening and drove me across town to Till's. "Nettie, sweetheart," Till said, meeting us at the door, "I can't believe you came." She took my arm and led me through the dim rooms lit by one floor lamp each, full of furniture old-fashioned as I am. Such a huge, old house it was, with its high ceilings and nooks and crannies, fringed throw rugs and radiators. Big and lived-in and pictures of friends and family on every wall. She sat me down in the parlor next to the heater, opened the drapes, and drew a chair beside me. We looked at each other a long time. She looked to me like she always did. "You must miss Fritzie in this big house," I said when Little Roy had gone out of the room to fetch coffee.

Till leaned over and patted my hand. "We talk more now than we ever did." She smiled. "Sometimes 'til one, two, three o'clock in the morning."

"Fritzie was never at a loss for something to say."

"'The soul recovers its plenitude in the grave'," she said. "The French writer, Victor Hugo, said that. 'There, everything is found again. Our health and all our mental faculties'."

"I wish I could believe that, Till."

"I wish you could, too."

"Art sends his love. He's not too steady on his feet since the stroke or he woulda come."

"I know."

The doorbell rang and I watched Little Roy go to answer it. It was almost time for the service and we were still the only ones there. I turned, curious to see who else would be coming and if I'd know them. Little Roy laughed at my face when she ushered Marie in. "It was a trick, Grandma."

I rose to greet my old friend, but the weight of all them years was a gravity pulling at me, slowing my mind and body like a stone sinking in the deep. My legs started shaking and my eyes tearing up. I had to let her come to me. "Nettie, sweetie. What is wrong, your legs no working? I am old woman, too, but I walk, drive, eat a little, dance a little. Now, boo hoo, I go on big trip alone."

I looked at Little Roy since she seemed to know everything that was going on. "Marie is moving to Florida next week," she explained. "She wanted to say goodbye."

"Moving? Florida? Why?"

"Florida is good place for old woman. Sunshine. Orange tree."

"How are you getting there?"

"Cadillac is good car." She frowned. "I am bit scary. Never such long trip take by self."

"You came all the way over the ocean by yourself and you were only a child! With no English, no money, no food. Tell my granddaughter how you did it and how you weren't even afraid."

"I never say no one be with me."

"Well, sure, there were other people on board the ship. Hundreds, probably. That's not what I mean."

"I no trip making without Ruth."

"Ruth? Who is Ruth?"

"Ruth is young woman no English having, no having even Polish. She is German. She have one coin, big enough buy loaf bread in Stüttgart. I have blanket. We help each other, laugh making, sick sharing. I no make it without her."

My hand landed on my breast. "This story you have never told me. All this time I thought you came alone. That you didn't need anybody to help you."

Marie put her head in her hands. "Nettie. Tillie. I be afraid I never see you again."

"There, there," Till said, "of course we'll all see each other again." The four chairs were set so close we could pat each other's knees. Outside, the pines scratched against the house and the leaf shadows from the street light danced on the walls. "This young woman has asked for a circle," Till said, nodding at Little Roy. "For old time's sake."

Without thinking, I held my hands to either side and they was filled with the hands of the others. Marie started to object. "A circle, not a seance," Till said, "a healing circle like we used to have."

Like Ivy in the old days, I couldn't keep the tears from coming. I blinked and saw Till. She had closed her eyes. So had my granddaughter. Marie bowed her head. "The spirits are listening," Till whispered. "Let us say the names of those we would send healing to."

"Art," I said, "my husband."

"Roy," my granddaughter said. "My dad." I raised my eyebrows. As if she saw me, she added, "For his anger."

Each of us said a name and each name was repeated by each of us. "Harold," Marie said.

Harold. Harold. Harold.

Till said, "Rosetta and Mrs. Jones."

"The waters, the earth and the air," Little Roy said.

The waters. The waters. The waters.

I said, "My blue spruce."

"The future," Little Roy surprised me with.

"The past," Till said.

We repeated the names of the dead, each of us saying and three times repeating. Dot. Ma. Pa. Stanley. Marie's daughter who she'd never named, and there she named her. When we were quiet again, when the words had flown into the air and left us, Till said, "There are two here the spirits have gifts for."

At that, my granddaughter stood up, breaking the circle, and ran into the other room. When she came back, she was holding two wrapped presents. "For Marie," she said.

"I no owe nobody nothing so far," Marie said, handing it back.

"Take it. It's a gift."

Marie scowled but opened the package. What was inside was also wrapped, in an envelope of gold paper. When she opened it, it was a stack of hundred dollar bills.

"To buy your bread on this trip. Know that your friends are with you," Till said.

"Till, you are not rich woman. Where you get this kind money?"

Till frowned. "Marie, don't try the spirits. Fritzie wants you to have it."

"Open yours, Grandma."

"What am I getting a present for? I'm not going anywhere."

"Just open it, Nettie," Till said. "I don't know why Fritzie was moved to give it to you."

It was a small framed photograph of Town of Pines. There was the courthouse, the main road, and there, the sparkling lakes. Fish Lake. Clear Lake. Stone Lake. Pine Lake. But where the woods should be, where there shoulda been pines lining the avenues and in the yards, was bare. "When was this taken? Where are all the trees?"

"They were all cut down in the first clearing."

"You mean the woods by the farm?"

"Second growth. Maybe as old as our grandparents."

"Well, I'll be damned. I wonder who planted 'em."

"Some plant self," Marie said, "some get planted."

"That tree outside my window seems like it's been there forever," I said, then winked at Till and Marie. "Just like us, I guess. Just like us."

Photo by Barbara Levine

Melissa Kwasny was born in LaPorte, Indiana, and educated at the University of Montana. She is a poet and a fiction writer. Her first novel, *Modern Daughters and the Outlaw West*, was published by Spinsters Ink in 1990. Her poetry has appeared in numerous regional publications. She is currently living in San Francisco, where she teaches in the California Poets in the Schools Program.